**ALTHEA HAYTON** is a womb twin survivor, writer and therapist, in that order. She began her writing career in 1991 with a book about addiction to food. Then, after several years writing about the grief associated with the loss of a baby before birth and the need for rituals of mourning, she discovered in 2002 that she is a womb twin survivor. At that time there was no information or psychological support available for womb twin survivors, so she began work at once to put this right. She started a research project by recruiting many hundreds of womb twin survivors by means of a web site and questionnaire. In 2007 she founded Womb Twin as a non-profit company with members, to provide information, help and support for womb twin survivors around the world. Althea was educated at Oxford University and is a qualified social worker and counsellor. She is married with two sons and lives in Hertfordshire, England.

## The Womb Twin series

## Other works by Althea Hayton

# A Healing Path
## For Womb Twin Survivors

**Althea Hayton**

**Wren Publications**

First published in 2012
by Wren Publications,
P.O. Box 396, St Albans, Herts, AL3 6NE
England

www.wrenpublications.co.uk

**ISBN  978-0-9557808-5-1**
Printed and bound in UK and USA by
Lightning Source:

Lightning Source Inc. (US)
1246 Heil Quaker Blvd., La Vergne, TN, USA 37086

Lightning Source UK Ltd.
Chapter House, Pitfield, Kiln Farm, Milton Keynes, MK11 3LW, UK

Cover image © Tina Wigan 2012, with permission

All other images © Althea Hayton

# Contents

# Acknowledgements

This book would not have been possible to write without the help of the thousands of womb twin survivors who have completed the questionnaire and shared their stories with me over the last ten years. I am very grateful for their openness and honesty and the way they have so willingly offered their stories for publication. I have kept their identities secret, but I have left their words largely unedited, which will explain the different spellings of some words.

I have been sustained in every way, over many years of research and writing, by my husband John. My gratitude to him is beyond words.

I am grateful to Dr Victoria Bourne of London University who kindly subjected the data I had collected, via the responses to the womb twin survivors questionnaire, to a statistical analysis, the results of which form the foundation of this book.

Many thanks to my editor Mike Groushko, who helped me to create this final book for adults in the Womb Twin series. I am grateful for his honest and sympathetic approach to this little-known and difficult subject.

I am grateful to my father, Edmund Wigan (1902-1970), who left me his portfolio of paintings and drawings. It has been my pleasure to include three of his many paintings of his own hands, as illustrations in the final chapter.

Last but not least, I would like to express my gratitude to Joe, Dee and Maria, three womb twin survivors who reviewed this book positively in its unfinished form and gave me the courage to proceed to publication.

# Introduction:

# A pathway to healing

Womb twin survivors are the sole survivors of a twin or multiple pregnancy. They started life in the womb as a twin but their twin died, either during pregnancy or around the time of birth. It has been discovered that womb twin survivors spend their lives constantly re-enacting the life and death of their womb twin. It seems that nothing is more important than that, even life itself. But once the real pre-birth scene is clarified and fully understood, the re-enactment ceases altogether, much to the benefit of the individual.

The brief life of a womb twin can be revealed, if we know where to look and what to look for. The results of ten years of research, clarifying the various physical and psychological effects on the survivor when a co-twin dies before birth, have been set out in a previous book, *Womb Twin Survivors, the Lost Twin in the Dream of the Womb.* In this companion volume, we will consider some of the ways in which those effects can be mitigated and healed.

**We will start out on the healing path** with an attempt to clarify your Dream of the Womb, which is the vague imprint of your life before birth. The lost twin in your Dream of the Womb was a real little person, with whom you had some kind of a relationship. Incredible though that may seem, as we continue to explore, you will meet other womb twin survivors and hear their stories. In these stories you may find an explanation of how you have felt all your life, but you never could understand why. We will gradually piece together the story of your life in your mother's womb and through your own intuitive sense you will be able to discover the true nature of your womb twin.

**The second stage** is to learn how the death of your twin (or more than one womb mate, if it was a multiple pregnancy) has become a template for how you have lived your life until now. The need to keep alive the lost twin in the Dream influences the tiny choices that womb twin survivors make every day, and many of those choices are self-sabotaging. This self-defeating lifestyle has within it a higher purpose that may not be immediately evident to you - it is a sacrificial act of love, to give everything over to a single task, which is always to keep your twin alive in your life.

**In the third stage** you will begin to realise the strength of your resistance to healing, despite the fact that being a womb twin survivor can be painful. You will discover the many subtle ways in which you have deliberately not realised your own potential as a person. You will see how a vague sense of something missing still drives you to fill that space inside in a variety of subtle ways. When you follow the steps on the healing path, the strength of your emotions will become more evident, as you re-experience your own pre-birth loss. Your own duality as a surviving twin will soon be clear to you, and the endless struggle between life and death that has characterised your life until now will be revealed, as you learn to recognise the Black Hole in which you have spent so much of your life so far.

**The fourth stage will describe the womb twin work,** where the Dream of the Womb will be explored in more detail. This is because only when the Dream of the Womb is fully clarified can there be complete healing. It is a journey through the Black Hole and out the other side. It can be painful. The work is specific to your personal story, so the biological nature of your twinship matters: were you once half of a monozygotic ("one-egg") twin pair, or one of a dizygotic ("two-egg") twins? Are you perhaps the sole survivor of a multiple pregnancy? We will explore the many differences that exist between these three groups of womb twin survivors.

**The final stage** on your healing path is the resolution of your Dream. You will find new ways to see the world and the people around you. As you step out on your new journey, you will find yourself beginning to use all your gifts and allowing your healing influence to spread to other womb twin survivors. Your new journey will take you into your future, where different and more appropriate choices will create a different kind of life for you.

Althea Hayton
St Albans, England, 2012

# STAGE ONE

## The journey begins

Come with me, sole survivor -
Come to where the healing lies amidst the pain;
Come to the darkest place where a tiny light shines;
Come with a million others who are searching for the one
Who will heal the screaming emptiness inside.

Bring a taste for paradox, for the healing comes through pain
And in your loneliness you'll find a new friend - once again.

Bring the worst that ever was - your Black Hole will give
The hardest lesson in how you could live.

Bring your non-existent, vacant self that mirrors cannot see,
For dissolution forms solidity.

Bring that empty space of pain within your soul
And it will fill itself with hope and make you whole.

# 1
# Your Dream of the Womb

As a womb twin survivor, you will not be surprised to know that we are all capable of some kind of awareness, even in the earliest stage of life in the womb. However, we lack the vocabulary to describe that vague and inchoate awareness. It would be inaccurate to call it a "memory" but it is not a fantasy or a product of the imagination either. The phrase, "Dream of the Womb" seems to be suitable.

> I want to thank you for the new awareness that I got and some language to use when talking about womb twin survivors. The words "Dream of the Womb" brought the images I have in mind to a place, in a sense. [Diannah, Canada]

## A neglected area

The brief lives of womb twins in the early stages of pregnancy and the extraordinary experiences of womb twin survivors have been sadly neglected and overlooked by the many writers who have theorised on the outworking of pre-birth experience in born life. Moreover, the notion that some people have been affected by the loss of a twin before or around birth remains unrecognised at this time by the many people in the world who are not womb twin survivors themselves. Even when the lost twin is known about, possibly as a tiny empty sac on an early ultrasound image, the fact that there

3

was once a twin is often deliberately concealed from the parents by medical professionals, in order to save the parents from distress. Little thought is given to the psychological effects on the sole survivor, for it is generally assumed that such an early experience could not possibly leave any impression. We now know that the sole survivor carries an indelible imprint of his or her early experience throughout life. In many cases this causes distress - although not always, as we shall see, but for those who do suffer, it is a needless burden that would have been greatly eased by this knowledge.

*I always knew I was a twin because I could see him, talk to him. He was always around. At first I didn't realise who he was, I was too young, but it became clearer as I grew older. Now, so many things are explained, things that always bothered me. But it's hard when there is no one to talk to. My Mum listens and tries to understand, but she just can't. I don't even understand sometimes. Anyway, I suppose I have to keep fighting and hope I can come to terms with it all one day.*
*[Ann, Ireland]*

# A real memory

In your Dream of the Womb is your lost twin. How you have responded to that experience in your born life depends on the exact nature of your womb story - was your twin your identical half or a fraternal (non-identical) twin, separate from you? Were there more tiny little embryos developing along with you, and if so, how many were there?

All the information is there, hard-wired into the neural network that makes up your brain. Your Dream of the Womb is like a giant jigsaw puzzle with no image of the completed picture. It is a multitude of vague impressions and physical signs. As a result of the Womb Twin Survivors Research Project[1] we now know that the impression of your pre-birth experience is very hard to access and make into any kind of sense.

*When I first heard of womb twin survivors, I immediately thought that it might explain some feelings I have and "memories" I have from being in the womb. I have always had an interest in twins, although I would not describe it as a "great" interest (meaning more than I assume and it appears most people have.) I have had and have feelings that many would define as and associate with the term "depression." As a child,*

*I remember being accused by my mother of being too sensitive, and I currently am very aware of my feelings and the feelings of others, which may or may not fit the definition of hypersensitive. I have "memories" and feelings from being in the womb and recurring dreams of being in the dark and being terrified of losing my life. I wouldn't say that I "hate goodbyes", in the way some people seem to hate them, but I think that I really steel myself against them and numb out many feelings that come up.*
*[May, UK]*

When that picture of your pre-birth experience begins to take shape in your mind, it will be remarkably accurate. The Dream was built as your brain was built. The whole experience is hardwired into the neurons of your brain. It is integral to your personality, written into your mind and seemingly inescapable. Your whole life so far has consisted of keeping your Dream alive - for in the Dream is your lost twin. Your pre-birth memory is entirely yours, and no one can tell you what you know or don't know about your twin or how real your feelings are. It is important for you to recognise that you are the world's greatest expert on your own experience of being yourself. At this stage, when things are so unclear and all you have so far is a dawning awareness that you may possibly be a womb twin survivor, you may have to begin by taking a close look at images of twinning, and see which ones seem to resonate with you. There is plenty of information of that kind in the companion volume to this one, *Womb Twin Survivors- the lost twin in the Dream of the Womb.*

## Cracking the code          **?**

As you explore these ideas, you will have to use your own intuition or "gut feeling." In the absence of other information, it will be the only resource you will have. You will develop a better understanding of how your own particular womb twin scenario has been repeated again and again in your life. It will work like breaking a code and you can decipher the code with the notion of a lost womb twin. The work proceeds by applying this idea to as many aspects of your life as you can, with as much honesty as you can muster.

*I feel that although I don't have memories in the strictest sense, I am developing an awareness of my twin.*
*[Breda, Australia]*

# One in ten

Dr Charles Boklage, Professor in the Department of Paediatrics in the Brody School of Medicine, East Carolina University, has provided us with an important statistic that has transformed our knowledge of the number of womb twin survivors across the world. Dr Boklage made a painstaking statistical study, published in 1995, of dozens of reports of the death of twins or multiples in the womb or at birth. The study involved gathering statistics from many thousands of pregnancies. Projections using these data indicated that one pregnancy in eight begins as twins. Furthermore, Dr Boklage concludes that, for every live-born twin pair there are 10 twin pregnancies resulting in only one baby - a womb twin survivor.[2] We already know that about 1% of births across the world are twin births, when two babies are born alive together. That gives us a minimum figure for the number of womb twin survivors, which is at least 10% of the world population. This important study has not been duplicated or disputed by any other researcher and has been quoted widely in the relevant scientific literature. If its conclusions are true, then at least 700 million people in the world are womb twin survivors. Dr Boklage, a father of twins himself, was astonished by his findings. He wrote, "The numbers estimated here for the frequency of twinning at conception and the prevalence of sole survivors of twin gestations are little short of astonishing at first consideration, and they are conservative, perhaps even minimum, estimates."[2]

As Dr Boklage notes, the 1:10 statistic may be a minimum figure. Wherever there is twinning, there will be womb twin survivors. That is worth bearing in mind when you are wondering about yourself and other members of your own family. There is probably at least one womb twin survivor in every family, and the one in your family may be you. In families where there are many pairs of born twins across several generations, it is possible that there are also many undiagnosed and unaware womb twin survivors. Even in families where twinning is rare or nonexistent, there may be several womb twin survivors.

Some womb twin survivors are aware of what they are, having been told about their twin. Others have not been told, but still have a sense of deep conviction about being a twin. Womb twin survivors are so often misdiagnosed, misunderstood, accused of being weird or deemed to be mentally ill, that most of them find it better to remain silent on the subject. Now you know how many womb twin survivors there are in the world, you no longer need to be afraid to talk openly about it. It will take a long time for other people to be convinced, but the more we speak out, the sooner everyone will realise this matter is real. Do not expect your close family to take it seriously. They may have their own reason for avoiding the subject, so don't push it, for their sake. Rest assured you are probably surrounded by other womb twin survivors and many of them are among your friends. If you mention your womb twin to them, they may feel able to tell you their own secret story. Then you will have an ally, who may be willing to accompany you along the healing path.

## Signs and physical indications of a twin pregnancy

Below is a list of signs and physical indications of a twin pregnancy. Just check any signs that you know were there when your mother was pregnant with you, were seen at your birth, or still remain in your body.

| Indication | Yes |
| --- | --- |
| Mother abnormally large in the first three months | |
| First trimester bleeding | |
| Complete miscarriage, but pregnancy continued | |
| Suspected miscarriage, but pregnancy continued | |
| Attempted abortion, but pregnancy continued | |
| Doctor or nurse suspected twin pregnancy | |
| Another person suspected twins | |
| Mother experienced infection during pregnancy | |
| Mother experienced severe physical or emotional trauma | |
| Mother experienced starvation through circumstances, illness or excessive vomiting (hyperemesis) | |
| Mother took hyper-ovulation drug (eg Clomid) | |
| More that one embryo transplanted after IVF | |
| Ultrasound evidence of second sac | |

| | |
|---|---|
| Birth was traumatic | |
| Breech birth | |
| Small for dates | |
| Placenta unusually large | |
| Additional sacs or cords found | |
| Foetus papyraceous | |
| Marks or lesions on the placenta | |
| Twin stillborn or died close to birth | |
| Dermoid cyst | |
| Teratoma | |
| Foetus in foetu | |
| Sexual organs of opposite sex | |
| Secondary sexual characteristics of opposite sex | |
| Cerebral palsy in the survivor | |
| Split organs | |
| Congenital abnormality | |
| Left-handedness or mixed-handedness | |
| Chimerism | |
| Mosaicism | |

As research and public awareness increase, we will discover more ways to identify womb twin survivors and help them to identify themselves. The list of signs and physical indications is just a beginning.

## The next step: The death of your womb twin

Now we have decided that the whole idea of being a womb twin survivor may not be a fantasy after all, this is where we will go to take our second step on the healing path, which will be about death.

8

# 2

# A matter of life and death

We now know that you have spent your life so far constantly re-enacting the life and death of your womb twin. The second step on your healing path is to recognise how existential issues - "matters of life and death"- have been worked out in the tiny choices you make every day. These choices have created your way of life, because your present existential position in born life accurately and directly reflects the life and death of your womb twin. Your Dream of the Womb is made up of millions of tiny details, hard-wired into your embryonic neural network. This part of your brain is the most primitive, but it orchestrates every other part. This is how your attitudes, feelings and choices have constantly repeated the original womb twin story that is the foundation of your Dream of the Womb. As you begin to explore the real nature of your womb twin and consider his or her brief life and untimely death, you will see with increasing clarity how the deep imprint of your pre-birth experience has been a major guiding force in your life.

## Two types of twinning

The two kinds of twinning differ according to how many fertilized egg (zygotes) were involved. As you move along the healing path, it is important for you to work out whether you and your twin were two halves of a single egg, or if there were two separate eggs (or more) and one of them was you.

Here is a list of the various terms commonly used to describe twinning:

**Twins arising from two separate zygotes are called:**
- Dizygotic
- Fraternal
- Non-identical
- Two-egg

**Twins arising from one zygote that split into two are called:**
- Monozygotic
- Identical
- One-egg

To keep things simple, from now on we will use the two terms **"Two-egg"** and **"One-egg"** for the two kinds of twinning. It is also possible that you had more than one womb mate. This means you could describe yourself as one of the following:

- One-egg womb twin survivor
- Two-egg womb twin survivor
- Multiple womb twin survivor

Finding out what type of womb twin survivor you are is a crucial aspect of your healing journey, so do give it a lot of thought. It may take a long time for you to come to a fixed conclusion, but the truth of your origins will eventually come clear in your mind.

## The death of a womb twin

We will now take a look at the various ways in which womb twins die.

### A SUDDEN AND UNTIMELY DEATH

If your twin died at birth or shortly afterwards, the event may have left you with a deep sense that your own life must also be short and your death untimely. Conversely, it may have left you with a sense of obligation, so that you live intensely - as if living for two. This may also find you living with no thought for the future.

**FADING AWAY**

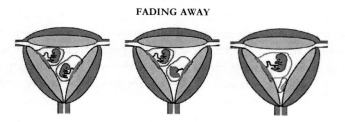

If your womb twin never made it to birth but died in the womb, it may have taken weeks, or even months, for death to occur. This may have been because your twin's placenta was not implanted properly, so there was insufficient nourishment and oxygen for survival. As you re-enact your Dream of the Womb, you too will probably have a sense of "fading away." This may be related to a problem with food and eating, or possibly recurrent chest infections, wheeziness and asthma. There is little reliable data at the moment, but there does seem to be some sort of relationship between anorexia and a womb twin who starved to death.

> *For the first time ever, I felt as if someone understood me. It was as if she was sitting inside my head, pulling out the threads of my tangled thoughts and rearranging them to make some sort of sense. I understood my feelings and inadequacies and the reasons for the anorexia. I felt that finally someone understood me, knowing how I was feeling, without thinking me "odd."*
> *[Teresa, UK]*

**UNABLE TO GROW**

The death of a womb twin may have less to do with the effectiveness of the placenta than with an intrinsic inability to grow. This can be due to some kind of environmental problem, such as a small or deformed uterus or the presence of fibroids that compromises good implantation. It may be that the mother's blood supply is insufficient to feed two babies. In that competitive environment, even a slight advantage of one over the other would decide who survives long enough to be born alive. Should both babies manage to survive to around 27 weeks, the birth may be induced early, to save at least one baby. One-egg twins in particular are subject to pre-term birth and in many cases only one baby survives the first few days. In your Dream of the Womb is your twin's inability to grow into a complete person. As a reflection of that, there will probably be some secret part of you that has always remained in a state of arrested development.

> *My daughter was a twin. I lost her twin at three months into the pregnancy but Liz survived to be born two months premature, in what was a very difficult pregnancy for me - I was in and out of hospital the whole pregnancy and she was induced, due to lack of oxygen and my high blood pressure. But somehow she managed to survive - she is a true survivor!*
> *[Una, Spain]*

### DOOMED TO DIE

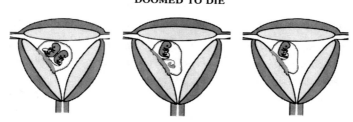

In "vanishing twin" pregnancies, twins or more can be seen on the ultrasound scan, but later only one remains visible. These tiny twins do not vanish - they die. Their little bodies, together with the membranes and the developing placenta, all disintegrate after death and the microscopic fragments that result are reabsorbed. There may be tiny traces left on the placenta to show your twin once existed, but that does not always happen.

If this is the story of your womb twin's life and death, it is important to know that your embryonic womb twin was always doomed to die, either as a result of some kind of abnormal development or because of a congenital deformity. There was never any capacity to develop normally. In that case, you may carry some sense that you too are doomed to die prematurely, and therefore you feel there is not much point in living. This feeling has been termed, "existential despair." If you suffer from the kind of depression that leaves you not caring if you live or die, then it could be because your womb twin never developed fully, had a very short life and was always doomed.

*Recently, I have had this sense that I'm essentially terminally ill at present. It feels as though the decision has been made - by my illness, by the effects of my illness on my life, by the resulting existential despair, and of course by a thinking, feeling me that just doesn't want to go on, doesn't want to rebuild, sees futility where others see hope and opportunity.*
*[Ned, USA]*

### HARDLY EXISTING AT ALL

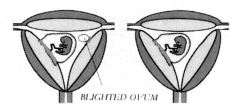

BLIGHTED OVUM

Your womb twin may have been a blighted ovum, which never developed beyond the earliest stages to become a functioning body and disappeared without trace. This happens in the first few weeks of pregnancy and in most cases there are no physical signs. Alternatively, you may be a chimera - that is, you may carry embryonic cells from your womb twin in your own blood or the tissues of your own body. The only sign may be found in the back of your mind - a feeling of hardly existing. Some womb twin survivors experience a prevailing feeling of invisibility, of non-being. If your womb twin only managed a brief existence before falling into total disintegration, then you might feel that you cannot allow yourself to exist fully in this world. It may also seem to you that other people don't exist either.

*When I was 12 I had begun having problems relating to other kids; a lot of them thought I was weird. Sometimes I felt like I did not really exist, that I was an empty shell, and sometimes other people were empty shells. I was in heaven at the age of ten when I met a distant girl cousin at a reunion who resembled me greatly. Everyone remarked that we looked like twins, and I wished she could have come home with me! Unfortunately, I never saw her again. I also had been aware of the presence of an unseen being everywhere I went, nobody dangerous or foreboding, just a gentle, constant presence. Due to my great fascination with twins, I sought out other twins hoping to be friends with them and*

*maybe their "Twin-ness" would rub off on me. All I ever wanted was to
be loved unconditionally and understood.*
*[Kat, USA]*

To have a sure sense of one's place in the world can be very hard if you are
a womb twin survivor who carries a vague impression of Something Vitally
Important, which hardly existed at all.

# The life of
# a womb twin survivor

The way you have chosen to live your life may not be what you truly wish.
You may feel compelled to exist in a certain way, as if some hidden force was
at work. That force may be nothing more than a desire to keep your Dream
alive. In your Dream is your lost twin, whom you once knew for a brief time.
Incredible though it may seem, the nature of that little life is known to you.
Furthermore, in some subtle way, it is the life you have been living.

## Too fast to live, too young to die

Some womb twin survivors live at such a pace they seem to have two
existences at once. They may take on so many activities that they fall into
periodic exhaustion. They may die prematurely, many of them at their own
hand. Suicidal thoughts are common among womb twin survivors. These
fast-living womb twin survivors may risk their lives once too often, for
example by driving much too fast, leading to a fatal accident. They may take
drugs to achieve a "high" but end up in despair. Elvis Presley was a womb
twin survivor whose twin was stillborn. Elvis died aged 42 after a hectic life
and meteoric career, both of which ended as a result of drug-taking and bad
eating habits

## Enfeebled

Despite being potentially perfectly healthy, some womb twin survivors
deliberately ruin their health and well-being. They find it hard to practise
regular self-care. They may eat in an unhealthy way, drink too much alcohol
or refuse to take any exercise. Consequently, their bodies become weak and
feeble and they are often ill.

*I know that my eating habits are killing me and I suppose deep down
that's what I am hoping for:- to die in a manner that nobody would
class as suicide, as this way of eating and being makes me so ill.*
*[Jules, USA]*

14

Even though such individuals are given plenty of healthy living advice and the support necessary to follow it, their way of life leads them directly and knowingly into an early grave. For instance, TV programmes about weight loss invariably demonstrate that when obese individuals choose to adopt a healthier lifestyle, most of them return to good health within a few months. However, despite their evident love of life and strong constitutions, almost all of them eventually fall back into their addictive eating habits and continue to risk their lives. It seems that such a strong willingness to die young and in this particular way, must be a reflection of a weak little womb twin starving to death, leaving the survivor with a lifelong feeling of guilt about food.

## Blighted

Some womb twin survivors do not seem to have the inner strength to cope with life. They are weak and feeble as children and often ill, so they remain isolated from their peers. The life force does not seem to be strong in them, as if they have in some sense opted out of a normal existence altogether. They carry a prevailing sense of helplessness, as if life is simply "all too much", and they would be better off dead. The true motivation becomes clear when individuals leading a blighted existence are encouraged to make a better life for themselves. They usually sabotage most or all of the opportunities that arise. If success does come it is short-lived, because some kind of self-defeating behaviour begins, such as simply not turning up for work or heavy gambling. The professionals involved are usually left with a sense of frustration, having encountered a very strong will not to succeed. They may not realise that some womb twin survivors have a higher agenda, which is to live a deliberately blighted life.

## Unable to get off the ground

There may be a part of you that never developed, which you might think of as your "inner child." If that is the case, you will have adapted your life to allow for this sense of personal inadequacy and however hard you try to move forward, you always fall back. Your life is littered with unfinished projects and broken dreams. Of course you have the capacity to finish the projects and make your dreams come true, but somehow you can never get going and make it all happen. If this is your story, then it is the lost memory of your twin that is driving it. Just a little bundle of cells - no more than that - your twin did not implant but drifted away out of the womb, leaving tiny traces of a tiny, brief existence in the very back of your mind. However vague the impression, the compulsion to hold back is extremely strong, as you continue to sacrifice your happiness and your future to preserve your Dream.

15

As you move further along the healing path, you will discover in yourself the will to grow and develop. Then your new life will begin.

## Not allowed to live

It is hard for most womb twin survivors to allow themselves to be fully alive, as if they need to give themselves permission to do so. Of course, if their twin was not permitted life, how fair is it to be the only one to have it - and have it to the full? If that is your story, then perhaps your very existence feels somehow wrong, as if you ought to leave this world and make space for others. You may have often felt suicidal, in the sense that life is painful. You may even feel that the world would be better off without you. For you, the whole business of being alive is probably negative.

Below will find a checklist summarising the points made in this chapter, plus some other common statements about death made by womb twin survivors as part of the Womb Twin Survivors Research Project. If you tick the statements that seem to apply to you, then a picture of your Dream of the Womb may begin to emerge.

| My life | Yes |
|---|---|
| I do not feel allowed to live | |
| I feel like I do not really exist | |
| I can't get started on what I want to achieve | |
| I can't get engaged in life | |
| I don't care if I live or die | |
| I don't see any hope for a better life for me | |
| I fear success | |
| My life is a constant struggle to survive | |
| I know that I could have a much better life if I tried | |
| I have often thought of suicide | |
| I have made one suicide attempt | |
| I have made several suicide attempts | |
| I don't want to be here | |

| | |
|---|---|
| I am trying not to die | |
| I hate my life | |

*I find that I can sometimes muster up enthusiasm for life and engage in it, but it soon passes and then I am left feeling "living-dead." I get suicidal quite frequently when all I can think is that this is as good as it gets - and it is terrible. Yet on the surface there is nothing wrong. [Deirdre, Scotland]*

| My death | Yes |
|---|---|
| I expect to die very soon | |
| I fear sudden death | |
| I feel like I am slowly dying | |
| I feel like half of me is dead | |
| I am afraid of dying | |
| I work with dying people | |
| I work with dead bodies | |
| I like to visit cemeteries | |
| I like to watch movies about death | |
| I like to read books about death | |
| I grieve for a very long time when someone close to me dies | |
| I grieve for a very long time when one of my pets dies | |
| I worry about dying in my sleep | |
| I have panic attacks, in which I think I am dying | |

## The next step: You are not crazy!

Your attitude to life and death will probably change profoundly as we go forward together. The next step will answer the question that may have been in your mind for years: "Am I crazy? The answer is that you are not crazy at all but a perfectly normal womb twin survivor.

# 3
# How crazy are you?

The first thing to understand as you take this third step is that you are not crazy. You are a womb twin survivor and that is why you feel as you do. You are an unusual person because you had such an unusual, very early experience. You can now relax in the knowledge that, possibly after years of struggle, your feelings are fully understood.

*In spite of all the work I've done to heal, there is still a deep grief, accompanied by deep fear of abandonment and rejection regarding men. Indeed I have been abandoned over and over again. Just knowing that there's someone who understands and cares and knows that I'm not crazy will be a big help.*
*[Beth, USA]*

## Obsession

Has any one ever told you that you are obsessed with the idea of being a womb twin survivor? Perhaps there is no physical evidence you are but you have always insisted on it. For years you have continued in your desperate search for information and reassurance that you are not crazy. Some people may see your endless search as some kind of insane fixation but it is perfectly normal for a womb twin survivor to devote a lot of energy to self-understanding. However much others insist that the early loss of your twin cannot possibly leave an impression in your mind as the survivor, you insist that it can. You may have learned to say nothing and try to look normal and cheerful but somewhere inside there is a psychic wound. Naturally enough, you will do whatever it takes to find healing but this is not an obsession.

# Personality disorders?

Various publications list the symptoms of personality disorders and all are based on the Diagnostic and Statistical Manual (DSM) produced by the American Psychological Association (APA) and now in its fourth edition.[1] The APA gathered this comprehensive list of symptoms into groups and created syndromes to describe clusters of symptoms that occur together. Each cluster is described as a specific disorder. The definitions are not very precise and it seems that there is a spectrum of different personality types, each one merging into another across the range. According to the results of the Womb Twin Survivors Research Project, many of these so-called "symptoms" seem to be a reflection of some kind of a pre-birth experience. We will now consider two personality disorders and see how they could be related to the loss of a twin or more, before or around birth.

## Bipolar Disorder
The term Bipolar Disorder is used to describe people who are subject to very exaggerated mood swings from mania to depression, in a set of symptoms that used to be called, "manic depression." The mood changes may happen over several months or they can occur extremely rapidly, within minutes. If you are subject to frequent mood swings you may have been diagnosed with this disorder. However, if the changes become exaggerated to the point where you are full of life one minute and the next you want to die, it may simply be your way to re-enact the life and death of your womb twin.

> *My twin brother was stillborn. I don't let many people into my private life and don't like to talk about it to anyone. No one understands how I can feel so attached to someone I never actually met but I feel him always. The fact that people dismiss my problems like this drives me insane. They have no idea how much it affects me. I have no self-esteem left and there's always something missing that I can never replace. I never feel at peace, barely rest and my mood swings are wild and erratic.*
> *[Barry, UK]*

If your despair becomes so deep that you try to commit suicide, then the people who care for you will send you for treatment, simply to keep you alive. Alternatively, your sense of aliveness may become so rich and intense that it develops into a reckless and hyperactive disregard for day or night, your requirement for sleep, your budget limits or even social norms. In that case, action must be taken by others for your own sake. They may insist, for your own safety and wellbeing, that you rest in a drugged sleep until the feeling passes. Either way, if that happens you will probably come to the attention of the medical professionals and be labelled as "mentally ill." It may be possible to avoid that label. If you have these symptoms and you know or genuinely believe you are a womb twin survivor, it is worth mentioning your lost twin next time you see your therapist.

### Borderline Personality Disorder

The symptom-set for Borderline Personality Disorder (BPD) consists of a particular cluster of nine characteristics. To be diagnosed as having BPD, you would have to display at least five of the nine. How many of these symptoms are to be seen your own character?

| Symptoms of Borderline Personality Disorder | Yes | No |
|---|---|---|
| Intense worries about abandonment and strong efforts to avoid it | | |
| Unpredictable, rocky relationships | | |
| Uncertainty about self identity | | |
| Reckless, risk-taking behaviour | | |
| Self-harming/self-destructive behaviour | | |
| Profound feelings of hollowness or emptiness | | |
| Highly volatile emotions | | |
| Short-term flights from reality | | |

*My mother had vaginal bleeding in her first few months of pregnancy. She also had extreme morning sickness. I have always felt that I don't belong and that something is strange and missing. It really bothers me when people don't like me for some reason. I can't accept it when people don't seem to like me. I was diagnosed with Borderline Personality Disorder at the age of 19 but the diagnosis changed to Bipolar then*

*to OCD (Obsessive-Compulsive Disorder) and also GAD (Generalised Anxiety Disorder) and ADD (Attention Deficit Disorder). I recently don't have a current diagnosis other than GAD and I accept that I have that and ADD. I feel that I don't deserve relationships with people when they are going well and I am constantly wondering what the person doesn't like about me, and that they just aren't telling me they are mad at me or dislike something about me.*
*[Sara, USA]*

Since 1980, various studies have concluded that Borderline Personality Disorder is to be found in about 6% of the population. The Womb Twin Survivors Research Project questionnaire survey results show that it is remarkably common among womb twin survivors. In the research questionnaire there were 77 statements, gathered from correspondence with many hundreds of womb twin survivors, about their psychological state. Twenty-four of these statements related directly to the nine symptoms of BPD, as described in the chart above. (The complete list of 77 statements can be found in Appendix 1.) Choosing only those respondents who had firm evidence of their twin - so there was no doubt that they were indeed womb twin survivors - an analysis was carried out to see to see how many symptoms each individual displayed. More than half showed the five out of nine symptoms necessary to be diagnosed with BPD and more than 10% displayed all nine. It seems there is certainly a connection between the list of nine symptoms of BPD and the psychological profile of the womb twin survivor.

*I had a twin brother die during my mom's pregnancy. I have had many circumstances through my life that have furthered my abandonment pain but the one before birth is by far the greatest and deepest. I also have been diagnosed with multiple illnesses, in my life that all correlate to the womb twin description. I have borderline personality disorder. I have been diagnosed with ADHD (Attention Deficit Hyperactivity Disorder), manic depression, panic disorder, major depression and others along the way. The most fitting is womb twin survivor/BPD. I have had a very hard time finding therapy through my life that helps. Now having been diagnosed with borderline, this has given the womb twin traits a more recognised label that I can work with.*
*[Annie, UK]*

In the absence of any other explanation for such a baffling, paradoxical and self-defeating set of psychological characteristics, it is small wonder that experts have grouped them as indicating a personality disorder. Once the diagnosis has been made, everyone feels better - except of course the individual concerned.

> *I was diagnosed with Borderline Personality Disorder after my husband left me. I went through a lot of counselling based on my diagnosis (BPD) and since my mother was a severe borderline, it was assumed that I inherited it from her. I was also diagnosed as manic/depressive during that time. I was so unable to cope that I didn't care what anyone labeled me.*
> *[Sandra, USA]*

# Young womb twin survivors

Parents whose children manifest such alarming symptoms as hallucinations, extreme sensitivity or withdrawal may be told that their child has a personality disorder. A favourite explanation by psychologists of how this disorder arises is that in some way the primary carers (parents or guardians) have failed to provide sufficient and appropriate care for the child. These unfortunate parents and guardians therefore have to take on the heavy weight of responsibility for the child's psychological state. In fact, the child was probably born that way. Everyone spends time in the womb and we are all influenced by what happened there. We are delivered ready-made at birth with our personality intact. Parents did not create and therefore cannot change the basic personality of their child, but they can be helped to work with it, hopefully to everyone's best advantage.

Only rarely do parents realise that some of their child's baffling psychological symptoms may be because of being a womb twin survivor, particularly if he or she is the only one in the family. If the child is terrified of being alone in the dark or talks constantly about wishing for a twin, it may seem very strange to parents who did not have a womb twin of their own. It would be very helpful if, as understanding of the psychological characteristics of womb twin survivors increases among professionals and others, the emphasis can shift at last from blaming the parents to healing the child. All that is needed is to provide parents with a clear and understandable explanation for how the child feels. If you are a young womb twin survivor and your parents do not understand how you feel, you may have to wait until the world becomes more aware of the issues at stake. If you are a parent of a womb twin survivor, then listen to your child, for there is much to learn.

> *My daughter is quick to understand, and obviously intelligent. Even as a small baby I remember her intense searching look, as though she were trying to communicate and I was too dense to get it. I wish I knew then what I know now.*
> *[Fran, Canada]*

It is now clear that the best way for parents to help their young womb twin survivors is to allow the lost twin to be a real person and part of the family. This will not foster a tendency to hallucinate or create delusions. Rather, it will provide a gradual process whereby the truth can be revealed and accepted: that the lost twin is no longer alive and physically present. There are some specialist resources and publications now available to facilitate this process with young children.[2]

> *After a tough start, losing his twin sister, at my son's last check-up we were told that has no deficits at all. I believe that his sister is with him all the time. Sometimes he will lie down on the floor and look at this one place on the ceiling and just talk to her. And this will last for about ten to twenty minutes. When this happens we are not a part of that world. We just lie down beside him and ask him to tell her that we love her and miss her. And she is celebrated on all occasions - she was and is a part of our lives. When he's done he is the happiest baby in the world. He just gets up like nothing happened.*
> *[Jan, USA]*

They may be born grieving, but young womb twin survivors can be given a special space to miss and mourn their twin in a healthy way. Gradually, as more and more parents help their children to go through the natural process of grieving for their twin while they are still very young, then perhaps some psychological problems, such as suicidal thoughts in children, may be reduced or even overcome altogether.

## Becoming sane

R.D. Laing (1927-1989) was a British psychiatrist who specialised in madness and was probably a womb twin survivor himself. He was convinced that somewhere behind insanity there is sanity. He wrote a book called *The*

*Divided Self*[3] which, when read with womb twin survivors in mind, seems to be redolent with images of the loss of a twin, and not simply in the title. Among other things, Laing writes, "The individual in the ordinary circumstances of living may feel more unreal than real; in a literal sense, more dead than alive." Many womb twin survivors share that feeling. A few years into his career, Laing began to study the origins of life in the womb. He got as far as seeing the placenta as "the twin," but he died in 1989, just as the wonders of ultrasound were beginning to reveal the astonishing number of twins that were lost in the early weeks of pregnancy. Had he been aware of this phenomenon, he may have found some of the answers he was seeking.

Until the people who set out to diagnose mental illness take into account the possibility of a lost womb twin, they will have missed an opportunity to discover the sanity that truly does lie behind some forms of seemingly insane behaviour. At various points in your life you may have been given a diagnosis about your own psychological state. No such diagnosis will help you to heal: only a full explanation will do that.

## The next step: Self-sabotage

The next step will consider self-sabotage and various other forms of self-destructive behaviour that are very common among womb twin survivors.

# 4

# Self-sabotaging behaviour

Womb twin survivors have a strong tendency towards self-sabotage and that probably includes you. This step will help you to see self-sabotage at work in your life and prepare you to make changes. The first step is to find out what your favourite forms of self sabotage may be. Self-sabotage can damage your life in three main ways: through your eating habits, how you use money and your attitude to your general wellbeing. Your self-sabotaging behaviour also has a negative effect on other people - even complete strangers.

The chart below offers a chance to learn more about your favourite ways to sabotage your life. To complete it, you can give yourself a score for how each type of behaviour impacts negatively on you and others. Your total score will give you an indication of where you are at the moment on your healing journey. For each activity, you can award yourself a mark out of five, with five being the greatest negative effect on your life and the life of others. When you have completed the chart, add up the individual scores to obtain a total. There is a blank space for other examples of your behaviour not already mentioned .

| Behaviour | Myself | Others |
|---|---|---|
| Eating habits | | |
| Over eating | | |
| Bulimia | | |

| | | |
|---|---|---|
| Binge eating | | |
| Anorexia | | |
| Other | | |
| **Using money** | | |
| Gambling | | |
| Over-spending | | |
| Excessive debt | | |
| Other | | |
| **Well-being** | | |
| Unhealthy lifestyle | | |
| Lack of bodily care | | |
| Other | | |
| **TOTAL SCORE** | | |

How did you do? Were there any surprises? Below is a space for you to record what seem to be your favourite forms of self-sabotage at the moment, and any further thoughts about that.

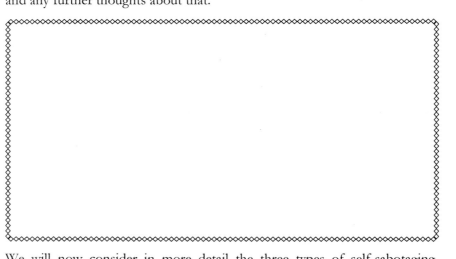

We will now consider in more detail the three types of self-sabotaging behaviour mentioned in the chart.

## Eating habits

We all eat differently. It seems that each individual requires an optimum amount of food and some of us need more than others. When food is scarce, some people quickly feel weak and ill while others manage quite well. We over-eat when the amount of food we consume exceeds the normal amount our own particular body may require in a specific situation. Some people have the kind of metabolism that allows them to eat a whole day's food in one meal, but others can't manage a lot at once and prefer several smaller meals. Some people can enjoy a big meal one day, but may not eat very much at all the day after. The trouble starts when eating big meals continues over a long period, regardless of hunger, personal metabolism or circumstances. To maintain a healthy life, feast times must be followed by a period of eating less, but some people turn their existence into one continuous feast and become dangerously obese. Some womb twin survivors eat quickly and constantly as a kind of protective mechanism against a lurking fear of running out of food. It seems that in their Dream of the Womb nourishment was in short supply. Somehow they managed to survive, but their twin weakened and died, unable to live on so little nourishment.

> *I had a lot of bleeding in my pregnancy with Eve. She was born with a node in the umbilical cord. She has had eating problems since she was a little child, always eating too much. I have to stop her - otherwise she would eat until she is sick. Nowadays she steals food and when she is caught, she cries a lot and says, "This feeling is stronger than myself."*
> *I feel there is a very deep sadness in her.*
> *[Dee, Belgium]*

### Binge eating

An eating binge is driven by an overwhelming impulse to stuff huge quantities of food into your mouth. Afterwards, it leaves you feeling ill and bitterly ashamed. Food is the friend that keeps you alive, but in a binge it is the enemy that seems to consume you, even as it is being consumed. A binge is like being caught up in some kind of perpetual present where there is a voiceless cry of pain and terror and things are going terribly wrong. In that strange moment, a prenatal memory has risen to the surface and driven all else aside. That is your Dream of the Womb.

## Bulimia

Some people want to conceal the fact that they binge at all, because they are so ashamed of themselves for doing it. To prevent weight gain after bingeing, a common practice is to get the food out of the body as fast as possible, by vomiting or taking laxatives to hurry it through the digestive system. Vomiting and purging can be extremely dangerous, leading to potentially fatal changes in the blood electrolytes. The result is weakness and malnourishment.

It is hard to be the well-nourished, strong survivor who inherited all the available placental blood supply after the death of a womb twin (or multiples). Bulimia expresses very well a prenatal story of inheriting a great feast in the womb and feeling terribly ashamed about eating it. It is a private, guilty feast, followed by a total rejection of all the food.

## Anorexia

Anorexia is self-starvation - a refusal to eat over long periods that causes drastic weight loss. It is widely supposed to be related to sexual anxiety and often starts in puberty.[1] Sexual anxiety is like a fear of growing up, and certainly the skeletal body of an anorexic individual bears little or no signs of sexual maturity. Anorexia is often described as a mental illness. However, from a womb twin survivor's point of view, it can be a way to re-enact the Dream of the Womb. In the Dream is the lost twin, who did not get enough nourishment to develop to full maturity. If you have begun to starve yourself and have become obsessed with any sign of weight gain, is it because you are trying to block your own development and fade away into a little wraith, just like your lost twin?

# Use of money

Some womb twin survivors use money as a means of self-sabotage. In the way you spend it, we may discover a pre-birth story of riches and poverty - of having everything you could ever need when your twin was with you and alive, but being left with nothing when he or she died. We will consider three kinds of financial self-sabotage in this section: - gambling, over-spending and excessive debt.

## Gambling

Gambling can be defined as an activity in which a person consciously risks

28

losing a certain amount of money in the hope of winning a larger amount back. It is a way to get something for nothing. If you win it will be at someone else's expense. If you lose, you lose everything. A visit to any gaming room makes it clear that the entire business is geared to making sure that the gamblers lose all their money almost every time. It is that "almost" that keeps hope alive. The gambler believes the next time it will all be different. But if you watch a gambler who has won a lot of money, he or she does not seem to be able to walk away with the winnings. Rather, the betting continues until everything is gone.

Gambling has a devastating effect on other people, particularly those who are financially dependent on the gambler. Consequently, the gambler is left ashamed, poor and at odds with others people. Persistent gamblers willingly throw away the chance for a happy life, but perhaps they are womb twin survivors. For them, riches may trigger a strong sense of survivor guilt, so they simply cannot allow themselves to be rich.

## Over-spending

If you are a womb twin survivor and your money is a burden to you, there are plenty of ways to get rid of it. You don't even have to buy anything - you can become a philanthropist and give it away to someone who has very little. That may seem healthy enough, but being over-generous is a form of self-sabotage. It is also common among womb twin survivors to spend too much on one item or buy lots of items that are not needed.

Money can mean safety and a secure future. When it is thrown away by over-spending, your future and your safety are put at risk. Why would you do that? Maybe it's because in your Dream there is no sense of a secure future. One way to keep that aspect of your Dream alive is to prejudice your own future by spending more money than you really have.

As soon as the wages come in, there is a brief sense of being rich. This is short-lived, for soon you have spent it all. Perhaps in your Dream there was an all-too-brief period when you had everything you ever wanted, but it went wrong and your twin died, leaving you with a sense of inner emptiness that no amount of purchases can fill, however hard you try.

## Excessive debt

Those who borrow more than they can pay back end up losing everything if the debt is called in. To borrow money to appear rich is to put yourself at risk of being made poor overnight. Excessive debt is the shortest route to poverty. Some people with enormous debts insist on remaining poor, adamantly refusing or subtly sabotaging all offers of help. It would seem that they are womb twin survivors. If so, they are not being stupid or inadequate. They are deeply bonded to their twin, who was once there in the closest possible human relationship, but was denied the gift of life. If you are a womb twin survivor and you make sure that you have insufficient resources to live out a full life, that probably seems to be a kind of rough justice, motivated by survivor guilt.

# Wellbeing

There are many ways in which you can sabotage your own wellbeing, but in this section we will consider just two: an unhealthy diet and not caring for your body.

## Unhealthy diet

As we have seen, food is an important aspect of life for womb twin survivors. However, if you eat symbolically to keep your Dream of the Womb alive, that will create health problems. Used appropriately, food can replenish your worn-out tissues, give you energy for life and provide bulk to keep your digestive tract healthy. Used inappropriately, food can give you health problems, including digestive difficulties, various skin ailments and stiffness of the joints. If you have been persistently eating an unhealthy diet until now, you will have already caused subtle changes in your body, as a result of which your health may have begun to fail. A healthy diet is hard to define, because people vary so much in what they need to eat and how healthy they are. Even so, if you know you have not been eating the best diet for your individual bodily needs, then an important part of your healing journey might be to find the right diet for you and stick with it. Health education programmes try to teach people the importance of a healthy diet and regular exercise, but the very idea is often met with resistance. Much of that resistance probably comes from the womb twin survivors in the population.

You may have already discovered how adopting a healthy diet and taking exercise can increase your available energy and reduce your medical problems. Nonetheless, after every attempt, you return to your old, unhealthy habits and you probably wonder why you always do that to yourself. As a womb twin survivor, you have a secret agenda: you must remain unhealthy in order to keep your Dream alive. In your Dream there is something about just managing to survive despite a poor food supply. This is probably a lost memory of your twin, who for some reason was not getting enough good nutrition to grow strong and healthy. He or she gradually weakened and eventually died. To follow a persistently unhealthy diet is a perfect mirror to that womb story. At first sight, stubbornly ignoring eating advice may look like self-sabotage, but it could also be interpreted as a loving act of self-sacrifice on behalf of your twin.

## Food allergy, food intolerance

About 2% of the adult population suffer from what are called food-induced allergic disorders. A very limited number of foods are responsible for these: peanuts, tree nuts, fish and shellfish.[2] The symptoms of food allergy are immediate, alarming and sometimes life-threatening. However, there are certain other very common foods to which some people have more-subtle bodily reactions that may include abdominal pain, bloating, dyspepsia or listlessness.[3] This is known as food intolerance. Some womb twin survivors, despite the fact that they know they are intolerant to given foods, continue to eat them nonetheless, deliberately perpetuating the effects.

> *My food problem is binge eating of all the foods I'm allergic to. I have always had food intolerances. I eat for comfort. I really wish to stick to my healthy diet, and when I do I am very strong about it. I take great satisfaction in not eating bad food. But then after weeks or months I binge eat and can't stop until I've had enough or I feel ill again. As I get older, the desire to stick to a healthy diet has worn off.*
> *[Ira, USA]*

If you are intolerant to some foods, you may have tried for years to work out what the problem truly is. The symptoms of food intolerance tend to vary, according to the state of your immune system. It can take a great deal of experimentation to find the right diet, but the results will be more energy and increased clarity of thought. The foods you have been bingeing on may be the very ones your body cannot cope with.

> *I have been gradually acquiring environmental sensitivities and allergies over the past 10 or 15 years. When I eat right, exercise and take care to build my immune system, I am not as troubled by them. When I am caught in a cycle of low self-esteem, I am more sensitive to soaps, perfumes, cleaners, pdust-mites etc. My emotional roller-coaster is hampering my ability to stay on a healthy eating and exercise plan.*
> *[May, USA]*

## Not looking after your body

If you feel unwell and have no energy, you will expend little or no effort on bodily care. Here is a chance to carry out a self-assessment. For each of the aspects of bodily care listed below, give yourself a mark out of five, with five being the highest level of self-care.

| Care of the body | 5 | 2 | 3 | 4 | 1 |
|---|---|---|---|---|---|
| Cleaning your body | | | | | |
| Washing your face and hands | | | | | |
| Bathing or showering | | | | | |
| Using the toilet | | | | | |
| Wearing clean clothes | | | | | |
| Appropriate clothes for the conditions | | | | | |
| Cleaning nails | | | | | |
| Cleaning hair | | | | | |
| Brushing/combing hair | | | | | |
| Cutting hair | | | | | |
| Skin care | | | | | |
| Prevention of foot/shoe fungus | | | | | |
| Appropriate shoes for the situation | | | | | |
| Brushing your teeth | | | | | |
| Visiting dentist | | | | | |
| Other | | | | | |

If you have scored less than two on any of the above, it may be because you actively hate your body. There are many ways to abuse it and neglect is one of them.

# The next step: Is addiction a choice?

The next step will address a controversial question: are addictions and compulsions matters of choice? Having now completed this fourth step towards healing, you may already know the answer.

# 5
# A matter of choice?

Self-sabotaging behaviour can become excessive. Then we may call it an "addiction" or a "compulsion." As you continue on your healing journey, it is time to consider what addictions or compulsions might be at work in your life. We have been told for too long that addiction is a "disease" [1] and that compulsions are due to some kind of "mental illness." We are about to discover that, for womb twin survivors at least, both are matters of choice, for they keep the Dream alive.

## Addiction

The idea that addiction is a choice has been widely debated. A book entitled *Addiction is a Choice*, published in 1999, begins with this sentence: "Today, just about everyone believes, or says they believe, that addicts - including regular smokers, heavy drinkers, frequent gamblers, presidents who seduce interns and people who run up credit card debts - can't help themselves." [2]

If addictions and compulsions are due to some disease, then surely addicts cannot control their behaviour. But we know, from countless cases of life-long recovery from addiction, that addicts can decide to gain control over their habits. The debate therefore should be not about whether addicts ever choose to become addicted, but exactly why they would choose to harm themselves in particular ways. Clearly, you selected your own particular addiction or compulsion according to your psychological and spiritual needs. No one forced you into it or made you carry on with it once you started. In other words, that "prison" of addiction or compulsion, in which you probably feel you must spend your life, is locked on the inside. The key is still in your hand. The womb twin work will show you how you could open the door to your healing - or not, as you wish.

### What is addiction?

If you are addicted, then your addiction to a particular substance, which we will call your favourite "fix," is related to feelings of helplessness and powerlessness.[3] You hold on to it to the neglect of everything else; build up tolerance to it over time; use it as a way to change your mood and get withdrawal symptoms if you stop. If you have ever been addicted to anything, you will probably be aware that there is a gradual progression into a darker and darker place, until death is near. It goes like this:

1. You try to control your use of your favourite fix, possibly with some therapeutic help or group support.

2. You manage to recover for a while by limiting the use of your fix.[4]

3. After a while, in some subtle way, you relapse.

4. You go on taking the fix in increasing amounts, knowing very well that an excessive intake of your chosen substance will harm your health, wealth or relationships.

5. You may overdose on your favourite fix. (Depending on which fix you choose, you are more or less in danger of death if you overdose.)

### The addiction danger spectrum

We will now describe addiction to a spectrum of favourite fixes in terms of how dangerous they are. The issue is, how likely is it that an individual will die if overdosing on each? The chart on the next page shows that illegal drugs are the most dangerous addiction and food is the least harmful. Your drug of choice may be legal (such as caffeine) or licensed (such as tobacco, prescription drugs or alcohol.)

**THE ADDICTION DANGER SPECTRUM**

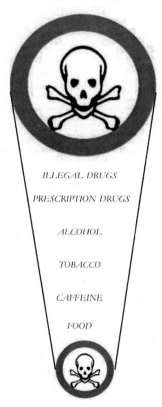

ILLEGAL DRUGS

PRESCRIPTION DRUGS

ALCOHOL

TOBACCO

CAFFEINE

FOOD

## Addiction to food

The very idea of food addiction has been controversial for decades. Abstinence is the usual remedy for addiction, but we all need to eat to survive. However, it seems that certain food ingredients are of their very nature addictive and that they can easily become the focus of binge eating. Among them are wheat, sugar, cow's milk and potato.[5] The reasons for this specific addictive effect are not clear and more research is needed.[6]

So what are your favourite "food fixes"? Try this checklist :

| Addiction to food | Yes |
|---|---|
| Food of all kinds | |
| Sugar (and sweet drinks) | |

| Milk and milk products | |
|---|---|
| Eggs | |
| Chocolate | |
| Wheat | |
| Corn | |
| Other | |

The most prevalent effect of addiction to food is obesity, which is generally associated with greed and a weak will. Massive weight gain obviously arises from bingeing and bad food choices, but this may not be greed. Obesity is the result of an addiction to food, so let it be treated with kindness, not with condemnation.

In her 2007 report on the subject, Julianna Kennedy wrote with considerable feeling: "I have a problem with food, I admit it - that doesn't mean I'm a 'glutton', it means I have a genuine problem just like an alcoholic does, but for anyone with a food addiction, life is much tougher. The fact of the matter is we, the morbidly obese, are hurting........Little is being done to help us, and we are living in misery until we die, after a brief life, barely lived."[7] That "brief life, barely lived" could be considered as a reflection of your womb twin's brief life. If you are morbidly obese, perhaps you are simply keeping your Dream alive, even as you are digging your grave with your teeth.

## Addiction to drugs

The drug you choose says a lot about you. For instance, a 1977 study of heroin and amphetamine users showed that their drug of choice was related to their psychological make-up. The amphetamine user coped with his difficulties with an inflated sense of self-worth and active confrontation with his environment. Meanwhile, the heroin user was consciously depressed and despairing and withdrew from an environment perceived as hostile and threatening.[8]

On the next page is a checklist of commonly used drugs, both legal and illegal. You may like to tick the ones that apply to you, if any.

| Drugs checklist | Yes |
|---|---|
| Hard drugs (heroin, cocaine etc.) | |
| Soft drugs (cannabis, etc.) | |
| Tobacco | |
| Alcohol | |
| Performance-enhancing drugs | |
| Body-building steroids | |
| Prescription drugs | |
| Slimming pills | |
| Pain killers | |
| Caffeine | |
| Sleeping pills | |
| Other | |

The commonest addiction of all seems to be caffeine, which is be found in tea, coffee and some soft drinks.

> *Eating is definitely a way to calm my system, to fill up the hollow feeling that is inside. I want to eat healthy food, but sometimes it just seems unbearable. When I want to do without coffee and wine I can manage for a few days and then the first cups of coffee begin to creep in again. In the "bad" times I start my day with coffee, no healthy foods, and end it with a few glasses of wine. Skipping both coffee and wine seems to be too difficult, so I do take coffee in the morning and no wine at all.*
> *[Jon, UK]*

Therapists who work with drug addicts often feel as if they are keeping their patients alive against their will, for deep down drug addiction is a matter of life and death. If you are, or ever have been, a drug addict, you may be familiar with a feeling of death being near. Death probably holds few fears for you, for it would heal your pain.

Out of all the addictions we have discussed, which three are the most important to you today? Overleaf is a chance for you to state them openly.

| My three strongest addictions are: |
|---|
| **1.** |
| **2.** |
| **3.** |

## Cross-addiction

Addicts in treatment who appear to make progress may be transferring their addiction to a type of fix that is lower on the addiction danger spectrum.[9] People who want to give up "hard" drugs may switch to "soft" ones such as cannabis. Illegal drug users may turn to prescription drugs in their search for a cure and so the addiction tendency remains. An alcoholic may stay dry by smoking more cigarettes instead. Eating sweet foods can help a smoker to give up, but this is another addiction yet to be conquered.

Clearly, addiction has nothing whatever to do with the type of fix, but rather it is the drive behind the need for a fix. It is known that addicts are trying to fill a sense of inner emptiness. Addiction is aa spiritual quest for wholeness. The addict is driven by a sense of emptiness, a void that demands satisfaction. [10]

Womb twin survivors can easily identify with that sense of lack, for it is the psychological gap left by the death of their womb twin. The desire to be whole and complete is probably so deeply engrained that it seems to be beyond your own power to control it. But what if this desire to be filled and whole is to compensate for the loss of your twin before birth?

## Giving up

How motivated are you to end your addictive behaviour? On the next page is a space for you to record how you feel today about the possibility of giving up your favourite fix. It may be interesting to read later, when you are further along the path to healing.

## Compulsive behaviour

Compulsions may not kill you, but they will rob you and those you love of a healthy and fulfilling life. A compulsion feels as if one is being taken over by some external force. It is urgent and impulsive; all other considerations are forgotten in that moment of overwhelming desire. It is well-known in psychology that traumatised people can feel a compulsion to repeat the trauma, either as the victim or the perpetrator. Some compulsive behaviour in womb twin survivors is probably driven by a trauma that took place early in life, long before memories could be properly formed.[11] If knowledge of the original prenatal trauma is not available, the compulsive behaviour may be diagnosed as Obsessive-Compulsive Disorder (OCD). If the traumatic event that is being endlessly recycled in your life is the pre-birth loss of your twin, then some of your compulsive behaviours make perfect sense. Womb twin survivors can remain "stuck" in the feelings related to their original experience and feel compelled to engage in some action that tells the original story. A study of your personal compulsions can take you straight back to the womb, so we will examine two kinds of compulsive behaviour in depth: the willing mutilation of your body and the accumulation of stuff in your home.

### Willing mutilation of your own body

Willingly mutilating your own body by some kind of self-harm is an almost perfect metaphor for the pain of prenatal loss, which is beyond words, so only actions can express it. Self-mutilation creates wounds and scars that take a long time to heal, for they are opened again and again. In a similar way, your primal wound will never heal until it is fully understood. Then it can be allowed to heal.

*Since about 13, when I went through puberty, I started attacking my face, picking at the skin and wanting to destroy my face. Perhaps I was trying to avoid having to look at myself and to be reminded on the most subtle, subliminal level, all those years, of my twin who didn't make it. Who knows, but it has helped with the self-destruction, which I've always carried out and am only now coming to grips with, in terms of kicking the habit of it. I am an attractive woman and know I have caused many loved ones much grief too, as they have for years tried to understand why I would want to destroy my face.*
*[Elise, Australia]*

Another form of self-harm is to willingly let other people inflict damage on your body. For instance, tattooing may seem innocuous, but it leaves a coloured scar that lasts a lifetime. Cosmetic surgery may be normal and necessary to correct some birth defect such as a harelip, but if you go back again and again for more surgery your body will be permanently damaged.

Here is a short checklist of some forms of compulsive self-mutilation. You may like to tick any of these that apply to you.

| Self-mutilation | Yes |
|---|---|
| Cosmetic surgery | |
| Tattooing | |
| Hair pulling | |
| Skin picking | |
| Constantly picking at scars | |
| Self harm by wounding, burning etc. | |
| Other | |

### Accumulating stuff

The Womb Twin Survivors Research Project has revealed that collecting large amounts of stuff is a common characteristic of womb twin survivors.[12]. If your home is cluttered with unfinished projects, unwanted pets you may rescue or unnecessary items that you constantly bring home, it is as if you are anxiously preparing for some disaster, such as a famine.

Hoarding and clutter could describe very well the story of the loss of a womb twin. Many womb twin survivors do not hoard at all, but then not all womb stories are the same, for womb twins die under a wide variety of circumstances. Perhaps the story is there to be seen amid all the muddle and mess, if we were able to read it. Perhaps hoarding is about having no space. If you clutter your home, the space gradually diminishes as time passes. In extreme cases there is eventually hardly any space at all and normal life becomes impossible. Perhaps in your Dream of the Womb your little womb twin is shrinking in relative size as you grow, until you fill up all the space and your womb twin is squashed into a corner and dies as a result. In your clutter is your womb twin's life story, played out in your own home.

## What are your compulsions?

Here are three checklists of some common activities, according to where they take place. You may find a few that you carry out to excess.

| Activities outside the home taken to excess | Yes |
|---|---|
| Working out in the gym | |
| Walking long distances | |
| Jogging | |
| Running | |
| Sports | |
| Work | |
| Over-commitment | |
| Religious practices | |

| Excessive household activities | Yes |
|---|---|
| Cleaning | |
| Cooking | |
| Remodelling the home | |
| Redecorating the home | |
| Moving house | |
| Checking locks | |

| | |
|---|---|
| Washing | |
| Throwing things away | |
| Hoarding | |
| Clutter | |

| Excessive leisure activities | Yes |
|---|---|
| Gambling | |
| Computer/video games | |
| Internet use | |
| Researching your family history | |
| Eating snacks | |
| Watching TV | |
| Shopping | |
| Sport | |

Having carried out these checks, you may have a clearer idea of your compulsions. It may help you to record the situation today, using the chart over leaf. Then you can compare notes later on, when you have moved on a little further along the healing path.

| My three strongest compulsions are: |
|---|
| 1. |
| 2. |
| 3. |

## Choices

It is vitally important, as we now prepare for the next step on the healing path, that you take responsibility for all your choices so far. Throughout your life you have been choosing to re-enact your Dream of the Womb. No one has forced you into it. No one has made you behave in the way you do, for your life path has been made out of countless personal decisions.

More often than not, self-defeating choices involve inaction rather than aon, which means staying the same rather than making a change. To choose not to act is a definite decision - you have to choose if you will make a decision or not. If you remain indecisive, then that is how you have chosen to be. There are many reasons why you have spent so much of your life in a metaphorical prison, but it has always been your choice. There is no escape from your personal responsibility for how you have elected to live your life so far. There are no excuses. In the meantime, as the pathway to healing opens up before you, never forget that all the choices are there, all the time. Then at last, using personal responsibility as the key, you will be able to set yourself free.

# Your womb story

We are now at the end of the first stage of the healing path. As we prepare to move on to the second stage, here is a chance to review the last five steps and begin to write the story of your life before birth - at least how it appears to you at the moment. Nothing can be sure or certain, because most of your ideas will be based on guesses arising out of your body memory and your intuition, neither of which can be relied upon totally. However, it may be useful to look back on it occasionally.

| My womb story | |
|---|---|
| **Type of twinning (One-egg, two-egg, multiple)** | |

**Signs or indications of twinning**

**Age of twin at death**

**Why your twin died**

# STAGE TWO
## Living the Dream

You are the one I need
The one that I don't know;
You are the one I look for
But I don't know where to go -

You are the one I know,
The root of my belief.
You are the cause of all my pain,
The anger and the grief.

The other half of me;
The face beneath the mask;
The reason for my living,
The questions I must ask.

I hope one day to know you -
Oh that would be so sweet!
When life is gone you will be there,
On that day we will meet.

# 6
# Self-isolation

In this second stage of the healing path we will examine the various ways in which you are living out your Dream of the Womb. This step will focus on self-isolation as a manifestation of your Dream. It is important to remember that things are not what they may seem: the Dream is not happening now, but is a memory of past events. The difficult feelings you may be experiencing are being generated within you, moment by moment, to keep the Dream alive. In fact, your attempts to live out your Dream of the Womb are based entirely on a set of foetal assumptions, which developed in your mind at a very early stage of your existence. They have about them a feeling of absolute reality, but they are only assumptions. Nonetheless, you have adopted them as a set of core beliefs by which you judge yourself and the world. It is time to question these beliefs and find the truth of how things really are.

This healing step will take a closer look at the foetal assumption we might express as: *I am alone.* Some womb twin survivors feel this way because they have isolated themselves from others. Overleaf there is a checklist of various ways to feel alone. See how many apply to you.

| Isolation | Yes |
|---|---|
| I find it hard to maintain a relationship for very long | |
| I sabotage my close relationships | |
| I feel invisible, unseen | |
| I feel different from other people | |

| | |
|---|---|
| Other people are not interested in knowing me | |
| I am very shy | |
| I don't go home to my birth family very often | |
| I fear rejection | |
| I don't want to be married | |
| I don't want to have children | |
| I have lots of friends but still feel alone | |
| I hate being alone | |
| I am a very private person | |
| I prefer to work in a partnership, not on my own | |
| I feel abandoned | |
| For me, loneliness and grief go together | |
| I always feel on the edge of every group | |
| I feel a sense of painful loneliness all the time | |
| I don't allow other people to get close to me | |
| I make a great effort to protect my privacy | |
| I put on a show and don't let other people see the real me | |
| I felt home a long time ago and have never returned | |
| Other: | |

We will now discuss some of these separately, as they apparently relate to very different prenatal experiences.

## Forms of self isolation

### Feeling abandoned

Feeling abandoned seems to be linked to a sense of being deserted by your twin who was once there, but went away. Someone who was present alongside you is now absent. You are left forsaken and alone. When you were a tiny foetus and you knew no better, you assumed this was The Way Things Are - an assumption that is now ever-present. This feeling is evidently most common among the sole survivors of a two-egg twin pair.[1]

> *I have a daughter who I think is probably suffering from the loss of her twin. I don't have any concrete evidence for this, only an intuitive sense. She suffers horribly and for no reason with feelings of inadequacy, self-criticism and loneliness. She also describes feelings of "not really being here," or disassociated from the world around her. She says she often feels like she is invisible. She has trouble relating to other people. She often makes friends and truly bonds with someone, only to discover the person is about to leave and move to another country or city. This has been happening since she was quite young. Now she is a beautiful young woman but she tells me she feels ugly, not good enough and the deep loneliness persists no matter how outwardly successful her life is.*
> *[Mary, Ireland]*

Perhaps your womb twin survived long enough to begin to respond, so that some kind of silent rapport started to build up between you. In that case, when your womb twin died and left you alone you experienced the event with a deep sense of grief. For the womb twin survivor, loneliness and grief always go together.

## An orphan

Some womb twin survivors feel like orphans, abandoned and un-wanted. Unfortunately, they may attribute this feeling to their relationship with their parents and family.

> *I was told at about eight or nine years old that my mum had miscarried my twin. This news was at the time devastating, yet somehow a relief. I always felt different, like something was always missing or I did not belong to them or perhaps they did not want me! The loneliness I have forever felt - always looking for that other person, yet somehow knowing that they are there but just out of reach.*
> *[Fran, Ireland]*

If you had such a difficult relationship with your parents that you had to abandon the family home and move away, that may be a reflection of your own prenatal sense of abandonment. Possibly your decision had nothing to do with your parents at all. In that case, part of your healing journey may be to take another look at why you find it so hard to be at home with your family. Leaving them feeling forsaken and missing you every day would be a way to silently communicate to them what it is like being you.

## Separate

If within days of conception you were half of a one-egg twin pair then you have been "hard-wired" for that very intimate relationship. Being by yourself is therefore against your deepest nature. Your core belief is that The Way Things Are is to have *a constant companion*. For you, life is supposed to be lived as half of a pair, not alone.

> *I can't say for sure if I was a twin or not but I've always felt alone, like my best friend is missing. I feel as though none of my friends know me or care to know me. I always want to be closer to them than they do to me. This has led me to distance myself from most people.*
> *[Summer, USA]*

The sole survivors of a one-egg twin pair do seem to feel more isolated than those of a two-egg twin pair. A member of the Lone Twin Network in the UK [2] made this clear. She wrote, "Someone asked me if I thought that being an identical twin had made a difference. All the other people in my group were non-identical twins. I have come away from the meetings with the impression that being an identical twin does seem to have increased my feelings of isolation." [3]

> *I was born with a teratoma tumor - a supposed dead twin limb or something like that. My mom says that it can't be possible for me to have had a twin in the process of my birth since after two weeks of me being conceived, that extra fetus disappeared. Apparently, the symptoms include a continuous feeling of loss, unexplained isolation and depression: symptoms I've come to experience.*
> *[Brenda, USA]*

## Feeling different

Feeling separate because you are different from other people is a painful, lonely feeling for some womb twin survivors. Others, of course, have no problem with difference, celebrating their individuality and rejoicing in variety. It seems that the brains of one-egg womb twin survivors are built around the idea of Someone Else who is almost exactly the same, so they have a problem with difference.

If you are a one-egg womb twin survivor, then you probably become very excited by the idea of being with other people who are of the same mind, who share interests with you or have the same opinions. This constant desire to be with someone similar to yourself is like a search for your twin - your lost half. One-egg twins are often called "identical" but in fact they not exactly alike. They are not genetically the same to begin with and tend to become less identical as times passes.[4] In fact, one-egg womb twin siblings are so different in their ability to survive that one may not make it through the whole pregnancy. If you are a one-egg womb twin survivor, then you were so very different from your womb twin - your other half - that you survived. If this is your story, then difference is probably a paradoxical idea for you. On one hand, you have a great need to find someone similar to yourself. On the other, in your Dream it was by being different that you survived. If you and your twin had been equally strong, then you would still be together. The very idea of the difference between you therefore, is associated with danger and death.

## Feeling set apart

If you have a problem with being different, you will nevertheless find some way to set yourself apart. For instance, if you insist on your friends being similar to yourself, you will not tolerate any differences that do exist between you and them very well. As a result, you may stand aside to such an extent that you won't join in any collaborative activity. You therefore work alone and play alone, become an outsider and make yourself, "different" in that way. Meanwhile, your friends will have a clear idea of the pain you feel about being different, for they will find it hard to reach you. Your self-isolation will have created an unbridgeable gulf, as painful for others as it is for you.

> *My mother told me at a young age, that I had been a twin. I thought of what it would be like to have known my twin and longed for a close relationship like what I had imagined. I found it difficult to have an intimate friend and felt very alone as a child even before having this knowledge. Around age nine or ten I became quite depressed and serious by nature. I felt very alone and my family did not understand me. I could not talk to my parents as they didn't know how to handle me, so they put me into counselling which did not help. I still struggle with loneliness, searching for direction, and often feel misunderstood. [Charlene, UK]*

## Fitting in

Alternatively, you may work very hard to overcome any differences, in order to remain friends with people. To succeed in this, you will have to become a forever-smiling, always-friendly enigma, sacrificing your own individuality for the sake of the friendship. This is how your very desire to fit in could become the problem. There would not be enough of the real, authentic You available for others to form the kind of deep relationship you crave.

## Fear of rejection

A fear of rejection is common among womb twin survivors. It is based on the foetal assumption that other people, having been friendly at first, will eventually turn away and lose interest. An expectation of closeness and friendliness is set up at the beginning, only to be disappointed as the other person stops responding. The end result is a sense of betrayal. This reflects exactly the story of a womb twin who begins life by being responsive, but who then ceases. The sole survivor's core belief is therefore: *Other people may be friendly now, but they will stop responding to me.* If this applies in your case, you may voluntarily withdraw from intimacy as a pre-emptive measure.

The choice of avoiding getting close to other people is common enough to have been noticed by psychologists, and there is now a diagnosis of Avoidant Personality Disorder (APD).[5] People with this condition include those who form good relationships, but suddenly leave them with little or no warning, devastating the partners, friends or family members concerned. Sufferers from APD are very sensitive to signs of potential rejection by others and this may be the story of your life. You may have a tendency to assume that other people are constantly judging you and finding you wanting. To be worthy only of such treatment is to be considered inferior and valueless, you convince yourself.

In the womb long ago, was this truly a rejection? If your twin stopped responding, it was not because of anything you did. Your twin was dying and after a brief life was no longer capable of a response. Sadly, those who are struggling to understand human psychology have not all been told about womb twin survivors. This is why the fear of rejection that leads one to reject others is generally misunderstood.

## Being invisible

An extreme example of withdrawal into self-isolation is to assume you are invisible, as if you have somehow ceased to exist. As your twin vanished from your life in the womb, so you "vanish" from the lives of others in your born life. If the mirror to your soul was a non-responsive twin who barely existed, then that is your chosen identity. If this is how you isolate yourself, you carry a basic assumption that you are *unseen* and *unheard.*

*I am usually quite amazed when people do listen to anything I say.
I guess the fact that it is so rare might mean that I've always been
accustomed to not being seen or heard. I have a very difficult time
claiming personal space when others are present - it seems that I've only
been able to have personal space ie., space of my own.*
*[Helena, UK]*

You can only be reassured that you do exist if someone else acknowledges you
are there. It is as if when you speak you need an echo. That womb experience
of being totally ignored has probably left you with an excessive hunger for
feedback from other people. Sadly, however, your acute desire for attention -
to be reassured that you are seen and heard - can act as a block to friendship,
for there is not enough space for a reciprocal relationship to develop. Your
craving for reassurance carries the risk that it will be experienced as selfishness
by the other person, who will probably reject you as a result.

## Healing loneliness

The sense of being alone that underpins the way you relate to people has little
to do with what is happening now. By now you will have understood that
your isolation has been self-inflicted. It is not true that everyone wants to
hurt you by abandoning or rejecting you. It is not true that you have to spend
the rest of your life alone. These ideas are based in a foetal misunderstanding,
created long ago. Your twin didn't reject or abandon you, he or she simply
died. As long as the memory of your twin remains within you, you can never
be truly alone.

### A letter to your twin

Let's imagine that you could send a letter to your twin. You could describe
your sense of loneliness, rejection and abandonment. Then, when the letter
is finished, you could write what you imagine would be the reply, if your twin
had lived.

### Making a reconnection

If you are to awaken from your Dream and find friends, then you will have
to move gradually towards other people. You could create for yourself a set
of diagrams according to your womb story.

**SET ONE: YOUR WOMB STORY**

*TWIN CONNECTION*

*RELATIONSHIP BROKEN BY DEATH*

*ALONE WITH MEMORIES*

**SET TWO: BEING ALONE**

*SEPARATED*

*ABANDONED*

**SET THREE: RECONNECTION**

*ALONE*

*DARING TO REACH OUT*

*MAKING CONNECTIONS*

Healing would mean allowing relationships to continue and deepen as time passes. It would mean changing your core beliefs, by awakening from the Dream and becoming aware that the world is full of other people who also need friends.

# The next step: Healing duality

As a womb twin survivor, you were not meant to be alone. One way to counter feelings of loneliness is to become two people in one. The next step will review how womb twin survivors develop a dual personality.

# 7
# Duality

In the beginning, it seems, we are alone. Floating in the amniotic fluid, surely babies know no other human person until they emerge into the light? Womb twin survivors have a different story - they know they are not alone. From the very start, there is that sense of two-ness. As we walk the healing path together, you will find that a sense of wholeness can only be discovered in relation to another living being much like yourself. In other words, the painful sense of isolation we discussed in the previous chapter will only be healed when your original sense of two-ness is restored.

> *My mother miscarried my twin and always I feel him around me. Twins are quite different from normal siblings. I have twin daughters that are three years old and each can't sleep without the other or basically function right until her sister is right by her side. They know when the other one is in pain - and even more so, they know when the other one needs her sister. It's scary to think that even when one twin is dead the one that survives still feels and knows when the other one is around. [Marta, USA]*

## The two-ness of things

It would seem that the world is designed around two-ness. In your life as a womb twin survivor, two-ness underpins everything. As we have seen, the search for your "other half" is driven by a sense of painful aloneness, which can only be healed by the presence of your shadowy lost twin. Your awareness of "being part of a pair" lies too deep for memory and can only be acted out in vague generalisations, but if we know where to look, we can find duality everywhere.

## Two the same

Womb twin survivors love to be one of a pair or a trio. They love being in a group, but best of all they love two-ness. As children they may show a preoccupation with twins, or often point out "two things the same." Later they may discover a great fondness for symmetry or balance. They may seek out opposite extremes to complete their lives, or they may want to have two the same of anything they like. Womb twin survivors love to find "soulmates." They are often deeply attracted to someone born on the same day or with the same name. This is how they recreate the original twin pair.

> *My mother always told me when I was young that I was supposed to have had a twin. Simple decisions take me forever. Picking out a shirt, I narrow it down to two or three, then it takes me forever comparing them. I buy one, and later on I think I should have gotten the other one. This is my dilemma for buying pretty much anything. If I really like something I want two. I don't know why, I have always been this way. If things aren't symmetrical it drives me nuts. I try to keep everything symmetrical, which is probably why I crave two of everything.*
> *[Chrissie, USA]*

We live in a world that celebrates The Individual. The Cult of the Self informs us that we will be happy only if we are free to express our individual desires, untrammelled by the needs and wishes of the rest of society. We are encouraged to know that we are "worth it" and we must think only of our development as individuals. It seems that we are being encouraged to separate ourselves from one another. There is another view, however. People who don't need people may willingly subscribe to the Cult of the Self, but womb twin survivors seek two-ness wherever it can be found. Their loneliness is rooted in a sense of half-ness, so they do not thrive in today's individualistic society.

## Being two people

Some womb twin survivors know how to be two people. They change their minds often and their style of dress even more frequently. They have a great many ways of altering their appearance, mainly with clothing, hairstyle and even makeup. As young children they may be very noisy and extrovert at school, but quiet and reserved at home - or the other way about. As teenagers they may be silent and withdrawn at home and the life and soul of the party when out with their friends. As adults, they may drive two very different cars or own two very different homes. They may have two different interests, such as motorcycling and nuclear physics, and as a result have two completely different and opposite sets of friends, who are of course carefully kept separate.

## Bodily signs of two-ness

When a zygote (fertilised egg) splits into two one-egg twins after the amniotic sac and placenta have formed, the split can go slightly awry and one twin may never develop. Occasionally, for reasons that are little understood, some of the organs are doubled in the body of the survivor. The most common forms of double organs are the uterus, kidneys, fingers and toes. In such cases, there is usually no other sign of the lost twin on the placenta or within the single amniotic sac.

> *I do believe I am a womb twin survivor. I only found this information after being diagnosed with having a duplex kidney. The doctor said that it occurs more frequently than you think and most people who have it, don't even know they have it. I have had a lifelong need to be searching for my soul mate, whom I can only describe as being alike to myself. I have been battling depression and loss for as long as I can remember. I am an artist and reflecting on my past works, I have been close to obsessed with mirror images, myself, reproduction, two sides to a soul and deep loneliness. I feel that the duplex kidney is proof that my twin's soul exists inside of me. When I asked my mother if she thought I was crazy to suggest that I am two people, she replied simply that she always knew I was two people.*
> *[Kim, USA]*

Some womb twin survivors gain a lot of weight and change shape entirely as a result, only to lose it again and "become a thin person." This may be repeated on several occasions during a person's life, with some people gaining and losing half their body weight each time. As a result some womb twin survivors have a fat self and a thin self, each with a complete set of clothing.

## Inner contradiction

Although womb twin survivors love sameness, they are essentially paradoxical people, full of contradictions. The inner inconsistency that is so much a part of their character can be a puzzle to parents or partners. Inner contradiction is treated as a kind of alternative reality, which feels more authentic than any other way of being. In trying to live out that contradiction, womb twin survivors can feel that they have lost their identity. To find out who they are, they seek out a way to be true to themselves, and it seems that the way to live out their own version of reality is to be two people at once.

> *My mother told me that I was twins while she was pregnant with me. What I wonder now is this. Did I absorb this person? Am I some rare case that is actually two people inside? Sometimes, I could swear that I am. I almost feel as though I definitely have a twin, question is, where did she go? I always wondered about the two sides of my head and face being pretty different - almost as if you could draw a straight line down the center and each side is a different person.*
> *[Rachel, USA]*

If your personality is full of contradictions, one way to maintain a sense of personal integrity might be to tell yourself you are always pretending to be someone; that you are in fact a sham. In other words, if you act as if you are strong and confident, you can believe inwardly that you are only pretending to be confident. Hidden somewhere inside you is the terrified little person whom you are carefully concealing behind your mask. But which one are you really - the confident sham or the shy person hiding behind the mask? If the shy person is your little twin, then clearly the confident person is you.

> *I do have a feeling though of being more than one and sometimes I wonder that in order to accommodate this sense of being more than one my mind has created this sense of "otherness" that exists within me. Instead of experiencing various emotions as being mine, it feels more like I am merely the messenger relaying what is taking place within because I don't feel connected to them as being mine.*
> *[Ned, USA]*

It is important to understand that if you are capable of acting strong, then you must possess some real strength to do so. If you can act confident, you must have some genuine confidence inside you to call upon. To resolve the internal conflict between the two versions of yourself, you have concocted a "false" self out of various real characteristics you already possess. In fact this is your true self: all of the characteristics of your "false" self are real and true and they all belong to you. It is like living in a hall of mirrors - you make a mask out of what is real and call it "false." Soon you just don't know how to distinguish between the two.

> *I am fascinated with images of mirrors and doubles, which is what led me to an interest in performing, especially on camera, where I can capture a double image of myself, a person who is both self and not-self. I live through this double image and work out all of my personal traumas through it. All of my narratives involve a relationship between two women, although I almost never have close female friends. My painting has also always been about self-portrait, and the creation of alternate selves. I am deeply empathetic and somewhat psychic, which I also attribute to sharing the womb with another person.*
> *[Anne, USA]*

## A paradoxical person

The paradox of your true and false selves needs to be resolved if you are to progress along the healing path. It is important to recognise how you have adopted some of your little womb twin's character traits - or rather what you imagine those to be - and added them to facets of your own personality, thus exaggerating them out of all proportion. They have been your way of keeping alive your lost twin in your Dream of the Womb. You are the strong survivor, the Alpha twin, but you probably keep forgetting that.

You may be able to think of times in your life when you have been paralysed by a sense of weakness or helplessness. As a result you were quite unable to function effectively and afterwards thought: "That wasn't like me, I wonder what came over me?" Perhaps you were adopting some of the characteristics of your twin, to keep your Dream alive.

## Alpha or Beta?  $\alpha$ $\beta$

An exercise may help to explain and resolve the conflict between the two opposing parts of yourself - the Alpha (you) and the Beta (your womb twin.) To do it, you will have to somehow imagine what your twin was like in body and personality. It will not be as difficult as you may think - in fact you may already have guessed what parts of your personality are "not you."

> *My Alpha side propels me forward into a course or job but I try too hard. I work too much - maybe under the idea that I need to achieve as much as I can before my Beta side kicks back in and causes me to crash. I am afraid to say "I can do this" in case one day I won't be able to, because I will probably fall into Beta after a while and sabotage my efforts. I get so frustrated. I am so sick of this perpetual cycle of achieve/ crash, achieve/crash. I just want to be me.*
> *[Kathleen, Australia]*

Here is a list of various opposing character traits, arranged on a spectrum from Alpha to Beta. You can mark where you are at the moment, somewhere between the two.

| Alpha | | | | | | | | Beta |
|-------|---|---|---|---|---|---|---|------|
| Strong | | | | | | | | Weak |
| Talkative | | | | | | | | Voiceless |
| Robust | | | | | | | | Frail |
| Obvious | | | | | | | | Unnoticed |
| Bright | | | | | | | | Fading away |
| Vital | | | | | | | | Inanimate |
| Alive | | | | | | | | Non-existent |
| Seen | | | | | | | | Vanishing |
| Substantial | | | | | | | | Insubstantial |
| Active | | | | | | | | Still |
| Noisy | | | | | | | | Silent |
| Visible | | | | | | | | Invisible |
| Secure | | | | | | | | Vulnerable |
| Present | | | | | | | | In another world |
| Capable | | | | | | | | Incapacitated |

| Intelligent | | | | | | | Unable to think |
|-------------|---|---|---|---|---|---|-----------------|
| Secure | | | | | | | Threatened |
| Resourceful | | | | | | | Helpless |
| Whole | | | | | | | Disintegrated |
| Autonomous | | | | | | | Dependent |

In your repeated attempts to keep your Dream alive you may have developed an exaggerated sense of weakness. If that has happened, you will probably try extra hard to compensate for your imagined Beta qualities, such as vulnerability or helplessness, by putting on a good show of being a competent, successful and generally effective member of society. Unfortunately, however, you are not some kind of supreme human being, but as frail as the next person, so your efforts to compensate for your imagined defects will eventually result in failure and collapse.

As a womb twin survivor, always remember that there was another little version of you who didn't make it into life. As you live out your Dream, half of you doesn't care about life and doesn't want to be here at all (that's your lost twin), but the other half wants to be alive and engaged with things here (that's you.) You are split, torn in two. You are two people, one feeding, one starving; one thriving, one fading. You are fighting with yourself. It's the way you are made, with two opposing sides.

## Healing your divided self

You are a paradoxical person and your route to healing will require you to resolve the paradox and discover your distinct individuality. Twins have to do this when they live in a pair, but you have not had that experience, as you do not have your twin here with you. After the death of your twin, you inherited all the space, nourishment and blood supply in the womb. You did not have to fight for it, or compete with anyone, for it was all yours and still is. Twins in a twin pair have to carve out their little piece of territory within the pair, so that they can each express their individuality. Twins, even one-egg twins, are never exactly the same — there is always something characteristic of one that is not the same in the other.

To find themselves within the pair, each twin has to discover what qualities he or she alone possesses and what qualities are shared between them. Your healing will be to find those individual characteristics that belong to you and give them full expression in your life.

At the same time, you will gradually discern some qualities that are not yours. You have adopted them as your own, in imitation of your twin. You have maintained them as part of your personality, even when they have caused you pain and suffering, in order to keep your dead twin alive in your life. You are not two people; you are an individual. You are a womb twin survivor, but whoever you may be, you are not your womb twin – you are the sole survivor. Trying to be two people at once is hurting you and preventing you from being the person you were designed to become. You are attempting to be more than you could ever be and as a result you are so much less that you are capable of being.

**Authentically you**

As we end this chapter, here are four things you can do to become more authentically you:

**Hand back the qualities** you have adopted as your own, but which belong to your twin. This will help you recognise when you are acting as if you were your own womb twin.

**Recognise that you fit somewhere** in the middle of the Beta to Alpha chart and that you are as frail and flawed as the next person, although you have your own strength and capabilities.

**Exercise the qualities that have been diminished** by trying to be two people – these may be related to strength or weakness. This will balance your personality towards an authentic way of being.

**Reduce the behaviour that exaggerates** some parts of your personality, so that you cease to be a person of extremes. You are not as strong or as weak as you have always assumed: you are a unique mixture of talents and flaws. That is the real you.

# The next step: Your true potential

Because you have spent so much of your life emulating your Beta twin, you probably have no idea what your capabilities are. You may have already been told that you could do better in your life, but something always seems to hold you back. In the next step on our healing path, we will discover what that may be.

# 8

# Your unrealised potential

In your life, as in the life of every womb twin survivor, there is a secret burden that is squashing you almost out of existence. It is like wearing a cloak of invisibility, such as the one depicted in the children's stories about Harry Potter. Under your personal invisibility cloak are certain parts of yourself that you carefully keep hidden and which are invisible, even to you. You badly need your cloak. As we saw in the last chapter, deep inside you is a sense of contradiction and that is what you are covering up. Your implacable nature is merely a design on your cloak. Underneath it, you are disturbed and confused, unsure who you are or why you are here at all. Your energetic pursuit of enjoyment is woven into the fabric of your cloak. You find contentment by avoiding anything that makes you feel unhappy, but underneath there is a sadness that runs so deep, it has enveloped your whole life like a grey mist.

This step will focus on what may be under your invisibility cloak - the hidden aspects of yourself that you cannot allow to grow or develop. We will uncover the reasons why, for the whole of your life so far, you have chosen not to realise your full potential as a human being.

**Unfinished**

In the womb there was another tiny human - or even more than one - developing nearby, but his or her life was cut short at some point. Your womb twin will always remain in your mind as an unfinished, incomplete little person who never got a chance at life as you did. Furthermore, you have identified yourself with your womb twin and that lies behind your dual nature. That Beta part of you feels like the Real You, but your Beta twin was never able to develop his or her potential as a person. So to keep your Dream alive, your Alpha qualities remain invisible, carefully hidden from view.

> *I often give heartfelt encouragement, but can barely recognize my own giftedness - I almost refuse to claim it. I actually find a deep resistance within me to my physical presence and have often commented how comfortable others seem to feel in their bodies.*
> *[Helena, UK]*

You are afraid of your talents and courage and need constant vigilance and self-discipline to restrain them. Concealing yourself under a cloak and withdrawing from human company feels like a very sensible thing to do if you are to continue to be like your Beta twin. You are determined not to let your full human potential be seen and realised, so all your gifts are kept hidden. Among those are your natural sociability and your ability to make intimate, equal relationships with other people.

## Healing

For you to be healed, the cloak has to go. No more concealment, no more pretending to be something you are not. Whoever you may be, you are not your cloak. To cast it off, you will have to recognise your own development, own up to your self-limiting ideas and distinguish yourself from your womb twin. Let's take each stage in turn.

### Recognise your own development

All your life you have been looking for someone to blame for your feelings of being "unworthy" or "useless." Long ago, when you were in the womb alongside your little twin, you did not even know you were a person. The only assumption available for you to make at the time was that you were just like your womb twin and therefore not a fully developed human being. That is why you feel so immature and undeveloped. Precipitated at birth into a world of love and encouragement, you decided to assume that you are a "barely human" individual only pretending to be fully human. Your cloak has been an ingenious solution to this problem. Your inner world of dreams contradicts things as they really are, but it can all make sense so long as you carefully conceal your gifts. Everyone else is acutely aware of the contradictions in your character and if you begin to wake up from your

Dream you will be able to resolve these by facing the truth of your own maturity and giftedness.

## Own up to your self-limiting ideas

Own up to the wasted years of your life. Face up to the squandered opportunities, the gifts left unrealised, the incomplete projects, the ideas still pending and the tasks that remain undone. Admit to the way you have let yourself down and not allowed yourself to live to the full. All your life you have been resisting growth and development. Your whole existence has been carefully arranged by you so that you never really grow up - you want to stay just the way you are. For you, this is vitally important for anything else would be a betrayal of your womb twin.

Own up to the shame. You are so much less than you could be. The way you are throwing your life away is frowned upon by your friends and family, who wish you to be fruitful and happy. You know you are only pretending not to be ashamed of the way you constantly limit yourself, for hidden beneath your cloak is a far deeper feeling of great guilt that you have "done something terribly wrong" for which you must be punished with a self-imposed life sentence of rigorous self-limitation.

> *I do feel abandoned, but also found by some presence outside myself - even, in a sense, deserving of abandonment. There is an intensity within me that seems to be searching for "normal," but at this point in my life the only thing that is normal is that I consistently provide space for others.*
> *[Lucy, UK]*

It is a very complicated situation you now have to resolve. You are a fully developed human person pretending to be a "hardly developed human being who is only pretending to be a real human."

## Split away from your womb twin

You are bonded to your undeveloped womb twin. You only feel right and safe when you are acting out your "hardly human" persona. At birth, you totally abandoned your beloved womb twin and gained all the freedom and space you needed to develop, whereas your womb twin had nothing – not even life. That explains the feeling that you have "done the wrong thing" by being born. Torn between loyalty to your womb twin and your natural desire for personal development, you have used your essential humanity to resolve the dilemma. You have sacrificed your completed personhood for your twin's sake. This is a loving, human thing to do and reveals what a wonderful person you have always been, right from the start. Your dual nature has stunted your growth, for you have tried to become your tiny womb twin. To develop your potential, you must begin to separate out what is you and not you. This will require you to split yourself into two and take full ownership of the half that is yours.

> *I am scared to admit to gifts and qualities because I always end up*
> *falling flat on my face. I cannot back it up with a sustained ability to*
> *carry out what I can do. It's like I have a host of talents but if I say that*
> *to someone and start work, I will burn out – this is not a fear, it is a*
> *fact of the life I have led so far.*
> *[Kathleen, Australia]*

## Three ways to limit your potential

We will now explore the three main areas in which that self-limiting foetal assumption of being "incomplete" and "unfinished" may have stunted your growth as a human person. They apply in your home environment, in your body and in your attitude to life. For each group there is a checklist to read and mark, to help you to identify your favourite ways to limit your own growth.

| Your home environment | Yes | No |
|---|---|---|
| Clutter | | |
| Hoarding | | |
| Messiness | | |
| A great many unfinished projects | | |
| Not cleaning your house | | |
| Not throwing garbage away | | |
| Too many animals in the home | | |
| Other | | |

Now could be a good time to take a look at the clutter and mess in your home and recognise what these things stand for. Clutter and mess block space, prevent creative activities and eat up energy better used for other purposes. You don't need your clutter or your mess any more - in fact the truth is you hate them. They are a way of concealing your true humanity, so cast them out. As you get rid of all the trivial things that tangle up your life, recognise your grief at deserting them. This is an echo of the grief you felt when your womb twin died. All you are left with now is emptiness, regret, sadness and a sense of being a traitor by being the only one to remain alive. Take another look under the cloak and realise that the useless little person who cannot maintain the home environment is not you but your little womb twin, struggling unsuccessfully to survive.

## Your body

There are dozens of subtle ways to limit your potential by not taking care of your body. Here is a checklist of a few of them. Which ones apply to you?

| Care of body | Yes |
|---|---|
| Neglect of personal grooming | |
| Lack of exercise | |
| Unhealthy food | |
| Taking on too many activities | |
| Not resting enough | |
| Not sleeping enough | |
| Not having enough play time | |
| Not treating illnesses and medical problems | |
| Other | |

If you neglect your health, you limit the length of your life, the amount of energy you have available and your bodily strength. We know an unhealthy diet and a general lack of exercise can lead to an early death. To live a fulfilled existence, you need long enough to bring your planned projects to completion. If you waste a large proportion of your life on meaningless pursuits and fruitless tasks, in the end there will not be enough time left to develop your gifts to the full. As we take this step forward, you could decide to stop wasting time and get on with living. There are many womb twin survivors who work so hard they become exhausted and can no longer function at their best. If you have been trying to do too many things at once and get so worn out that you can't do any of them properly, it may be time to stop and reconsider. You could think about letting go of your impossible dreams, and stay only with the possible ones that you do have the time, talent and tenacity to bring to fruition.

## Your attitude to life

The most self-limiting attitude anyone can adopt is negativity, which has more to do with *I can't* than *I can*. Here is a checklist of some of the many ways in which negativity may be expressed:

| Attitude to life | Yes | No |
|---|---|---|
| Cowardice | | |
| No goal in life | | |
| Hatred | | |
| Fear of change | | |
| Envy | | |
| Low self-esteem | | |
| Regretting past mistakes | | |
| Worrying about your image | | |
| Blaming other people | | |
| Lack of enthusiasm | | |
| Other | | |

There are two ways of viewing the world - optimism that sees the potential in everything and pessimism that sees only hopelessness. Take poverty, for example. For some womb twin survivors, their poverty is more of an attitude of mind or spirit than about money. To feel poor is to live an empty and meaningless existence. Surrounded by the trappings of wealth, the spiritually poor, financially rich people of this world wait for the happy life and the inner joy promised by advertisements. This always eludes them.

Here are the stories of two old women living in the same retirement home. Although their lives are so similar, one feels rich and the other feels poor.

**Mabel feels rich**: Mabel now in her eighties, does not consider herself poor. She lived through poverty and privation during the Second World War, and lost everything in the London Blitz. She now lives in a warm and comfortable retirement home with every amenity provided, but she misses the closeness of her supportive group of friends, many of whom have now died. Her childhood was difficult, but she accepted her lot and did not waste energy in regrets. She never married, but is rarely, if ever, alone. In her new life in the retirement home, she makes little trinkets and crochets woollen rugs to raise money for charity. She welcomes every morning "as a gift."

**Mary feels poor**: Mary, now in her seventies, was fostered by her grandmother as a child. As a result she had a better life than her three siblings, who grew up in their difficult family home. She is well-aware of this and claims that she was "spoiled." She had a good job and a busy social life, but ended up as a drug addict. She overcame this habit, but then became an alcoholic for many years. She never married. She still suffers from depression and a feeling of being abandoned. She lives in a warm retirement home with every need met, but she suffers from arthritis. As it is painful to walk, she stays alone in her room, mostly lying in bed. She wants to die because she feels her life is not worth living. She greets every morning with a sigh, as yet another empty day of a meaningless existence.

What would it take to change Mary's negativity into the joy of living that Mabel experiences? Clearly, Mary needs to let go of her negative attitude, which has become a self-fulfilling prophecy.

## Let go of your limitations

The clutter, self-neglect and negativity in your life have weighed you down and limited your growth. It is time to put that burden to one side.

### Self - forgiveness

As you reach a clear understanding of how you have deliberately limited your potential in a dozen different ways, the first and most important thing is to forgive yourself. As an embryo with a very primitive brain, what on earth were you supposed to assume when confronted with a tiny human person developing alongside you, who never made it into the world alive and fully developed? Of course you identified with your womb twin! You could not help it: you made the only assumption open to you - a foetal assumption that feels like absolute truth because it has been in your mind for so long. Now is the time to forgive yourself for creating that cloak of pretence.

It was a way to adapt to a very difficult situation. Torn in two, how were you to find wholeness and integration except by hiding your true nature? Now you understand why you did this, you could forgive yourself for the hurt you have inflicted on yourself and others. Only the people closest to you can see what is under your cloak, but they have forgiven you, again and again. Can you forgive yourself for being afraid to display your gifts to the world? It is a normal fear for womb twin survivors, and one of the many things that sets them apart.

Now is the time to cast off your invisibility cloak and let the world see all of you. Rest assured other people guessed long ago that you are a perfectly normal person in disguise, so they will not be surprised. They will be delighted to see you a little more clearly.

## The next step: Something missing

Behind your reluctance to develop your own potential is a deep sense of lack. There is something missing in your life that has left you feeling empty and unsatisfied. The next chapter will explore the many ways in which womb twin survivors express a sense of inner emptiness.

# 9
# Something missing

A lifelong sense of something lacking is a common characteristic of womb twin survivors. It is reasonable to miss someone who had been there beside you all your life but the idea that a womb twin survivor may miss a twin who only existed briefly in the womb may seem unreasonable to some. For womb twin survivors, however, it is a real feeling. Here are some statements to check through. See if any of these describes how you feel:

| Something missing | Yes |
|---|---|
| I feel incomplete but I don't know why | |
| I feel unsatisfied but nothing helps | |
| I have been searching for Something or Someone all my life | |
| I feel empty inside | |
| There is something missing in my life | |
| I feel a deep sense of loss | |
| I am longing for my twin | |
| I feel as if I have lost part of me | |
| I am filled with a nameless yearning | |
| Other | |

In this chapter we will look at three ways in which that sense of Something Missing may be expressed in your life: a nameless yearning, a fruitless search and a feeling of inner emptiness.

## A nameless yearning

Much of your life until now has been driven by a nameless desire for *Something* or *Someone* who you believe will restore you to wholeness and make everything right. The brief time in the womb with your twin has created your sensation of incompleteness. This is because there once was a real sense of wholeness that existed when your twin was alive and both of you were together.

> *I feel like I am missing something big. Even though I know I had a twin, there is still something I'm missing. My mother delivered a foetus before me. The doctor verbalized concern (he swore). My mother asked what was wrong. She heard something drop into a bucket at the side of the bed. A nurse whisked it away. I don't know how developed the foetus was.*
> *[Marylin, USA]*

You cannot miss something you never had, so the very fact that you have missed your twin all your life is as much a proof you once had a twin as any physical sign.

> *This idea explains me in the greatest of detail all so perfectly, everything that has always had me in a state of confusion as to why I am here. The deep feeling of loss always, since I was about three. The extreme need to create my twin and allow her to be there, inside of me. The extreme feeling that there was something missing in me. Always, always searching to fill that hole in me with something that never seems to work or satisfy that strong need.*
> *[Frances, USA]*

The nameless yearning in your life now has a name - your missing twin. It always helps to put a name to things, so even if you have no idea if your twin was male or female, try to find a name for him or her. Most womb twin survivors know their twin's name already or pick one almost instantly when they think about it. If nothing springs to mind at this moment, don't worry.

Just come back to this spot when you have found one. On the opposite page is a space for you to write the name of your twin, perhaps for the first time in your life.

**I name my twin:**

## A fruitless search

Womb twin survivors are often restless. They constantly switch jobs, move house or change their mind about things. They move from one relationship to another and do not allow matters to remain the same for very long. Just when it's time to settle down, they are ready to move on. This characteristic restlessness is driven by the nameless yearning described above. You may recognise it in your own life. It is self-defeating, for when something good is at last within your grasp you let it slip through your fingers.

> *I was adopted by my older auntie as a newborn. At the age of 18, I had a dermoid cyst removed that contained hair and teeth. During the years leading up to this, I was always searching, but attributed it to me being adopted and searching for my parents. However, upon learning the truth about my birth, I continued to search but didn't know what to search for or why I felt the continued need to search. A coworker spoke of vanishing twins upon learning of me being a lefty. They really became interested once I shared the story of the dermoid cyst. Since I've been reading and researching this, it feels right.*
> *[Stacey, USA]*

It appears the endless search must be fruitless, for the happiness in your Dream of the Womb cannot be allowed and the Someone you seek must never be found. All your life you have been on a fruitless search for your lost twin. That is entirely understandable and not some kind of character defect. As we move on, you will learn more about your lost twin and be able to make him or her more real in your life. Soon you will be able to reformulate those vague feelings in your Dream of the Womb as a real memory .

73

## An inner emptiness

Some womb twin survivors feel as if there is an empty space inside them. In such cases, their restless activity is more related to filling the void within, than to searching endlessly for *Something Out There.* The emptiness inside acts like a vacuum, drawing into it anything that might possibly fill it up, but it cannot be filled. There is an unsatisfied feeling nothing can assuage.

### Emptiness and addiction

Inner emptiness is the energy behind addictions of all kinds. Addictions are known to arise out of a feeling of unmet emotional needs. The empty sensation inside can be confused with hunger, and it has been pointed out that the feelings of hunger associated with eating disorders originate in spiritual rather than physical needs. Naturally enough, if your "hunger" is not about food, then food will never satisfy it. The same argument can be applied to alcohol. In alcoholics there is an overwhelming need for drink that arises whenever that cavernous space inside opens up. Despite a concerted effort to drink less or give up altogether, the inner hole requires filling and only alcohol will do. Many drinks later, it is quite clear alcohol will not fill the hole, because it never had anything to do with drink, or the lack of it, in the first place.

For tobacco smokers, there is comfort in the nicotine "hit" but it is short-lived. Even after 60 hits a day, the emptiness remains. Sex addicts seek comfort and connection in sexual activity and may truly find them for a few moments, only to be left afterwards feeling lonelier than before. Self-harmers may experience a momentary respite when they break their skin to make it bleed, but the empty space inside remains as big as ever. If you have been addicted to anything and ever tried to stop, you will know the sensations of emptiness that return once the fix is no longer available. The fix only masks the neediness. It never truly satisfies it, for the real need is for your twin.

> *I've always felt that I should have been a twin, but I'm not sure why. When I go to the grocery store, I usually purchase things in twos or in multiples of two. I've always felt different from everyone in my family. I do tend to overeat, mainly to try to fill the void I feel deep inside.*
> *[Tracey, USA]*

74

# Filling the inner hollow

The inner emptiness that womb twin survivors experience is similar to being left alone and bereft. It is related to missing a specific form of very intimate relationship. Womb twin survivors move from one close relationship to another, sometimes briefly feeling a sense of absolute one-ness with the other person that brings completeness and the sense of being "filled up". Inevitably, though, these relationships end with disappointment. No individual, however close and loving, can replace your lost twin.

## Imaginary friends

The need to find a surrogate twin is often expressed in the notion of imaginary friends. It is very common for womb twin survivors to have an imaginary friend. If you used to have one, or have one today, he or she probably is or was very similar to how you imagine your lost twin to be.

> *Other than the story of my actual birth, and the inconvenience it caused her, my mother has never discussed her pregnancy or my birth with me. Even then she has only related trivial details. I know that I have always felt something was missing, even as a child. I don't make friends easily - I want them and always have, but I have this feeling of searching for something, some quality that I can't find or define. Fairy tales and stories with long-lost siblings or enchanted family members always fascinated me as a child. I had imaginary friends, usually a girl with a name similar to mine, but the specifics varied as my needs varied - sometimes she was older than me, sometimes younger, but usually close to my age.*
> *[Cassie, Canada]*

To have an imaginary friend is often dismissed by professionals as a perfectly normal form of play that the child will "grow out of". For womb twin survivors however, the friend has been created to replace the missing twin.

Parents should be alert to this possibility, particularly if the need for an imaginary friend continues into adolescence or even adulthood. Some parents believe that to mention the lost twin would be to place a burden on their child. In fact, it is a great relief for a womb twin survivor to know the adoption of an imaginary friend is a normal response to feelings of inner emptiness, not a sign of immaturity.

*I have always had dreams of me around age three playing dolls with another little girl with my same features. Now age 22 I still have them and feel as though I lost a part of me I cannot seem to find. I asked my mom today if I was a twin and she told me when she was six weeks pregnant with me the nurse heard two heartbeats and said it was twins. But at 12 weeks my twin was gone. They assumed it was an echo of my heartbeat. When I was born I almost died due to an extremely oversized umbilical cord. Also they found traces of a second cord and placenta in my mother's womb. My mother never told me this until I asked her, five hours ago.*
*[Sandy, USA]*

If you talk to your image in the mirror when you have a problem, you are not deluded. You just want to share your life with someone who really understands. You are not being over-dependent if you long for Someone close enough to you to understand what you mean without you having to explain all the time; or so empathetic that he or she knows how to help without your having to articulate your needs. All these character traits are normal - for a womb twin survivor, that is.

## Making a life jigsaw

You are longing for something that will restore your sense of wholeness; you yearn to find that missing piece in your life and you wish the emptiness inside could be filled. The only thing that could satisfy all these longings would be to have your twin back. That situation will never occur again, so you must make the best of what you have.

There is much in your life already that could contribute to your healing but as yet there are only tiny fragments. However, if you were to pull all those fragments together, you may be surprised at how much you already have. To help you to do this, it's time to make a "life jigsaw." Your life jigsaw will consist of various relationships and will grow ever larger as your healing work continues, should you decide to create one.

There are four steps to this process - to find the gaps in your life, discover what you already have, find a pattern and make a plan to change things.

## Step 1: Find the gaps

For the first part of this exercise, you will create a series of jigsaw pieces that represent what seems to be lacking in your life. It is safe to assume that what you are missing is more than the physical presence of your twin. It probably has more to do with the quality of the twin-twin relationship.

| **Qualities of the missing twin-twin relationship** | |
|---|---|
| Shared experience | Empathy |
| Understanding | Loyalty |
| Reliability | Personal attention |
| Company | Shared feelings |
| Friendship | Safety |
| Intimacy | Reassurance |
| Other | |

Choose from the list above (or from some other ideas) the three words that sum up what is missing most in your life. You can write each word in one of the three empty jigsaw pieces below.

**THE MISSING PIECES IN MY LIFE**

**Step 2: Discover what you already have**

This is not intended to be a "count your blessings" exercise, however much it may feel like one. It is specific to the gaps in your emotional life. What do you already have that could be a substitute - not an ideal replacement, but a good enough match - for those missing qualities?

> *I didn't have affectionate love from my parents after the age of five, but luckily, some of my friends' parents were hippyish and hugged everyone, so I got human warmth in a small way which I think helped me a lot. [Stephan, USA]*

The chart below lists some of the aspects of relationship that may already be helping to fill the emptiness inside you. You may like to write in the appropriate places the names of the people who are providing each kind of support, help and comfort.

| Shared experience | |
| --- | --- |
| Empathy | |
| Understanding | |
| Loyalty | |
| Reliability | |
| Personal attention | |
| Company | |
| Safety | |
| Friendship | |
| Intimacy | |
| Reassurance | |
| Shared feelings | |
| Other | |

**3. Find a pattern**

Did you find little or nothing on the chart above that fills your inner emptiness, even slightly? Perhaps you have turned away from sources of human comfort and denied yourself what you really need, just to keep your

Dream alive. You may be seeking out the qualities you require through some kind of fix. What is your chosen way to deny yourself more than a small fragment of the relationship qualities you crave so much? Perhaps your usual pattern of relationships is a vague reflection of the original relationship you once had with your twin. If you can make out your personal pattern as the healing path proceeds, you may begin to break that pattern and discover new means to gain fulfilment.

**Step 4: Make a plan**

Your plan for healing your life will be to find new and healthy ways to fill the empty spaces inside, just a little. There are two important principles to accept now, as we move forward. There can never be a replacement for your twin, so stop looking for one. There is no single person alive today who can provide all the qualities you are looking for. There will always be a gap in your life, but let's try to make it as small as possible. A new search can begin now for new companions and friends, any one of whom may provide just one of the qualities you crave. To make a start, you could write in these jigsaw pieces the kind of people you are going to seek out to help you.

**THE PEOPLE WHO WILL HELP ME TO HEAL**

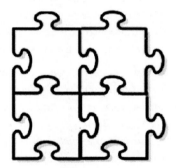

# The next step: Strong emotions

The next stage of the healing path will take us directly into the empty space inside you that was created by the death of your twin. As we move on, you are about to discover that this space is not as empty as it may first appear, for it is filled with your strongest emotions.

# 10

# Your emotional life

As we come to the final chapter in this second stage of the healing path, it is important that you begin to understand how your emotional life has been affected by the loss of your twin. You have probably spent a great deal of time and energy trying to work out where your most painful feelings have come from. If you are lucky and have already received appropriate help, you may have found the root cause – the death of your twin. If you have never considered your feelings before, then as you read on you will see with increasing clarity how your emotional life was formed.

*Mum was seven months when she went into labour. They gave her medication to stop the labour and I was born on time - well, nearly two days late. She said delivering the afterbirth was as painful as giving birth but thought nothing of it. At a doctor's appointment six weeks later she asked what was put into the bucket in the delivery room and was told it was another baby that had only developed to about four months then died and was delivered along with me. I got very emotional when I heard about womb twin survivors. I am very sensitive and emotional. Films make me cry, even the news sometimes. I don't mind being alone in the dark now I am an adult but as a child I was afraid and used to sing myself to sleep at night. All my life I have been searching for something, not knowing what it was. Now I have heard of womb twins I hope I can eventually understand why I am the way I am.*
*[Maureen, USA]*

## No emotions

You may have cried a lot as a child and did not know why, but today as an adult you probably conceal how hurt and upset you are every time your hopes are dashed and your expectations disappointed. Some womb twin survivors are quite unaware of their own emotions. For them, this is a self-defence measure against the hurt that lies in the Dream of the Womb. The mind simply shuts down the pathways that process emotions, resulting in a stoic, emotionless state. Today you can choose to live as a machine without feelings and without any need for other people. In your self-sufficient little world, no one can get to you. You will be immune to emotional pain. If your emotional state does not quite fit with the life you are leading, so that for instance you have a stable family environment, but feel depressed and lonely, it may sound crazy to speak about your feelings, so you don't. That doesn't mean you don't have them - you just don't have the words.

> *I am a man and I was a twin with the twin dying in the womb. My family never spoke about the twin with me and I don't even know if it was a boy or girl. I have felt restless and alone, even when with my wife. I was a teenager before things emerged that I had been a twin, but sadly my Mum died before she could tell me a lot of information. Her last 11 years were in a wheelchair following a bad stroke, so her memory was mixed. My Dad I never stayed in touch with, so beyond knowing I was a twin I know very little else. I never used to think that it mattered until recently when during the past year I started counseling with my partner and I started to look at my emotions. I looked up missing twins when they die in the womb and people's descriptions of how they felt were very close to how I feel. I know I need to take this more onboard. [Paul, Canada]*

You probably yearn for a world where there is no pain and all is as it should be, but again and again your expectations are dashed. However, if you pretend to have no feelings you cannot be hurt.

## The primal wound

As a womb twin survivor, it probably seems to you that some kind of primal wound lies below everything you feel, do and say. If you examine your own feelings carefully you may discover that deep sense of wounded-ness. It is always there; a kind of "floating" emotion that constantly seeks out places to come to rest, none of which are entirely appropriate. The wound is of course the loss of your twin. This complex feeling is very hard to put into words.

*I lost my twin at birth and I found out about this when I was seven. Since then, I don't think there has been a day gone by that I have not thought about him, what he would look like, act like, type of job he would have, would I be the same person etc. I am now 30 years old and I can't talk to anyone because they would not and could not understand how it feels to grow up knowing there is something missing from your life, only to find out the thing that is missing is the other half of you. I cannot talk to my parents because it is too upsetting for everyone, so I have been alone with this for 23 years. It hurts, really hurts.*
*[Mark, USA]*

## Your emotional profile

To establish your own emotional profile, we will start with a list of the six main emotions. On the whole, how intensely do you experience your emotions? For each one listed here you can give yourself a score from one to five, with five being the most intense. Just put an X in the appropriate square:

| Your emotional profile | | | | | |
|---|---|---|---|---|---|
| **Emotion** | **5** | **4** | **3** | **2** | **1** |
| Anger | | | | | |
| Anxiety | | | | | |
| Grief | | | | | |
| Guilt | | | | | |
| Love | | | | | |
| Other | | | | | |

Womb twin survivors vary a great deal in terms of their emotional profile. For example, if you feel annoyed about finding yet another table to complete, remember that it is only put there to help you. If you easily feel guilty, remember you don't have to do this exercise. If you tend to be anxious, do not worry about your score. Clearly, your emotionality - that is, how intensely your emotions are experienced - varies across a spectrum, from very little feeling at one extreme to very intense feelings at the other. We will describe this spectrum in more detail by focusing on just one of the emotions listed above - anger.

## Anger

For womb twin survivors, anger is a common problem. It arises mainly out of disappointment and vulnerability.

### Disappointment

There is a different emotional outcome for those whose womb twin was miscarried and left the womb altogether and for the others, whose womb twin died and was around for a while as a dead, unresponsive presence. The survivors of a miscarriage are left feeling forsaken and the victim of a catastrophic event. It is different for womb twin survivors whose twin died a little later and remained in the womb somewhere alongside. In this situation the body gradually disintegrates until it is quite gone, eventually leaving nothing to show that it had ever been there. If that is your story, in your Dream of the Womb there is a vague sense of *Someone* who once did respond, but who eventually stopped responding. An expectation of an instant response, created during the brief life of your womb twin, would now be disappointed. You were left alone and vulnerable, feeling a sense of lack - an empty space where that beloved *Someone* ought to be. Your dreams were thwarted. You lost something very valuable. It is a loss that cannot be restored, so only resentment remains.

### Vulnerability

Anger is a primitive survival mechanism that enables us to respond to threat with aggression. Vulnerable people have a problem with anger. If you feel vulnerable most of the time, you will imagine yourself threatened more often than if you always feel strong. The more vulnerable you perceive yourself , the more "trigger-happy" your anger will be.

> *I constantly have fear that one day I am just going to have to live my life alone. Even though right now there are good people around me who love me, I still feel that one day they will use me and abandon me. Because of this sometimes I distance myself from my husband thinking that one day I will have to just live alone. A lot of times I want to share myself with others but I feel so afraid. I feel like that once they know me, these people*

*will use my vulnerable side for their advantage. In past such things have*
*happened and I feel like I probably created these things.*
*[Siobhan, Ireland]*

Clearly, anger has its place in your life but where it is denied or exaggerated, we can see that a self-sabotaging choice is being made. As always however, we can find an intelligent, rational and loving reason for this choice if we look. A deep sense of extreme vulnerability may seem inappropriate or even crazy to you, but in your Dream of the Womb you have someone to protect – your fragile little womb twin. You identify with your tiny twin so you feel small, fragile and at risk. At the same time, you are the strong survivor and protective of your twin. This is why you feel both vulnerable and protective at the same time. The general result is anger, expressed in a variety of ways. So that you can see clearly what form your anger takes, we will consider a spectrum of ways to express it.

### 1: NO EXPRESSION OF ANGER

Some womb twin survivors are inwardly angry, but prefer to remain unaware of that fact. If this is how you deal with your anger, it is extremely rare for you to lose your temper. When things don't go your way or people behave badly, you feel disappointment, not rage. For you, the free expression of anger against any individual is forbidden, so you keep the lid on it. What anger you do express is probably a cool, diffuse, negative emotion, hardly worth classifying as anger at all.

### 2. ANGER RELEASED ONLY WHEN PROVOKED

Do you find expressing anger very uncomfortable, so you go out of your way not to be provoked? If this is your story, then the anger is already in you, but you would rather not to acknowledge it. You try to keep the lid on your anger, but you know that lid could be easily be lifted off by a sudden outburst, which you prefer not to express.

*Since I was a child I have always been angry about my father. My father*
*was always drinking and that made me very angry and aggressive. When*
*he came him drunk he sometimes teased me and my brother. Then I felt*
*the anger coming up. But I never expressed it.*
*[Ken, Belgium]*

84

Once anger has been provoked, it may seem you have good reason for it. On reflection, though, perhaps there was nothing that ever warranted such an angry response. It's that Dream again - that sense of vulnerability is probably related to your tiny lost twin who was too weak to survive, and that sense of weakness has become part of your character, even though you know you are the strong survivor.

### 3. APPROPRIATE ANGER

If you suppress your feelings in order to behave reasonably, but you are prepared to express yourself before you become extremely frustrated, then there will be no build-up to the resulting explosive outburst. For those who tend towards the extremes with their anger, this would be the position to aim for as the healing continues. If you release your angry feelings from time to time, they will not build into a rage.

### 4. SIMMERING RAGE

You may believe that taking the lid off and giving vent to your feelings is the only way to be truly honest about how you feel. In that case, you are easily annoyed about things and always ready to complain. Anger for you is a form of self-defence, because when you are angry you feel vulnerable. The simmering rage you feel is always close to the surface, but somehow you manage to keep yourself from becoming thoroughly enraged.

### 5. BOILING RAGE

At the extreme end of the anger spectrum, pain and vulnerability are at their height. Rage is the natural, angry response to being hurt. You are filled with pain that is almost beyond endurance. You badly need to express it. You use your rage to communicate your hurt to the world, so that you can be understood and feel "heard". Unfortunately, if you have little control over your temper and are easily enraged, you may find that you hurt the people you love, again and again. You probably end up apologising profusely, not sure why you have done such a thing. It may help you to know that you express your rage and pain in this way because you want the rest of the world to absolutely understand how you feel.

## Healing emotional pain

Emotional pain consists of intensely experienced feelings such as shame and depression, plus an anguished sense of helplessness and disorientation. Emotional pain can be healed, simply by understanding. As a womb twin survivor, you now know that your emotional pain belongs in your Dream of the Womb. Today the loss of your twin has left you with a sense of lack tied up with one of doom and guilt, that you were somehow to blame.

As you live out your perpetual guilt trip, feeling as if you are responsible for running the world, watch out for self-pity. That is how you are keeping the pain alive - believing no one understands how you suffer, which is why it hurts so much. Now you understand that the pain is in your Dream, you don't have to feel it any more, it is over.

- **You can set yourself free**

- **The pain will just fade if you don't keep awakening it**

- **Remember that no one is hurting you**

- **You yourself are keeping the pain alive**

- **You are making yourself unhappy**

## The next stage of the journey: Ways to heal your life

We are the end of this stage of our journey. Hopefully, you now understand a little more about how your attitudes, behaviours, feelings and beliefs originated in your Dream of the Womb. As we reach the third stage of our healing path, we will consider some of the ways in which you can start to heal your life. We will begin in the depths of your Black Hole.

# Stage 3

# Ways to heal your life

In the dead heart of a small part
That lies somewhere in the back of my mind,
There is a hurricane that roars endlessly, silently screaming.

In the still centre of the rage that does not speak,
In the sharp cutting edge of unfeeling coldness,
In the clamped, fettered silence,
In the empty, desperate, jolly laughter,
There is a body lying somewhere offstage

The people walk past it unseeing;
The birds peck at the eyes uncaring.
I dare not look - for it is myself.
My eyes are blinded by crows,
My flesh falls raggedly crumbling,
I am dead.

Teach me to live;
Teach me to live -
I cannot live
Without you.

# 11

# Making friends with your Black Hole

The term "Black Hole" describes how it feels inside to be a womb twin survivor. This chapter will explore in depth how you hold on to the difficult feelings that lie in your Black Hole and what triggers a Black Hole moment. We will discover where the pain that lies in your Black Hole comes from and how you can reduce it until it simply fades away.

## A pool of pain

The Dream of the Womb consists of the vague and primitive impression of your experiences in the womb, which still remains in the back of your mind. Within the Dream are various illogical and irrational feelings that seem to have nowhere to rest. Among them are sorrow, searching, yearning, bewilderment and nameless fears. The overall result is a pool of pain and that is your Black Hole. The negative energy is a pool of personal pain that lies deep within your soul. It is a vague memory of your first trauma, which was the loss of your twin.

Because you have been keeping your twin alive in your Dream of the Womb, you have kept your pool of pain topped up. Every time you engage in negative thoughts and self-defeating behaviour, this pool gets deeper. This is how the pool is filled with the kind of emotional pain that can last a lifetime, despite your great efforts to heal it. It could be that you, too, have experienced

89

many years of such unexplained pain, but never fully understood it until now. The pain belongs in your Dream of the Womb, and at least some of it is much, much older than you.

### Draining the pain pool

Once personal pain develops beyond a certain point, there is a need to release it. You have probably developed all kinds of ways to achieve this, but they only provide temporary relief. The trouble is that, however awful the feelings may be in your Black Hole, they lie at the centre of your Dream of the Womb. It seems the Dream must be preserved at all costs, to keep your twin alive. That is why your Black Hole, with all its negativity and pain, must be so carefully maintained.

## Black Hole moments

It is important to learn to recognise Black Hole moments when they occur and to know what triggers them. When a Black Hole occurs, it feels like your worst nightmare come true. Suddenly, a moment comes when the world seems a hostile and terrible place. All sense of reality and time fades. You are left faced with an unbearable feeling that you instantly try to avoid with some kind of distraction or denial.

The Dream of the Womb varies for each of us and so does the nature of everyone's Black Hole. To help you to recognise your personal Black Hole moments, below is a checklist of some of the feelings that can arise when they occur. Tick any of the feelings you regularly experience in such circumstances.

| Black Hole moments | Yes | No |
|---|---|---|
| About to die | | |
| Vulnerable | | |
| Abandoned, totally alone | | |
| Loss of identity | | |
| Falling to bits | | |
| Overwhelmed | | |

| | | |
|---|---|---|
| Torn in half | | |
| Going crazy | | |
| No good, useless | | |
| Imprisoned | | |
| Unheard | | |
| Lost | | |
| Non-existent, unreal | | |
| Other: | | |

## Black Hole triggers

The second step is to recognise what triggers a Black Hole moment in your life. Remember that things can either change very suddenly or build up slowly over time, but the end result is always the same. Back comes that horrible feeling and you are thrown into your Black Hole once more.

Black Hole triggers are not always related to your environment or to the people around you. You may be in the same situation, with the same people, every day for weeks. Then one day everything just becomes unbearable and the Black Hole is there again. The triggers come from deep inside you and that is very important to know. Next time you have a Black Hole moment, take a look at where you are and what has been going on. Did anyone do anything to make you feel so bad? Or did you feel bad already and this was just one more reminder of how you always feel?

> *I was born into this world a murderer. My twin came out first but he had the cord wrapped around his neck. He would have been called Jack. He had no chance. My life has been one train wreck after another. The inner turmoil is so deep inside I don't even realise that I do it. Death follows wherever I go - or do I follow it? The constant guilt I carry - why me and not Jack? He has every right to be here too!*
> *[Zach, USA]*

There may be another way to look at your life. Try playing "*What if?*".

- What if no one is trying to hurt you?
- What if you are in fact already filled with pain?
- What if you are not your Beta twin, invisible and hardly alive?
- What if you are in fact the strong Alpha survivor?

91

- What if you are not abandoned, alone or rejected?
- What if you drive people away, so you remain alone?

## The source of your pain

An important step towards understanding your Black Hole is to discover why those bad feelings arrived inside you in the first place. Where did they come from? It is possible that at least some of the pain in your life is self-inflicted. The case study that follows illustrates how a womb twin survivor worked hard, at great cost, to keep her pain alive.

### Jo's story

Jo is a recovering addict. Sometimes the sheer hopelessness of the situation overwhelms her and she just stares at the wall in despair. She spends a great deal of time asleep in order to escape. During this time she closes off. She wants to be alone and sees people as little as possible. She feels better for a while, but then a dark cloud settles over her mind. Her life is filled with a deep-seated pain that will not go away.

"I help people as often as I can," she says, "but I find I get terribly used as I don't want to get hurt any more." At one time she thought she might be possessed and sought spiritual healing. "All I can remember when I was a child was a bright light following me", she recalls. "I used to run to my mum for a cuddle or put my head under the bedclothes". One of the first things Jo looked for was a brother. "I know intuitively my twin is male, because of that male energy that pushes me on. I do not like being here, being alive. Even at my happiest there was that underlying problem. But in my reality of pain and understanding of pain, I would know something was very different if all these negatives stopped operating in my life. How wonderful it would be to breathe easy, and wake up without the thought of death constantly on my mind!"

*What if?*

- What if, like Jo's, your pain is self-inflicted?
- What if you too are deliberately maintaining your Black Hole?

## Super-sensitivity

One way to keep up the level of pain in your life is allow yourself to be easily hurt or afraid. That means being super-sensitive. According to Elaine Aron, author of *The Highly Sensitive Person,* to be very sensitive is to be aware of subtleties, but also easily over-stimulated.[1]

Super-sensitive people teeter all their lives on the edge of their Black Hole. An innocent look or gesture can be magnified into rejection, a lost object can signal that the world has fallen to pieces, and the briefest parting can feel like total abandonment. If you are a super-sensitive womb twin survivor, it probably seems as though there is a constant risk of falling into your Black Hole and being lost forever, like your own womb twin.

The level of sensitivity appears to vary among womb twin survivors, but they do seem to be much more sensitive than people born of a single conception. This is probably because of the additional stimulation of the foetal brain by one or more other active and responsive embryos or foetuses developing nearby. It seems that the more stimulated your brain is before birth, the more sensitive you will be to everything around you. It may sound like a disability, but in fact super-sensitivity is one of the great gifts of being a womb twin survivor. It means you are strongly empathetic and intuitive, which is an advantage. The difficulty is that you have been using your empathy in your search for painful experiences to keep your pool of pain topped up. It is highly likely that you have taken on other people's pain without ever realising it.

## Ancestral pain

Some of the pain that lies deep inside you may not be yours. If your mother was bereaved or traumatised when you were in the womb, you may have received a dose of stress hormone directly via the placenta and umbilical cord. The pain you carry may be your mother's grief when your twin died. But the pain, grief and trauma may have happened many generations ago and been handed down via the womb twin survivors in every generation.

A super-sensitive mother would have been acutely aware of her own mother's pain. If her mother was also a womb twin survivor, she may have been aware of pain in the previous generation. Womb twin survivors are, in a real sense, the bearers of ancestral pain. It is important for your healing for you to know whether or not you are carrying pain that belongs to another person. If you have tried very hard to heal your inner wounded-ness with no long-term good result, that may be a sign the pain does not belong to you.

Perhaps you do manage to climb out of your Black Hole for a while, the pain does go away, but then returns in another guise to push you back in.

If it feels like the healing has begun but still the pain won't go away, then that pain is probably not yours. People in your generation can inflict their pain on you by abusing you, but that does not happen to everyone. The trouble with being empathetic and super-sensitive is that you become like a sponge. You can easily absorb other people's pain and carry it about with you, in the name of trying to help. Perhaps you believe you can take the pain from the other person so he or she doesn't have to suffer it. That is not true and the only result is two people in pain. With your pool of pain filled to the brim, you will be so disabled by what you are feeling that you will be unable to help anyone effectively.

## Reducing negative energy

Your Black Hole is a pool of negative energy, but you can turn that energy into positive thoughts and ideas. Just struggling always to think positively will not be enough, but you can counteract negativity. For instance, if you make it a habit to turn difficult problems upside down, approaching them from a completely opposite perspective, it is amazing what new insights can come. So use this strategy often.

In trying to keep your Dream alive you have probably deliberately enlarged your Black Hole so that it appears to dominate your life, whereas in reality it is only a small, empty space where your twin once was. Here are three simple exercises to help you to reduce the negative energy in your Black Hole. They are all to do with how you handle emotional pain –

- Insulating yourself from the pain of others
- Celebrating super-sensitivity
- Handing back ancestral pain

### Insulating yourself from the pain of others

If you are a womb twin survivor you are probably super-sensitive, even if you do not realise it. In that case so, you are in danger of unwittingly absorbing the feelings of other people because of your empathetic nature. In other words, if you have been among people who are hurting, you may soak up their pain and willingly pour it into your own Black Hole. Empathy is a wonderful gift, but it can be draining and exhausting to use it to take on responsibility for other people's "stuff," with no possibility of ever resolving it.

Here are some ideas that may help you :

- **Listen** to your own feelings and work out which of them are appropriate for your situation. If they seem inappropriate, they have probably been taken on.
- **Notice** particular people from whom you easily pick up negative energy by means of your own empathy.
- **Imagine** a one-way barrier between you and such other people, through which your kindness and empathy can reach out, but no negative feelings can enter from outside.
- **Begin** to notice as soon as negative feelings arise in you, and remind yourself that they do not belong to you. In your mind's eye, hand them back and feel the strength and effectiveness of the one-way barrier increase.
- **Check** if there are difficult feelings inside you that do not belong to you, if and when you are unable to sleep at night. If you find any, you may not know where they come from, but you can simply disown them and allow them to fade away.

### Celebrating super-sensitivity

It is time to see your super-sensitivity as a gift, not a problem.

| Sensitivity | Gift |
| --- | --- |
| You notice people who are in trouble or in pain and who may need your help. | Kindness |
| You are acutely aware of the feelings of others | Empathy |
| You are acutely aware of negativity among people | Peacemaking |
| You can literally feel the pain of others | Healing |

Gifts are no good if they are not used, so it is worth finding positive actions that exercise them. Many womb twin survivors deploy their special gifts to become carers, healers and helpers. They make kind and thoughtful family members, too. Simply by using their gifts, they transform negativity into positive action. If you can spend time sending positive actions outward to others rather than gathering negative thoughts to yourself, then your Black Hole will run out of energy and simply fade away.

### Handing **back ancestral pain**

The next exercise will require you to do a bit of detective work. If you know nothing of your ancestors (even your own parents), just read a bit of history and find out what difficult times your family may have lived through. War, epidemics, massacres, natural disasters and enforced large-scale population movements can leave a deep imprint on whole societies. Super-sensitive womb twin survivors in the population are more likely than others to be traumatised by such events. They in turn will communicate their trauma to their children. Now is the time to put an end to this inter-generational recycling of suffering: you don't have to feel the pain any more.

> **Always remember**: The pain never did belong to you. No one inflicted the pain on you. You soaked it up. Carrying the pain of others does not help anyone.

> **Another more-practical** step would be to take a walk somewhere alone. With every step of your walk chant, I don't have to feel the pain any more. By the time you have said this again and again for an hour or so, it will be imprinted into your brain - hopefully forever.

## The next step: You and your womb twin

The nature of your Black Hole varies according to what is in your Dream of the Womb, and the substance of your Dream depends on the real nature of your womb twin. Your individual Dream of the Womb was formed according to the difference between you and your womb twin, so that is what we will consider in the next step along the healing path.

# 12

# Bridging the Alpha-Beta gap

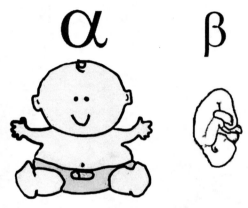

Experts have noticed that in any pair of twins, even when they share identical genes, there is a more-dominant (Alpha) twin and a more-compliant (Beta) one. This step on our journey will clarify the difference between your Alpha and Beta characteristics and explore the nature of your personal Alpha-Beta gap. The theory behind this stage of the healing path is that, in keeping your twin alive in your life, you are perpetuating characteristics in yourself that do not belong to you. This may be preventing you from living to the full. When a twin dies, the sole survivor may take over the belongings, tastes and even the personality of the dead twin, as if to preserve the memory. It is reported that one teenager, following the sudden death of his twin, underwent a radical change of character: "As the months passed, this bereaved teenager also assumed some of his brother's qualities. Having been the less responsible and tidy of the two, he became increasingly dependable and orderly." [1] This tendency to adopt the characteristics of your own lost twin also applies when a twin dies in the womb, or around birth. In your existence as a womb twin survivor, you are keeping alive two versions of yourself - an Alpha version and a Beta version.

## Alpha or Beta?
It is important to determine whether you are an Alpha or a Beta womb twin survivor. If one twin is too damaged or sick to make it through pregnancy the Alpha twin almost always survives. However, in the case of an abortion or an accident at birth, it is possible for either to survive. These diagrams on show two such womb twin stories through the three trimesters. of pregnancy:

## AN ACCIDENT AT BIRTH

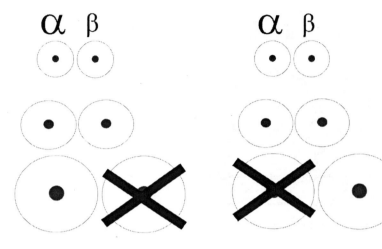

*THE ALPHA TWIN SURVIVED*          *THE BETA TWIN SURVIVED*

## AN ABORTION OR MISCARRIAGE IN THE SECOND TRIMESTER

*THE ALPHA TWIN SURVIVED*          *THE BETA TWIN SURVIVED*

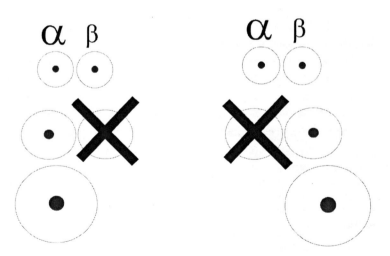

We will now consider what Alpha and Beta twins are like, both in the womb and later on in born life.

## The typical qualities of an Alpha twin

Alessandra Piontelli's book *Twins: from Fetus to Child* describes how she studied the behaviour of twins in the womb and noticed that they differed markedly in character in ways that persisted after birth. She realised there was always one twin who was dominant - the Alpha. It seems that these characteristics tend to persist into childhood and even into adulthood, as the following table indicates.

| Quality | Notes |
|---------|-------|
| Initiative | Evident in the womb, as the Alpha is almost always the first to make a move. In born life the ability to get things going, make things happen or trigger a reaction in others |
| Strength | In the womb, Alpha swims around strongly and may attack or grab anything that comes within range. In born life a tendency to respond to restriction or outward control with resistance and frustration. |
| Activity | The Alpha shows high levels of vitality and energetic activity in the womb and after birth |
| Tolerance | The Alpha is well able to adapt to extremes of temperature, hunger or exhaustion. Able to digest any kind of food without ill effects. A strong immune system. Ability to recover rapidly and completely from disease. High tolerance to pain. |
| Dominance | The ready expression of the will in expectation that it will be carried out. Degree of its expression varies, according to the nature of local competition and other factors that affect the Alpha's desire to dominate. |

**The typical qualities of a Beta twin**

The Beta twin, when observed on the ultrasound scan, is the one who remains quiet until stimulated by the Alpha. This tendency persists into childhood and adulthood.

| Quality | Notes |
| --- | --- |
| Stillness | In the womb, the Beta has a tendency to spend long periods resting or inactive. In born life a tendency to sleep a lot. A love of peaceful, slow places and activities. |
| Obedience | In the womb, a tendency to react slowly and only when provoked. In born life a ready responder, but only if provoked. Prefers to be a follower, not a leader. |
| Intolerance | Low coping threshold. Reduced ability to withstand extremes of temperature, may become exhausted by too much activity and feel ill if there is insufficient rest overall. Slow to recover from disease or injury. Low tolerance to pain. |
| Gentleness | In the womb an evident feebleness of movement. In born life patient, not often angry; accepting of dominant others. |
| Submission | Tolerance of dominance, in the knowledge that there is insufficient personal strength to fight and overcome. The ability to let go of one's own will to allow the will of another to be carried out. |

Beta womb twin survivors whose Alpha twin died in the womb may spend a lot of energy struggling to be like an Alpha in order to keep the Alpha alive. As a result, they may become exhausted and have to rest. Healing for "pushy" Beta womb twin survivors is to accept their in-built limitations.

### Simon - a pushy Beta

Simon, a Beta womb twin survivor, is filled with a sense of privilege at being allowed to have life when his Alpha twin didn't survive birth, owing to a cord accident. He tries to keep up with everyone else by running that little bit faster. Until he faces the difficult fact that he truly is a Beta womb twin survivor, Simon will continue to stretch his abilities to the maximum in order to be equal to the Alphas, often to the point of utter exhaustion. Nevertheless, he feels proud of the fact that, despite his in-built inadequacies, he can do as well as the Alphas - sometimes perhaps just a little better. When he manages to excel, he feels like an Alpha for one wonderful moment, but he knows he can't follow it through, so he pulls back to his usual position of being a bit behind the others.

### The false Beta

If the Beta twin dies in the womb and a lone Alpha twin is delivered into the world, then survivor guilt dampens the Alpha's ability to express his or her qualities. It is this difficulty in giving free rein to such Alpha qualities that characterises most Alpha womb twin survivors - they are acting like "false Betas". False Betas are not hard to spot: they are healthy and strong, but needlessly depend on other people. They are talented individuals who sabotage their successes. They are often victims of long-term abuse and bullying, as they are so submissive that no matter what is inflicted upon them, they will pay the cost of maintaining the relationship. If you are acting like a false Beta, you have identified yourself with your own weak and helpless Beta twin. Your healing will be to acknowledge your Alpha gifts with gratitude and use them responsibly. To begin to do that, you will first need to discover the Alpha-Beta gap in your life.

## The Alpha-Beta gap $\qquad \alpha \longleftrightarrow \beta$

The size of the Alpha-Beta gap varies according to what developmental stage your twin reached before death. It is measured according to how much of the pregnancy you spent in the womb after the death of your twin. In the diagrams that follow, the length of the black line represents the Alpha-Beta gap in the life of the survivor. The longer the line, the greater the difference between you and your womb twin in terms of physical development.

If some of the terms in the diagrams are unfamiliar, they are explained in the glossary (pages 280-281.)

## VARIATIONS IN THE ALPHA-BETA GAP

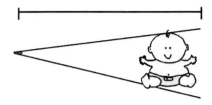
**A blighted ovum** creates the largest gap, for the twin never developed. The same applies to an enclosed twin (dermoid cyst, teratoma) or cells from an enclosed twin (chimera, mosaic.)

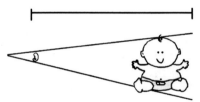
**Death of a twin at about 5-8 weeks** (a "vanishing twin" pregnancy) Creates a slightly smaller gap because there was a little time when the twins were alive together.

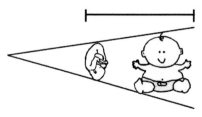
**Death of a twin in the second trimester** Creates a smaller gap, because the twins were alive together for nearly three months.

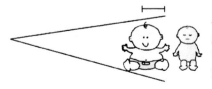
**A stillborn twin** creates the smallest gap, because both twins were alive together for almost the entire pregnancy.

The Alpha-Beta gap describes the difference between you and your twin. If there is a big gap, then there will be a big difference between who you are and who you could be, as the following case study illustrates:

### Stella's story

Stella is tall, well built and athletic but she says, "Often inside I feel very small, almost invisible". In moods like that, she can scarcely do anything. She feels helpless and "no good" at those times. Even though she is keen on sport, she does not play consistently well. This is a matter of great frustration, both to her and her sports coach. It seems that Stella has identified herself with her Beta womb twin brother, who was miscarried at around 12 weeks. She is living out the memory of a little, helpless Beta individual while at the same time being a naturally strong and capable Alpha survivor. Her Alpha-Beta gap defines the difference between how she is and the person she could be if she allowed herself to reach her true potential.

The size of an individual's Alpha-Beta gap is evident in many ways, not least in the stories emailed to the Womb Twin Survivors web site. Womb twin survivors who are living as "false Betas" feel so non-existent that they sometimes find it hard to use a capital I when nominating themselves in writing. They are also acutely aware of their own Alpha-Beta gap. The following story (left unedited) illustrates this.

> *i need to stop feeling as though i am wasting your time and appreciate the fact that you want to hear what i have to say. Survivor guilt! I have it full-fledged and take it to the extreme. From the alcoholism to the low self-esteem to the black hole of screaming pain. I am living the false Beta life too, on the side. I am a diagnosed genius who has been self-assassinating for years. I was noted in kindergarten for intelligence and took special tests but was desperately afraid of the examiner. Then I switched schools and although everything else was wonderful, bright and shiny, I was noted for not fulfilling my potential.*
> *[Rachel, USA]*

# What is your womb story?

Your womb story varies according to what actually happened to you. Overleaf are a few of the different scenarios that can develop in the womb, in the three trimesters of pregnancy. Among them you may find one applicable to you. The whole story is there in your Dream - at the very beginning, you and your twin were together for a while, then things began to change. So your womb story starts with you and your twin alive together, but then your twin died, either very soon or much later.

**BLIGHTED OVUM**

**DEATH AT 4-6 WEEKS : "VANISHING TWIN" PREGNANCY**

**DEATH/ABORTION IN THE SECOND TRIMESTER, TRACES OF BODY REMAIN**

**MISCARRIAGE OR ABORTION, BODY OF TWIN EXPELLED FROM THE WOMB**

**ENCLOSED OR ABSORBED TWIN (TERATOMA, DERMOID CYST, EXTRA DIGITS, PARASITIC TWIN)**

**STILLBIRTH OR NEONATAL DEATH OF TWIN**

## Making your own womb story

You did not have a fully functioning brain for most of your time in the womb, so any memories that may still exist will be extremely hard to recapture and understand. They are only vague feelings and impressions, with no sense of place and time. Therefore it might help to make sense of the jumble in your head to create a drawing describing your own womb story. This will put the events into chronological order.

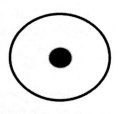

You do not have to be a great artist, as you can represent yourself and your twin like this. The black dot can represent your body and the circle your amniotic sac.

If you enjoy drawing you could be more technical and make a storyboard like the one below, which shows (1) identical twins sharing the same sac, (2) one dies away, and (3) leaves a sole survivor.

**1**  **2**  **3**

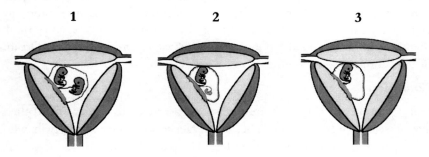

It is very important to create a womb story that is as accurate as you can, grasping at every clue you can find. You may spend months or even years, grappling with tiny details. It is like trying to do a huge jigsaw puzzle without the whole image to refer to. Keep at it, for one day you will find an explanation that makes perfect sense.

> *Apart from helplessness, my life is dominated by fear. Fear of loud noises, fear of the dark, fear of flying etc. Most of my fears take on ridiculous size when I'm alone, and I loathe being alone unless I have specifically chosen it. I would really like help on finding out the gender of my twin. Initially, I assumed we were identical; that's the way I want it to be. However, a few things have made me wonder. I feel very angry at men in general, and don't want to have had a twin brother!*
> *[Kathy, UK]*

# Bridging the gap

Having found your own Alpha-Beta gap, the next step is to bridge it. You can do this by means of a Me/Not-Me exercise. Put simply, this will show you the times when you are not being your authentic self. You are an Alpha survivor, so you are not being authentic when you act like a false Beta. The same applies if you are a Beta womb twin survivor acting like an Alpha. As you begin this exercise, you will encounter three major problems:

## Paradox

If you are trying to be both your womb twin and yourself at the same time, things can get difficult. In attempting to be two people and believe two things simultaneously, the only way to keep your Dream alive will be to indulge in paradoxical thoughts. For example, you may get the feeling that in some way you "don't exist", while of course being aware that you must exist to think that thought. This is a kind of mental gymnastics - a sure sign of your Dream of the Womb at work

## Confusion

Many womb twin survivors are not sure who they are. They spend their lives in search of themselves. They are in fact seeking their womb twin, who is a separate person, but somehow feels like part of their most basic self. A fraternal twin of a different sex is in some way part of you, so you are unsure about your gender. An identical twin feels like the other half of you, but is also a separate individual. If you are not sure who you are or what is really going on, then that is the Dream of the Womb *par excellence!*

## Concurrence

There was no sense of time in the womb. Vague impressions are all jumbled up and in a mess. Everything is happening at once. You may feel as if you are somehow dead, yet obviously still alive. You may feel as if you are in a state of perpetually dying or fading away. Alongside this is a grim determination to stay alive against all odds, confounded by terrible guilt for having already survived. If you had an identical twin, it feels as if half of you were here, but somehow at the same time not here.

**The Me/Not-Me exercise**

This is simple enough to do in a few minutes, but also worth a great deal of time and thought if you have time to spare for this kind of thinking.

1. **Notice** the contradictions in your life and record them.

2. **Look at** the following list of character traits. Tick any you possess and note down any others that occur to you and seem relevant.

3. **Write each one** of these character traits on a slip of paper.

| Trait | Yes | No | Trait | Yes | No |
|-------|-----|-----|-------|-----|-----|
| Initiative | | | Surrender | | |
| Strength | | | Dominance | | |
| Activity | | | Stillness | | |
| Tolerance | | | Obedience | | |
| Gentleness | | | Intolerance | | |
| Other | | | | | |

4. **Divide** the papers into two piles: *Me* and *Not-Me.*

5. **Examine** the *Not-Me* pile. They will form a description of how you have tried to live out the un-lived life of your womb twin.

6. **Ask someone** you trust to describe you honestly, if you are still not sure who you are.

7. **Observe yourself** deciding this person is wrong, because he or she can't possibly know what it is like being you on the inside.

8. **Write down the truth** of how you feel on the inside (you need not tell anyone this.)

9. **Write a description** of each "version" of you.

10. **Decide now** - which is the real you?

# The next step: Your personal boundary

Because you have been living your life as if you were your own Beta womb twin, you have not maintained a firm personal boundary. If you are to move into your Alpha space you will need to strengthen your boundary. The next step on the healing path will show you how to do that.

# 13

# Maintaining your personal boundary

Some womb twin survivors have a real problem with maintaining their personal boundary. To have fulfilling relationships and maintain some kind of control over yourself and your life, your personal boundary must remain firm and strong at all times. It is the limit of your personal field of operation. It marks the limit of your capacity to influence others and be influenced by them. It is the arena within which all your energy, motivation to act and capacity to reach out to others can have some effect. Like the borders of any country, if your boundary is left weakened or loose you will be at risk of invasion or exploitation.

## A firm personal boundary

Here are some typical characteristics of a firm personal boundary. You can find out how firm yours is by giving yourself a score of one to five (five is high) for each characteristic.

| Characteristic | 1 | 2 | 3 | 4 | 5 | 6 |
|---|---|---|---|---|---|---|
| Maintaining your energy levels | | | | | | |
| Awareness of your personal power | | | | | | |
| Saying no to other people | | | | | | |

| | | | | | |
|---|---|---|---|---|---|
| Getting what you want | | | | | |
| Taking responsibility | | | | | |
| Self-esteem | | | | | |
| Self-confidence | | | | | |
| Being in touch with reality | | | | | |
| Self-control | | | | | |

As your healing progresses, your personal boundary will strengthen, improving your relationships. You will find yourself better able to respect yourself and others. If you have a clear idea of who you are as a separate and distinct individual, then your boundary will be strong.

# A loose personal boundary

If you have a weak sense of who you are as a separate individual, then your personal boundary will be loose. One sign of this might be putting others before yourself, to the extent that you almost "disappear" as a person in your own right.

> *I feel lost and alone and want someone to look after me and show me the way. I'm fed up with being the strong one, the capable one that people turn to when they need an ear, help, whatever. What about me, I want to scream!*
> *[Marta, USA]*

**Over-giving**

If your personal boundary is loose, you will keep on expending energy on others without making sure you have enough resources to continue. That will eventually leave you exhausted and burnt out.

If this is the story of your life, then think of the safety talk given on aircraft: when the cabin air loses pressure and the all-important oxygen masks come down, we are instructed to put on our own mask before helping others. Constantly giving to other people without some measure of self-care is self-defeating, for eventually you are left unable to help anyone, including yourself.

### Over-responsibility

If you feel very guilty about saying NO to other people, you will be constantly meeting their demands, catering for their every need, rescuing them from disaster and supporting them in their weaknesses. That can be a sign of a perilously loose personal boundary.

> *I have always felt like I have to live for two, and try twice as hard to do everything in life. I try to do everything for everyone else. I feel like I cannot be myself and that I have to be who they want me to be. I feel I have to help everyone. If I let them down, it is my fault that they are not the best they can be in life. I have a hard time saying no to people. I want to be helpful to others by taking the pain from them. I often worry about everyone and everything until I am depressed.*
> *[Amy, USA]*

The danger of a loose boundary is that you are at risk of being eclipsed. You will become some kind of "servant" or "slave" whose life consists only of meeting the demands of other people. When you help and support others, you make a valuable contribution to society, but if you give too much the cost will be too high. Allow yourself to take a rest sometimes and ask for support when you need it. This will maintain your personal boundary, your sense of yourself and your available energy for making a difference in the lives of others.

### Dependency

Dependency is taking more from other people than you give back. If you are a dependent kind of person, you may imagine you are protecting yourself from being drained by other people. If you feel unable to cope with the demands of others, it may seem entirely logical to ask for support from individuals who appear stronger than you. However, if you depend on others for help and support, your personal boundary will not be firm enough to keep you feeling confident and strong.

## The membranes in a twin pregnancy

As a result of the Womb Twin Survivors Research Project, through which many hundreds of womb twin survivors have shared their stories, a new idea related to personal boundaries is beginning to emerge. It seems that how you manage your boundary is rooted in your very first relationship, which was between you and your twin. Your personal view of how to handle intimate relationships probably reflects the arrangement of membranes (the chorion and the amnion) in the pregnancy that produced you.

## The chorion

The chorion is the outer membrane that encloses the whole pregnancy (the foetus, the amniotic sac and the umbilical cord.) The placenta develops from the chorion. Where there are twins, there can be one or two chorions. Two-egg twins each have their own chorion. Most one-egg twins share a single chorion, but in about one-third of cases one-egg twins develop in two separate chorions. [1]

## The amnion

The amnion is the membrane that surrounds the amniotic sac, which is filled with fluid. This sac was your first home - the watery world in which you developed, hidden in your mother's womb. In twin or multiple pregnancies. it is usual for each baby to have his or her own amniotic sac. In some one-egg twin pregnancies, however, one sac is shared by both.

## The membranes in twin pregnancies

The following set of diagrams illustrates the ways in which the chorion and amnion are arranged in "vanishing twin" pregnancies.

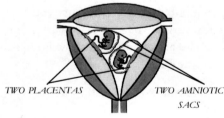

*TWO PLACENTAS*    *TWO AMNIOTIC SACS*

**TWO CHORIONS, TWO AMNIOTIC SACS, TWO SEPARATE PLACENTAS**

- Most two-egg twins
- Some one-egg twins

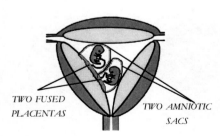

*TWO FUSED PLACENTAS*    *TWO AMNIOTIC SACS*

**TWO CHORIONS, TWO AMNIOTIC SACS, TWO SEPARATE PLACENTAS WHICH HAVE FUSED TOGETHER INTO ONE**

- Some two-egg twins
- Some one-egg twins

111

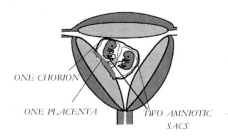

**ONE CHORION, ONE PLACENTA, WITH TWO AMNIOTIC SACS, ONE FOR EACH TWIN**

- Some one-egg twins

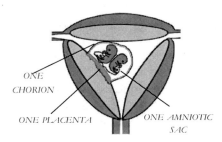

**ONE CHORION, ONE PLACENTA, ONE AMNIOTIC SAC**

- Some one-egg twins

When you were a tiny foetus you knew no other situation except the one that existed in the womb. Naturally, you assumed that this situation was The Way Things Are. This was a foetal assumption, the basis of your Dream of the Womb. Your intimate relationships in born life seem to reflect your Dream of the Womb, particularly in the way the pregnancy membranes were arranged. Below is a set of diagrams that show how this may work in different kinds of twinning. In each case, the grey-tinted circle represents you, the sole survivor. The white circle represents another person with whom you now have a close relationship. The two circles are arranged to show how the personal boundaries of the two individuals interact.

**A "VANISHING TWIN" PREGNANCY WITH SEPARATE SACS AND PLACENTAS**

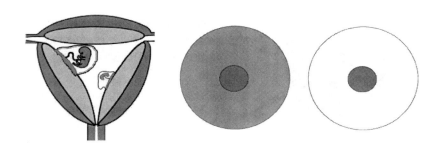

The foetal assumption you would have made, while developing in this situation, was: *in close relationships I have my own space and so does the other person. We do not need to spend much time in close contact.*

### A "VANISHING TWIN" PREGNANCY WITH SEPARATE SACS, PLACENTAS AND CHORIONS BUT THE PLACENTAS HAVE FUSED INTO ONE.

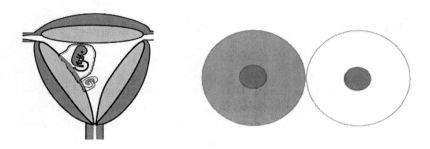

In this case the placentas have fused together. If this is your story, your foetal assumption would have been: *in close relationships I have my own space and so does the other person. We need to spend a lot of time in close contact with each other.*

### A "VANISHING TWIN" PREGNANCY WITH SEPARATE SACS, ONE PLACENTA AND ONE CHORION

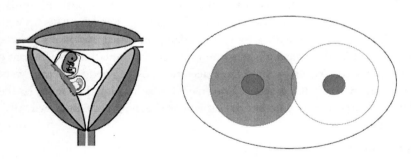

In this case, there is only one chorion, which encloses both sacs, and a shared placenta. The foetal assumption would have been: *in close relationships I have my own space and so does the other person, but we are very close and we occasionally enter each other's personal space. We spend most of our time in close contact with each other, in a world of our own.*

113

**A "VANISHING TWIN" PREGNANCY WITH A SINGLE CHORION, PLACENTA AND AMNIOTIC SAC**

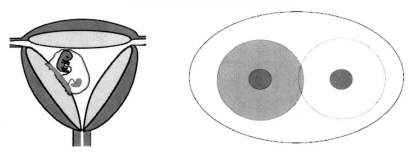

In this case, everything is shared. There is no barrier of any kind between the two twins. The foetal assumption is: *in close relationships I share my space with my twin. We spend a lot of time in each other's personal space. We spend most of our time almost merged into one entity.*

# Invasion

It may sound far-fetched to say that the way you set your boundary between yourself and others depends on how the membranes were arranged in the first few weeks of your life. However it does explain some aspects of human behaviour. If a person with a sense of entitlement to "invade" meets up with a womb twin survivor with a loose boundary, then that survivor's private space is at risk of "invasion" of some kind. In this situation, bullying and abuse may occur. You may encourage neediness, or be needy; you may want to be rescued, or be the rescuer. You may choose to play the victim or the bully. It all depends on whether or not you are keeping your Beta twin alive in your life.

### Reclaiming your personal space

If you take on the identity of your own Beta twin you may adopt Beta characteristics, such as feeling weak, insubstantial or "falling apart". In that case, you are unlikely to claim all your personal space. An important healing step therefore is to reclaim any personal space you might have relinquished in order to "become" your Beta twin. Boundaries and relationships can be complicated by a common tendency among womb twin survivors to identify

114

themselves with their lost Beta twins. You may have noticed this already in yourself. Identification with another person means you almost "become" that person and believe you have the same attributes. If you have a loose personal boundary, you may not be sure about your own identity. As you live out your Dream of the Womb, where your twin was as close as can be, you can get so muddled up with other people that the two personal boundaries intersect. Then you will not be sure where the other person's boundary starts and how far your boundary can extend. Here is an exercise that may help to make this clear:

## A personal space exercise

This is a physical exercise. To do it you will need a private, clear area, large enough to stretch out both arms at the same time.

- Find something to stand on, such as a small mat, and say out loud, *"This MY place, it belongs to me".*

- Standing on the mat, spread your arms out on either side, as far as they will go, stretching your fingers out. Say three times, gradually getting louder, *"This is MY space."*

- Revolve slowly on the spot to create a space around you at arm's length. As you do it say, *"All this is my space, I claim it as mine."*

- Notice the feelings that come up.

- Now revolve again and again, as many times as you need, remaining in place on the mat, repeating words like: *"This is my space, it belongs to me; I cannot make it any bigger or smaller, this is all I have. It is all mine."*

- Once that idea feels secure in your mind, stand still, strong and tall. Stretch out your arms, but this time put your palms outwards, creating a wall around you. This is your personal boundary.

- Very slowly, claiming every inch as your own, say: *"This is my space, no one can take it away from me, or give me any more. It is all mine."* Do that often. It helps.

## A firm boundary exercise

A second physical exercise can make it clear how to keep your boundary firm in the presence of other people. For this, you will need another person to help you.

- You have the right to claim as much space as your personal limitations will allow.

- You may not have always claimed it, so now could be the moment to start.

- All you have to do is to carry out the boundary-claiming exercise again as described above, but this time there will be two of you - if you can find more people to do this, so much the better.

- As you each claim your personal space in the room, you will see how you characteristically interact with other people. Do you let yourself be invaded or are you the invader?

*I recently felt given the insight that I had a womb twin. I have been in caring roles all my working life, although I've recently gotten much better at understanding and setting boundaries. This has helped me begin to separate out what I and others are responsible for.*
*[Laura, USA]*

## Maintaining a firm personal boundary

The best way to maintain a firm personal boundary is to practise creating relationships of mutual respect:

| R | Rights |
|---|--------|
| E | Equality |
| S | Separateness |
| P | Power |
| E | Empathy |
| C | Consideration |
| T | Trust |

The respect has to be mutual to really work - that is, each person must respect the other person's boundary in the same way.

**Rights**: You cannot claim any rights for yourself unless you take responsibility for the effect of your claim on other people. An important aspect of mutual respect, therefore, is to balance the rights of all the various individuals involved in any situation, including your own.

**Equality**: However worthless and useless you may feel compared with others, the truth is that we are all of equal worth. You may be an Alpha twin stuck in your Beta space but that does not affect your true personal worth. A climate of mutual respect, where everyone's boundaries are carefully maintained, must be based on the principle of equality among people.

**Separateness**: Womb twin survivors easily find themselves trapped in the pain of other people and assume responsibility for the wellbeing of others. If that is your problem, then keep reminding yourself you are a separate individual, operating in your own personal space.

**Power**: In a relationship of mutual respect, there must be a balance of power. If you manage to overpower another person, you will certainly reduce the extent of his or her personal space, but that space can never be yours – it has been stolen. Conversely, if you feel overpowered or dominated by another person, then you have chosen to let them dominate you. Never forget that if you don't use all your personal space no one else can use it.

**Empathy**: Mutual respect is not possible without empathy on both sides. Empathy is the ability to imagine accurately what it feels like to be the other person and to understand why he or she is feeling that way. To keep your boundary intact and allow other people to maintain their own boundaries, you must be sure that you do not steal their space or invade their privacy, however well-intentioned you may be.

**Consideration:** Womb twin survivors are gifted with strong empathy, intuition and great sensitivity towards other people. This gift is dangerous, however, if it is not used with consideration. Impulsive reactions can send you blundering into the private space of another individual and having to apologise. Equally, impulsive openness can allow someone to claim your private space. You may find it hard to retrieve it if that happens.

**Trust:** Trust is an essential ingredient of respect. Unfortunately, some womb twin survivors find it hard to trust. Deep down is the memory of being closely bonded to your twin, only to find yourself alone when your twin died. The foetal assumption is: *Love and friendship is a thing that leaves. It won't last.* Claim as much personal space as you are allowed and you will feel less vulnerable.

## The next step: Shame

For the next step you will need all the personal strength you can muster, so work hard on your personal boundaries before moving on. When you feel grounded enough, turn the page and we will take a look at shame.

# 14

# Healing shame

The healing step will examine the shame in your life as a womb twin survivor. The image above is intended to clarify the difference between shame and guilt, because the two are often confused.

> **Guilt** is the knowledge that you are personally responsible for some kind of wrongdoing. The man on the right in the picture above is reluctant to speak about some wrong he has done.

> **Shame** on the other hand, is social. It is about your standing in society. The man on the left in the picture has covered his face so he cannot be seen.

This chapter will focus on the many kinds of shame that womb twin survivors can feel.

## Assumptions and decisions

John James, who has written extensively about womb twin survivors, describes a series of "decisions" that may be made by womb twin survivors long before birth. These underlie the foetal assumptions they appear to have made. These decisions fuel the particular kind of shame that may haunt your life and the lives of many womb twin survivors.

Which assumptions did you make, that even today keep you feeling guilty and ashamed about being a womb twin survivor? Here is a list and you may like to tick any you have experienced:

| Shameful assumptions made by womb twin survivors | Yes |
|---|---|
| I took all the nourishment and my twin starved | |
| I was responsible for my twin's death | |
| I failed because I could not keep my twin with me | |
| I blame myself for my twin's death | |
| I was not worthy, so I had to remain on earth alone | |
| Other | |

Healing the shame you feel will mean emerging from behind the false self you have created. It will require courage, because your whole self will then be in full view. Shame can be caused by feeling bad about not being your true self and failing to fulfill your potential as a human being. This awareness of falling short of what you could become has been called "existential guilt." If you feel ashamed of not being fully you, it follows that healing this shame will be the start to becoming your authentic self. If that seems too difficult for you at the moment, please return to the previous step and continue to strengthen your personal boundary. Eventually, you will be able to build relationships around you based on mutual respect. Then you will be ready to start.

# Experiencing shame

## Selfishness

Shame is selfish. This may seem an extraordinary claim to make, but shame is a bad feeling that most of the time is carefully avoided by the individual concerned. It is widely believed a prevailing sense of shame in an adult is due to some kind of painful humiliation in early life. However, for womb twin survivors, shame is not of this kind: it is like a self-inflicted wound. Shame is a cover-up - the reason for personal pride. Pride is the cover for shame, for it demands your public image remains untarnished and acceptable to all. Shame is all about self-protection. It is the constructed image you project to the world, not the truth.

It takes a lot of energy to maintain such an excellent image but if you spend a great deal of time feeling proud of yourself, you are wasting energy. You may like to believe that you are keeping up an image of being a "strong person" but perhaps that mask of yours is not as effective as you believe.

*Two healing challenges:*

1. **Hear the truth spoken in friendship.** Find someone who will, in kindness, speak the honest truth to you about how you come across. Listen and let this person speak for as long as needed, without any interruptions. Then write down what has been said and read it carefully. What have you seen in what you read that you should be ashamed of?

2. **Speak the truth in friendship:** Do the same for someone else, remembering always to be kind. Notice how good that was for you.

By means of this difficult exercise, you will have learned how selfish it is to keep pretending to be "wonderful" when you know the truth can heal you and everyone else as well.

### Hatred

Shame is bound up with hatred. The best way to get people to hate you is to shame them - which means exposing their vulnerabilities to public view. If you have ever had your own vulnerabilities exposed, you will know what being bullied feels like. Everyone hates a bully. A bully will pick up those secret aspects of yourself that you think you have managed to conceal, expose them in public and ridicule them. Shame lies behind self-hatred. If you were to fully accept yourself in all your human frailties and failures, there would be no need for a cover-up. The thickness and size of the mask you wear is an indication of how deeply you must hate yourself. If there were no self-hatred, there would be no need for that mask.

The courage to own up to your faults is a great virtue. It acts like a bottomless hole in your life into which you can pour away all your self-hate, until all that is left is the kind of vulnerability that is actually a great strength. Don't let anyone convince you that openness is "naïve" or "dangerous". Being frail and flawed is simply being human. If you have a firm personal boundary and always try to create relationships of mutual respect, your capacity to be vulnerable will be your greatest strength and asset. After all, if you totally accept yourself, what weapons are there for a bully to use?

#### Mike – living a life of shame

Mike thinks that shame is an inevitable aspect of his personality. He believes that being molested at around the age of 13 by a schoolteacher is the cause of his persistent feelings of shame about his body. He has only recently felt able to tell anyone about these incidents. He was bullied at school and called "Weed" because he was naturally thin and not very muscular. He and his identical twin were delivered prematurely and only Mike survived. Shame is like a prism through which he sees the world and himself in the world. He regards himself as bad, dirty, worthless, hopeless and incapable of ever "growing up" into a "real man." He often interprets personal remarks as insults, even when they clearly are not. He wants to be accepted "just as he is." He describes every passing reference to his bodily form as "humiliating".

## Taking things to extremes

Any activity can be made shameful if you take things to extremes. Shame can be disguised as rage, greed, violence, addiction, compulsion, impulsiveness or disobedience. You may already be familiar with the shame that goes with being "over the top" in the way you behave. Rather than admit that you have been greedy or histrionic, you may look for ways to justify your behaviour. What is your favourite response when someone suggests you have gone too far?

| Favourite justifications | Yes |
|---|---|
| I am being unjustly accused/judged | |
| I was only trying to express my true feelings | |
| I needed to vent, or I would explode! | |
| I feel very hurt/abused/insulted by what you have said | |
| I can't help being this way | |
| It's who I am  - can't you accept me just as I am? | |
| Other | |

## Paralysed with shame

There can be an opposite effect: there is the fear of shame arising out of saying or doing "the wrong thing" that can be paralysing. Rather than experience the shame of admitting that you have done the wrong thing, you do nothing. You don't even try, out of fear of failure or inability to cope.

Is that your story? If so, you may have found your own way to justify your inaction or mistake, so you don't have to feel ashamed. What is your favourite way to insist that nothing is ever your fault?

| Favourite excuses | Yes |
|---|---|
| I thought it was the right thing to do/say at the time | |
| It was not my fault it didn't work | |
| It was your fault for making me do it | |
| I couldn't help it | |
| You do it - you are the expert | |
| I haven't got around to it yet | |
| Other | |

If you invent things to feel ashamed of, then you can hold yourself in a perpetual cycle of remorse, regret and sorrow that you will find hard to acknowledge publicly.

## Invented shame

The criminal who repeatedly offends; the child who consistently opposes the parent or teacher; the resistant, difficult adult who refuses to change; all these are manifestations of invented shame. Clearly, there is no logical reason to go on doing something that heaps blame and shame upon you, unless of course you want it to be that way. The criminal can choose to go straight, the child can begin to obey and the adult can decide to be more friendly and cooperative. If this does not happen, it is probably because the idea is to trigger punishment, admonition or blame, so that the sense of shame increases. A subtle form of invented shame is to assume that whenever something bad happens it is all your fault - when clearly there were other people involved.

Invented shame can, if you choose, keep you stuck in a loop of compulsive activities of which you are ashamed. You can spot a compulsive activity by asking yourself, "Why did I do that?" If there is no sensible answer, then you are dealing with a "shame trip". If your life is driven by "musts" and "shoulds," then take a second look, for you will find invented shame lurking in there somewhere. Nothing says that you "should" do anything. You have absolute power over your own life and how you live it. You are totally responsible for everything you believe, feel, think, do and say. Invented shame enables you to feel powerless and helpless when confronted with your own compulsions. Perhaps you need to feel that way in order to emulate your weak little Beta twin and keep your Dream alive.

> *I feel like I have to get things right the first time. If I mess up, and I mean normal mess-ups, I feel guilty and stupid. I feel bad for little, normal things - like if I use the last of the toothpaste and someone goes in the bathroom before I can replace it, I feel really guilty.*
> *[Cherry, USA]*

If you take on responsibility for the happiness and wellbeing of everyone around you, then in a sense you are adopting other people's shame as your own burden. Womb twin survivors, because of their need for invented shame, often create codependent relationships with addicts. They easily fall into a kind of "shame game."

### Michael and Marsha - a shame game

Michael was a heavy drinker who often vomited or passed out at parties because of an excess of alcohol. Marsha, womb twin survivor and his ever-capable wife, took charge in these circumstances. She would make apologies to the hostess, mop up the vomit, take Michael home, undress him and put him to bed. She also would wash his clothes immediately, even when it was late at night, to keep the smell of vomit out of the house. By morning, apart from a hangover, Michael would seem oblivious of the embarrassment and trouble he had caused his wife, but Marsha would feel deeply ashamed.

To cover her husband's shame, Marsha had become the obedient Beta "servant", who willingly cleared up the mess for her Alpha "master", so that in the morning the whole sorry episode could be forgotten. But why was she not ashamed of her own collusion with her husband's bad behaviour? It was demeaning for her to have to involve herself in the mess, but she didn't seem to care. How can that be, unless she had willingly taken on the burden of her husband's shame? They both had their part to play. The husband adopted the role of the helplessly addicted alcoholic, while the wife became the suffering codependent partner.

Healing for Marsha and Michael has been slow, but good progress is being made. After a period of abstinence and resolutions to change, Michael began to drink heavily again. This time, Marsha warned him that if he fell down drunk, he would lie in his own vomit until he woke up. She would leave him there and he would clear up the mess for himself. To carry out her threat, Marsha had to use her Alpha quality of strong-mindedness, leaving her drunken husband insensible on the floor and going home. To Michael, this seemed like a betrayal, but eventually he realised the excessive drinking was his problem, not his wife's. Since Marsha's warning he has not passed out at a party.

Perhaps, like Michael and Marsha, you are stuck in a codependent relationship. Maybe you cover up for another person, who behaves badly, but refuses to own up to it. If so, you have been taking on the other person's shame. Your healing will be to recognise you don't have to carry that shame any more. You can hand it back to where it belongs. In the world of addiction therapy, handing back the shame is called "tough love" and it is the most effective cure for addiction. It requires the giver to risk the entire relationship for the sake of truth. It confronts the other with his or her shame in an atmosphere of absolute love and trust. That is how it brings healing to everyone involved.

## Healing shame

As a womb twin survivor, healing for you will be to unravel the knot of your invented shame and rediscover your real, original womb experience. Only then will you be able to understand, accept and forgive those deeply-held feelings of helplessness and emotional need. They are characteristics adopted from your own lost womb twin.

### Healing through mortification

It may seem to you that the only way to overcome shame is to balance it out by a process of atonement or reparation. The thinking goes something like this: *If I make some kind of personal sacrifice, then that will be a way to make amends for what I have done.* But what if your sin has been to be alive on this earth? How can you make recompense for the fact that you have life? There is one way to do that - the most fitting kind of reparation would be not to live. Many womb twin survivors yearn to die. Suicidal thoughts are remarkably common among them, according to the Womb Twin Survivors Research Project.

Another way to make amends for the sin of being alive is to "be dead inside." The original meaning of the word mortify was to kill or subdue. We use the word these days to describe extreme shame in a way that is connected to death. To feel mortified is to feel totally humiliated - in a way, "ashamed to death." To avoid such a terrible feeling you may be motivated to work extremely hard, win awards, gain prestige or increase your status in society. In that way, you might be able to prove that you are worth the great gift of life, which you alone inherited when your twin died.

### Truth heals shame

Healing shame is easy: just add truth. Putting truth into shame means not being afraid to reveal the soft underbelly of your personality. Once you are no longer afraid to admit the truth of your faults and inadequacies, you will feel your personal power and strength increase. With this new power you will be able to make amends, put things right and develop new resolutions. You will not have to go on constantly breaking rules of your own construction in order to give yourself something to be ashamed of. Shame overcome by personal honesty is one of the most potent forces for good in society.

## The next step: Resistance to healing

Your feelings of shame at not using your talents to the full and guilt about being alive at all may be so strong that you are still resisting healing. It could come for you if only you would allow it into your life. In the next chapter we will reflect on what healing could mean for you and why you may not wish to have it, after all.

# 15
# Resistance to healing

We have been on the healing path for a long time now and are now exactly halfway. Despite all the excellent work you may have done, your resistance to healing is probably at the maximum at this stage. The image above is a development of the previous step. Despite your shame at covering your Alpha self with Beta energy, you find it hard to let go of the Dream.

If you have begun to feel that healing will never come or you are ready to give up, take heart. Doing the womb twin work is like crossing a great chasm on a flimsy rope bridge. The only way is to keep your eyes fixed on the firm ground on the far side. The first stage is relatively easy, as you are on a downhill path, but once you reach the centre, the bridge is at its most unstable. It tends to swing wildly from side to side whenever you try to move. Things feel very uncertain, but you will have to hang on, stay calm and move forward inch by inch. That is where we are at the moment. What remains is an uphill climb, but rest assured the way will become firmer and stronger as we proceed.

## Taking stock

As you pause to take a breath at this mid-point of your healing path, you may like to take stock of your progress so far – or the lack of it. You may be reading casually through these steps for the first time, with a view to "following the path, one day". Are you ready now to continue with the work, or do you want to rush to the end, let it all be over quickly and thus avoid the pain of actually doing it?

# Blocks to your healing

There are many blocks to healing that you may have carefully created. Your worst enemies are impatience, apathy, despondency or over-confidence, depending on the kind of person you are. If you feel unable to overcome these obstacles, you will carefully ensure you will never be healed of the pain and suffering of being a womb twin survivor - and that is exactly how you want things to be. Here are some of the things womb twin survivors say when they are resisting the womb twin work. You may like to tick any that resonate with you (there is space to add more, if necessary).

## Impatience

| Blocks to healing | Yes |
|---|---|
| I want healing and I want it now! | |
| I have done so much work I should be healed by now | |
| I have been in the Black Hole for too long and I want OUT! | |
| I want all this to be over – and soon! | |
| Other | |

## Apathy

| Blocks to healing | Yes |
|---|---|
| I don't have the energy to do this work | |
| I am too overwhelmed to do this | |
| I can't handle any more pain | |
| I don't care about healing any more | |
| I am stuck | |
| Other | |

## Despondency

| | |
|---|---|
| Maybe this is as good as it's going to get, so I'll stop now | |
| I'll never be healed – if such a thing is ever possible | |
| I'm not getting anything out of this | |
| I can't see a way forward to anything better | |
| I get out of my Black Hole for a while, but I'm soon in it again | |
| Other | |

## Over-confidence

| | |
|---|---|
| I am healed already | |
| I am working really hard to heal myself | |
| I am in more than one kind of therapy | |
| I have put my life on hold to concentrate on this healing work | |
| I am sure I can go on with this in my own way with no help | |
| Other | |

- You could learn to see signs of your resistance when you are with your own therapist - if you have one.

- You may make half-hearted little jokes about your most painful memories, or carefully disguise your feelings, even to yourself.

- You may miss therapy sessions or "forget to mention" certain things during them.

*I really want to move forward in my life but I feel like I'm caught in a spiral. I get strong and begin to move powerfully forward and then I get stopped by feelings of being incomplete and therefore unworthy of having the things in my life that I want. I take two or three steps forward, am inspired and people are enrolled in my project and then I just stop taking action that will move me forward. I fall back a step or two and find myself drifting and feeling incomplete. Before long nothing is happening to move my business forward and all momentum of business building is gone...*
*[Mary, USA]*

128

**IN AND OUT OF THE BLACK HOLE**

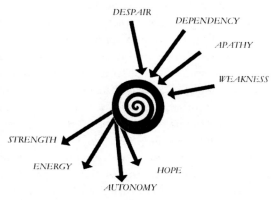

It can be helpful to stand back and consider what is going on when you feel that darkness coming over you. If you have made friends with your Black Hole, you will have learned you are in full charge of the process of entering and leaving it. When you enter your Black Hole to revisit those lost memories of your twin, you are resisting healing. You may want to heal and have a better life, but the Black Hole will always beckon you back.

Next time the darkness comes, take note: is this just an excuse not to heal your life? Are you allowing yourself to sink into the pit where you can say, "I don't have the strength to get myself out"? Are you simply becoming your Beta twin when you do that? What would happen if you changed your mind and decided to be the strong Alpha survivor instead? Try it next time!

# Disintegration

Healing and personal growth require a change of behaviour and attitudes. However, the process of change can cause anxiety in those womb twin survivors who have disintegration as a factor in their Dream of the Womb. If you fear change, it may be that in your Dream is a lost memory of your twin falling to pieces somewhere nearby. In that case, you may associate change with disintegration, misery and death - not with healing, growth and a better life. You may also have a deep sense of things being "not quite right". This can be expressed in a bodily way as vague, minor physical ailments that resist all treatment and make you very worried about any change in your health or wellbeing. Your sense of inner disturbance may frighten you, because it feels as if you are somehow falling apart inside. In that case, your fears may be expressed in erratic mood swings or sudden bursts of irrational rage.

An inner sense of being "in a complete mess" can be expressed in the home environment, usually in one of two opposite ways: either by deliberately creating a messy, cluttered home or by being excessively neat and tidy. If this is your story, then somewhere in your Dream there is a vague sense of Something disintegrating. This may be a lost memory of a blighted ovum, which never really made it into any kind of ordered existence. Perhaps there is a vague impression of a foetus papyraceous - a foetus that was developing quite normally, but began to disintegrate after death until it was just a bag of bones. Perhaps there were two or more womb twins present, falling apart after death in their own way. Any of these lost memories would be enough to create a sense of inner confusion and chaos in the mind of the sole survivor.

You may notice the way you are maintaining needless chaos and confusion in your life. Perhaps it is simply not completing one project before you start another, or having too many projects on the go at once. Perhaps you find it hard to set priorities and end up doing things in the wrong order. Perhaps on some days you don't know how you feel, or even who you truly are. It is important to realise there is a rational, intelligent and loving reason why you would allow chaos to reign in your home and in your life. It may be a big problem for you, but that doesn't make you a crazy person. When you are confronted with the chaos in your life, you tend to tumble into your own Black Hole.

## Feeling stuck

"I can't do this!", you cry. You have identified a bit too much with your Beta twin and lost sight of your own self. Reclaim it by asking yourself, "What would an Alpha twin do now?" The Alpha twin inside you would say exactly what your friends say all the time to encourage you: "Tackle one small area of your life now and you will sort it all out in time." For you, the sole survivor, chaos does not mean death. Chaos is not your story – it is your womb twin's story. Messiness may briefly impair your ability to function normally, but order can soon be restored. Allowing a little creative mess is an excellent idea and great fun. A fear of chaos will hold back your creative talents. Your present way of living which seems so habitual and resistant to change, is your only way to keep the Dream alive.

Regardless of the many choices available to you, there is only one you can actually bring yourself to make: to stay stuck. The idea of feeling "stuck" is a problem many therapists encounter and which you will probably recognise in yourself.

> *My thoughts have been so negative eg. "I wish I was dead." I felt drained and went to the gym. I still ran all the negative thoughts. When I ask myself, "What do I want instead?" the answer is "To be left alone to die," or "I wish my heart would stop." I'd love to feel I'm moving forward. I still think of suicide more than once daily. I won't do it but it would be nice to be free of that thought. Sometimes I think I've got to take my crap to the grave rather than be free of it.*
> *[Andrew, Ireland]*

- Are you a voluntary inmate in a prison of your own construction?
- Do you feel as if you are in a pit and lack the capacity to climb out?
- Are you so weighed down by pain and suffering you have no energy for anything, other than some kind of dull and pointless existence?
- Does it sometimes seem that you have no choices in life at all?

If this is how you feel, then you are stuck. Intrinsic to the sensation of being stuck is the notion that you have no idea how to get unstuck. There are just two options open to you at this point. You could solve the problem and become unstuck, or you could remain stuck while pretending you are trying very hard to get unstuck.

In staying stuck you will naturally resist healing, because the re-enactment of your Dream of the Womb continues to be the principal task of your life. Even if you see your marriage failing, your health breaking down or your future in ruins, you will hold fast to the way things have always been and refuse to make any changes. That has probably been normal life for you, as a womb twin survivor, but it no longer has to be that way.

## A healing challenge

As an example of how you may be resisting any forward movement, see how many excuses you can find not to take up this challenge: **Just for the next three weeks, try solving your Problem of Being Stuck.**

Deep down, you know exactly what your principal problem is and exactly what to do to solve it, however hard you are trying to convince yourself that you do not. It may be an overwhelming sense of despair, against which you feel unable to summon up any hope. If you want to solve the problem, you will need to prepare carefully and take action courageously.

### Prepare carefully

- Know what your problem is
- Observe the situation that creates the problem
- Notice how you are making it happen, every time
- Ponder on the problem of solving your problem
- Assess the possibilities of ever solving your problem
- Consider the range of choices available to you at this moment

### Take action courageously

- Take control of your own process of problem-solving
- Exercise your power of choice to decide whether to try and solve the problem or not
- Inch forward, making sure at all times that you are in control of the process

If you can solve all your problems in this way for three weeks, then surely you can solve them for ever – that is, once you have woken from your Dream of the Womb.

## Permission to grow

We will now consider three areas of the healing process that you may have allowed yourself to engage in so far. They are personal development, life lessons and personal growth experiences.

### Personal development

| Area of personal development | Yes |
|---|---|
| More qualifications | |
| Better employment prospects | |
| Improved living environment | |

| | |
|---|---|
| More money | |
| Increased knowledge | |
| Extensive reading | |
| The widest possible range of interests | |
| Travel to as many places as possible | |
| More personal challenges | |
| Seizing every opportunity | |
| Having a wide range of experiences | |
| Meeting as many people as possible | |
| Other: | |

## Life lessons

How hard is it for you to learn the following life lessons? (Five is high.)

| Life lesson | 1 | 2 | 3 | 4 | 5 |
|---|---|---|---|---|---|
| Learning from experience | | | | | |
| Developing wisdom | | | | | |
| Reflecting on personal experience | | | | | |
| Learning from mistakes | | | | | |
| Recognising how little you know | | | | | |
| Letting other people teach you | | | | | |
| Developing your creativity | | | | | |
| Developing your practical skills | | | | | |
| Knowing where to find things out | | | | | |
| Acknowledging your learning difficulties | | | | | |
| Accepting maturity and old age | | | | | |
| Other | | | | | |

**Personal growth experiences**

On the same scale as previously, how well are you talking advantage of opportunities for personal growth? (Again, five is high)

| Growth experience | 1 | 2 | 3 | 4 | 5 |
|---|---|---|---|---|---|
| I am discovering my in-built talents and gifts | | | | | |
| I have found that I learn more easily when I don't try so hard | | | | | |
| I am opening my mind to my inner experience | | | | | |
| I am developing my in-built talents by practising them. | | | | | |
| I am learning by helping others to learn | | | | | |
| I am beginning to trust my intuitive sense. | | | | | |
| I am healing myself by helping others to heal | | | | | |
| Other: | | | | | |

Lastly, you could write a message to yourself. giving yourself permission to grow:

# The next step: A healing bond

The next step is a particular effective way to break out of being stuck. It is time to start forming a healing bond, which will move you on to the next stage of healing.

# 16
# Building a healing bond

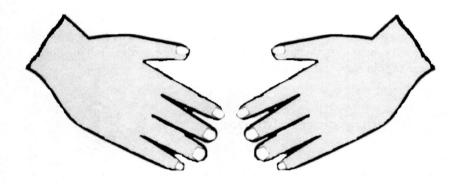

One simple action on your part could open the door to healing today, if you are prepared to try it. The image above shows two hands, reaching out to each other. It is easy to imagine that, if only the left hand will reach out a little further and the right hand will dare to take hold of the left, the result will be a handclasp - a new connection. Womb twin survivors cannot heal themselves in isolation. As we saw in a previous chapter, isolation is very painful for womb twin survivors. You are probably already aware you are not built to do anything completely alone. To begin to heal your life you will need to create a special kind of healing connection - a healing bond.

## Creating a healing bond

So far, in trying to keep your twin alive in your Dream of the Womb, you have probably sought to recreate in every close relationship the kind of bond you once had with your twin. If so, it is time to replace the lost twin connection from your Dream with a healing bond made with a real, living person in today's world. The Womb Twin Survivors Research Project has revealed that making a healing bond with another womb twin survivor is the fastest and most effective way to heal yourself.

Sadly, people born of a singleton conception find it very hard to understand the inner experience of the womb twin survivor, however carefully it is explained. Only another womb twin survivor has sufficient empathy to enable a new healing bond to develop. Reaching out to other womb twin survivors will help you to heal all of the five problems that are characteristic of womb twin survivors. These are:

135

- Your painful loneliness
- Your dual personality
- Your undeveloped potential
- Your sense of something missing
- Your strong feelings

All these can be overcome, at least in part, by creating a healing bond with another womb twin survivor. We will now explore each of these characteristics in turn and see how making a healing bond can help.

## Healing your painful loneliness

Unhealthy relationships are those that mirror your womb experience. As a womb twin survivor, you will constantly try to duplicate the relationship you had in the womb with your twin and in that way keep your Dream alive. The trouble is that the womb experience is not a snapshot, but a complete story, which began with connection, but ended in isolation. If you attempt to create a twin connection from your Dream in your born life, then the story of that relationship will inevitably be played out over time in the same way. However deep the bond may be at first, it will end in disaster, leaving behind only isolation, pain and sorrow.

> *I was in a relationship with another twinless twin for five years. We were the best of friends. We often joked that we were more like brothers and sisters instead of lovers. But our similar traits destroyed us. Our relationship was extremely unhealthy. I miss him so much. I feel like I am losing my twin all over again. He filled that void that was empty for so long. I cry at the drop of a hat whenever I think of him or wake up after dreaming of him. I am still in love with him. We were supposed to be forever, get married next fall and never let go. I want to go back to him, to feel complete again but he was so bad for me. I just want the pain to stop.*
> *[Becky, USA]*

For a practical exercise that may help, look back over your life and find a relationship that ended in painful isolation. This may be an example of trying to create a twin connection from your Dream.

Here are some of the ways in which recreated twin connections may end. They reflect several real situations in the womb when a twin dies (sudden

136

death, slowly fading away etc.) See if the story of your chosen relationships is on this list. If not, you can write in the space provided.

| How a relationship ended | Yes |
|---|---|
| The other person abandoned me | |
| The other person came too close to me | |
| The other person drained me dry | |
| The other person refused to merge with me | |
| The other person asked too much of me | |
| The relationship died, long before we parted | |
| The relationship just faded away | |
| I tried to make connection but failed | |
| The other person wasn't interested in me | |
| The other person was not my type at all | |
| There was too much conflict | |
| There was too much pain | |
| I had to work hard to make it work | |
| Other | |

The way to create a healing bond with someone that will not end in isolation for you both is to consider your immediate reaction to this person:

1. Does it feel as if you have found a soulmate?
2. Is there anything about this person that makes you feel uneasy?
3. How trustworthy is this person?

## The soulmate

An instant "meeting of minds and hearts" experienced by both sides of a new friendship is a sure sign that here is a reflection of a relationship that once existed in the Dream of the Womb. But there is a danger that you will drift into re-enacting the whole womb story between you, for example feeling "abandoned" every time the other person doesn't answer the phone or reply to an email. To maintain the relationship, recognise that your new friend has a separate life from you and may have very good reasons not to

137

respond, which have nothing to do with how much he or she wants to be your friend.

## Uneasiness

If something about your new friend makes you feel slightly uneasy, take heed of that feeling. The uneasiness is probably your intuition, picking up on something negative. However charming your new friend may be on the surface, this could be an attempt to drag you into his or her Black Hole. Make sure that the other person is aware of how he or she is turning you into his or her own Beta twin and you will be able to keep the relationship alive, to the benefit of both of you.

## Lack of trust

Your new friend may test your relationship again and again because he or she is lost in the Dream and is unable to believe that any close relationship can last. In that case, building a healing bond requires at least one of you to trust in the ability of the relationship to survive. That will be a challenge for both of you but this in itself can build a healing bond.

# Healing your dual personality

You may have experienced significant changes of mood or personality throughout your life, as you try to be both Alpha and Beta at once. This is true for most womb twin survivors, as we have seen in previous chapters. The best way to heal the split inside your personality is to recreate the original twin pair with another womb twin survivor in an atmosphere of mutual acceptance. We now know that when pairs or groups of womb twin survivors come together, there is a delightful sense of being understood without having to explain.

An atmosphere of acceptance builds very quickly at first, but at some point somebody's Black Hole will begin to dominate the relationship. That person will "split into two" and make someone else responsible for living out the life of his or her "other half." For instance, your friend may accuse you of being a "control freak" in not letting him or her decide what happens next. In the face of such an accusation and to keep the relationship alive, you would probably surrender control out of simple kindness. But in the process you would also "split into two" and adopt the character of your Beta twin. Very soon, you would start to resent not having the power to decide and you would want to become the Alpha twin once more. At that point you could begin to make a healing bond by reclaiming your Alpha energy. If you do not seek to dominate, but rather to share, you can create a relationship of mutual respect that will be your healing bond.

# Healing your undeveloped potential

One of the most joyful aspects of being with other womb twin survivors is that everyone feels stronger by being together. Never forget that we are self-healing organisms. However hard you try to sabotage your own personal development, you can't help growing and developing as time passes. But you can slow the process down almost to a stop by refusing to learn from other people and by not helping others to grow.

## Refusing to learn from others

If you find it hard to learn from others and prefer to teach yourself, then you are missing out on the chance to grow with the help of someone else. Certainly you will learn at your own pace if you teach yourself, but you will only try things for as long as they remain interesting. If that is what you choose to do, there will be no stimulating challenges to help you to discover the true extent of your abilities and no structures to keep you on track until you have completed the task. In short, if you only teach yourself you will greatly lessen every chance to learn and grow.

*I've been told that I don't have enough passion for anything. I start something and it can take me days, weeks even months to finish what I started because I get bored so easily.*
*[Alan, USA]*

Do you often resist the chance to learn something new?

| Excuse | Agree | Disagree |
|---|---|---|
| I won't be capable of doing it properly | | |
| I don't need to know about it | | |
| I know I will fail, so I won't bother | | |
| It sounds like a boring idea | | |

| It will be bad for me | | |
|---|---|---|
| Other: | | |

### Refusing to help others to grow

In a healing bond where each of you encourages and stimulates the other, you will discover not only the joys of being helped with your learning, but also the delights of seeing the other person grow. The best teachers let their pupils teach them. The worst teachers think they have nothing to learn.

There are many ways to help other people to learn and grow and all of them require empathy, enabling you to imagine what it is like not to know or understand. Empathy helps you to remain patient when the other person does not seem to want to listen to you or doesn't want follow your advice. Listening is another vital component in a healing bond. When both parties listen to each other carefully and give each other space to speak, they will both develop in patience and understanding.

## Healing something missing

You have probably been trying to heal the hole in your life since you were a small child, perhaps by creating a surrogate twin in the form of an imaginary friend.

> *My mom started bleeding when she was three months pregnant with me. I had an imaginary friend that only I could see. I don't remember her now, but my mum said they couldn't even sit down on some chairs and she used to sleep in my dresser. I am thinking this was my twin and I was manifesting her in my mind.*
> *[Michelle, Canada]*

If as an adult you still have an imaginary friend, it may be that even now you only think of yourself as "half of a pair". That is absolutely normal for a womb twin survivor. If you find a new friend who is also a womb twin survivor, you can talk about your mutual need to be "twins" to each other. That can be your healing bond. As you develop a shared relationship of mutual support, you will feel stronger. Your new friend can become your surrogate twin, but be careful - if you allow the story in your Dream to dominate your relationship, it will not last. Keep openly sharing how you feel about each other as the relationship develops. Eventually the healing bond will free both of you from needing to turn everyone into a twin replacement.

## Healing strong emotions

If you are a super-sensitive person who carries the feelings of others, you may have a problem with expressing your emotions appropriately. Three ways in which you may be managing your strong emotions are repression, rumination and release. A healing bond can help in each case.

**Repression**: You may repress your feelings to the point where you are unaware of having any. If this is the situation, another womb twin survivor with a strong intuitive sense will soon recognise that something is wrong. He or she may even pick up and personally experience the same strong feelings that you have suppressed so carefully. A healing bond with another womb twin survivor can help both of you to express your feelings more appropriately.

**Rumination**: Perhaps your problem with expressing your emotions is because you think of little else. If this is your story, you ruminate on your feelings endlessly. You are the kind of person who holds a grudge, never forgets or forgives and in a sense is always "picking at sores". In a healing bond with another womb twin survivor, your friend can learn to see you have a pain inside you that won't go away. At the same time, you can learn that you are holding on to it.

**Release**: One of the problems of denying feelings, or exaggerating them through endless rumination, is that one day you will have to let them loose in an emotional outburst. If you do this unthinkingly and indiscriminately, you could destroy a relationship almost at once. In a healing bond, where these things are discussed fearlessly and openly, you can find ways to express your feelings in a less-destructive way.

## Developing a healing bond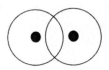

Your womb twin work will be most effective when carried out with the help of a healing friend, best of all another womb twin survivor. This connection will be one of equal sharing. Everything will be split 50:50. Another womb twin survivor in search of a healing bond could help you to create a relationship of shared power, for he or she will need that 50:50 balance as much as you do.

## Negotiation

Once you try to set up an equal relationship, your attitude to personal power will be visible to both sides. If the healing bond is to work, there must be absolute freedom of activity for both parties. Everything must be equally negotiated. If either party goes too far or leans too much on the other, then it will be time to complain or pull away, depending on who does what to whom.

## Hope

A healing bond must be able to survive negative feelings such as anger, despair and anguish. These feelings are discovered and experienced in an atmosphere of hope. This is an act of trust on both sides. Your healing friend must trust you to be able to survive expressing your pain and you must trust your healing friend to be able to survive witnessing it. That means both of you putting your Dreams to one side and starting to believe that your friend will stay and not forsake you.

**An exercise:** When you have found a healing friend to work with, stand facing one another with your arms outstretched before you with fingertips touching. Then move slightly backwards. You are now literally keeping each other "at arms length".

Move back and forth, negotiating the distance between you, until you are both happy with how close you are to each other. This will be a compromise reached by both parties in a process of give and take.

You will both need to practise this frequently if the womb twin healing work is to be successful between you.

# The next stage: The biology of twinning

The next stage of our healing path will take us deep into the biology of twinning. Your Dream of the Womb will be revealed to you in more detail and the way forward will become much clearer.

# STAGE FOUR
## Three pathways to healing

Half-ness is a divided soul;
I walk on a one-legged limp.
I see one-eyed with no depth of vision,
I cannot tell how near you are to me.

One side is emptiness and death;
An un-slaked thirst; a mirage of completion:
A cracked box, empty and crumbling into dust.
What was there was something: nothing now.

The other side is yearning and pain;
Tears for two and anguish for more than myself.
An empty chair at the feast of life.
My voice is stilled by the sheer silence of you.

The treasure chest stands between us;
My life, my voice, my strength, is there
Locked away for you for many years:
I want - I may and now I will.

# 17

# Twin myths as an aid to healing

GEMINI    NARCISSUS    CHIRON

An exploration of ancient myths and legends will take us deep into human psychology. Until the rise of the modern scientific study of mental processes about 100 years ago, these tales were the only way to describe the various aspects of the human psyche. In some of them, womb twin survivors can be discovered. Twinning has been part of human existence throughout the ages, so we can safely assume that womb twin survivors have existed in large numbers in every generation, even in ancient Greece. In this chapter we will consider the Greek myths of Gemini, Narcissus and Chiron, as described in more detail by Roger Graves in his book *The Greek Myths.*[1] The Womb Twin Survivors Research Project revealed three distinct groups of womb twin survivors, each of which corresponds closely to one of the characters described in these three ancient myths.

## Gemini – the two-egg (dizygotic) womb twin story

  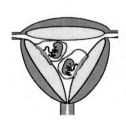  

GEMINI SYMBOL   TWO-EGG TWINS   TWO-EGG WOMB TWIN
SURVIVOR

The myth of Gemini tells the story of warrior twins, Castor and Pollux. They were fraternal twins from two different fathers, one mortal and the other immortal. The two brothers were inseparable and loved each other dearly. One day Castor (the mortal twin) was killed in battle, leaving Pollux (the immortal twin) as the sole survivor. Pollux was so stricken with grief that he asked Zeus to let him sacrifice his own immortality and join his brother in death. Zeus, impressed by the deep love the two brothers shared, lifted Pollux to heaven to be beside his twin forever. They shine today as the brightest twin stars in the constellation of Gemini. The Gemini myth describes the story of a lost twin from a two-egg (dizygotic) twin pair. Within the myth are the three special characteristics of two-egg womb twin survivors – the pain of abandonment, duality in difference and self-sacrifice.

## The pain of abandonment

All Pollux wanted was to be reunited with his twin. The pain of abandonment for the two-egg womb twin survivor is a vague sensation of *Someone* who was always there somewhere close by, but is now gone. To be the only one left is very painful. If you are a two-egg womb twin survivor, it feels as if the many experiences of life are meant to be shared.

> *My frustration is that our relationship ended SO suddenly, even though in hindsight it was in trouble, but she forced it to a crisis. I left and ran. Then when I came back she never gave me a second chance. Just gone. And I realised today I am still hanging onto her. There is part of me that still thinks we will get back together. I don't know how to let her go.*
> *[Joe, Australia]*

## Duality in difference

If you are a two-egg womb twin survivor, you probably find no difficulty in making a close bond with someone who is opposite to you in character. You may spend so much energy making up opposite ways of being that you lose all sense of your own identity.

> *Oftentimes I find myself making up different lives for myself, others, or made-up people. And for some reason the question about having irrational feelings of non-existence really stood out because when I was little (and even now) sometimes in the mirror I look and think to myself, "Is this the person that everyone sees? Is this me?"*
> *[Naomi, USA]*

### Altruistic self-sacrifice

Pollux was immortal, but was prepared to sacrifice his gifts in order to become mortal and die. In the same way, the sole surviving two-egg twin is willing to sacrifice strength, success and potential to emulate his or her Beta twin. The two-egg womb twin survivor is always ready to help others, to the point where that altruism may develop into a caring compulsion. If this is your story, it could be that your compulsion to care becomes self-defeating, if the sacrifice is so great that exhaustion or illness results. But for you, the two-egg womb twin survivor, no effort is too much to rescue and save people who are less fortunate or able. Any individual in need quickly becomes your weak and helpless little Beta twin, from your Dream of the Womb.

> *I was born at six months of pregnancy, a fraternal twin female. My sister was born dead. All my life I felt different from others, and could identify with sadness easily. I realized I was always empathetic towards others to a great degree, and sensitive to others' distress. I used to save the little kid in the playground, then after the "rescue" I would get depressed when the big kids went after me instead, and then not understand why I was so sad.*
> *[Yolanda, USA]*

# Narcissus - the one-egg (monozygotic) womb twin story

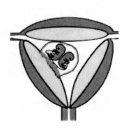

NARCISSUS SYMBOL      ONE-EGG TWINS      ONE-EGG
WOMB TWIN SURVIVOR

The symbol for Narcissus is a mask with a double face, one joyful and the other sad. This illustrates the deeply contradictory nature of the monozygotic (one-egg) womb twin survivor. The Greek myth describes the life and death of Narcissus, a beautiful youth. Many of the water nymphs in the country where he lived fell in love with him, especially Echo. He heartlessly rejected them all. As a punishment, the gods put a spell on him, to make him fall in love with the very next person he saw. Unfortunately that person was himself, in the form of his own reflection in a clear pool. Narcissus lay by the pool for many months in a trance-like state, pining away for love of his reflection. Eventually he died.

The Narcissus myth seems to be based on the story of the lost twin from a one-egg twin pair. Within it are the three special characteristics of the one-egg womb twin survivor - the Bubble of Oblivion, inwardly focused energy and contradiction.

## The Bubble of Oblivion

In the myth, Narcissus came to live in a world where the only other person present in his life was his unattainable reflection in the water. The name Narcissus is derived from the Greek word *narke*, which means "deep sleep." Clearly, Narcissus had no desire whatever to wake up from his trance, lest he lost sight of his precious reflection. For the one-egg womb twin survivor, the thrall of the Dream of the Womb is like a deep sleep. The Bubble of Oblivion is a recreation of the single chorion, the outer membrane that once enclosed two one-egg, embryonic twins, of whom only one now remains. With this in mind, the story of Narcissus, deep in loving contemplation of a mirror-image of himself, begins to make sense.

> *It is very confronting to even begin to see that I have protected myself and built up these walls, that I hide away from people and prevent myself from really having close friends. I stay very separate and protect the boundaries of my personal space. It seems so final, the feeling that I will always be alone, always. I am always searching for someone to fill the gap but they can't.*
> *[Steven, UK]*

## Inwardly focused energy

For Narcissus, all his physical and emotional energy was spent in maintaining his Bubble of Oblivion and keeping alive the precious image of himself in the pool. Similarly, the one-egg womb twin survivor is focused utterly on the missing twin, who would restore wholeness, but who will never be found. This constant inward focus may seem self-centred, but if you are a one-egg womb twin survivor, you will know that what others may call "selfishness" is in fact an attempt to heal your primal wound.

> *Sometimes when I protect myself, it is perceived by others as being selfish. Sometimes I feel smothered, put upon, confused and a whole list of things by my family. I need to take time to identify the problem and*

148

*decide if I want to continue the relationship. I have withdrawn from some of them permanently. That has caused their feelings to get hurt but I am not responsible for their feelings, only how I deal with my own. [Trish, USA]*

## Contradiction

In the myth, Narcissus is in many ways a contradiction, particularly in the way he manages his feelings. He is heartless and rejects the love of the beautiful nymphs who surround him. Yet his capacity for loving is so great that he dies out of unrequited longing for his precious reflection. He is heartless yet broken-hearted, all at once. In the Dream of the Womb, where there was once a pair of one-egg twins, there is now a sole survivor. To keep the Dream alive, somehow it has to be possible to be two people at once. For the one-egg womb twin survivor, being two very different people is a rational way to resolve the inner contradiction.

*My son is so easy to love but there are long periods when he withdraws into a stony-faced silence. Sometimes I do not know him as my son. At those times it is like someone else has entered the room and taken his place. It breaks my heart when that happens. [Meg, Ireland]*

## Chiron - the multiple womb twin story

 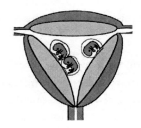 

| CHIRON SYMBOL | MULTIPLE PREGNANCY | MULTIPLE WOMB TWIN SURVIVOR |

The symbol for Chiron is a key, suggesting the wisdom that unlocks many mysteries. In the Greek myth, Chiron was the most renowned of the centaurs, creatures that were half man and half horse. He was immortal and one of the wisest beings on earth. When his mother gave birth to a centaur, she was so ashamed that she abandoned him. Chiron was forced to grow up alone in a dark cave but his great wisdom and learning brought him fame.

He made friends with many of the ancient Greek heroes, such as Achilles and Jason, and taught them how to hunt and fight. Chiron was wounded with an arrow smeared with venom so poisonous that it could never heal. He retreated into his cave, seeking out ways to ease the continuous pain. In the process he learned about healing and became a famous healer himself, but only death could take away his own pain. Meanwhile, Prometheus, the Titan who stole fire from Mount Olympus to give to humankind, wished to be immortal. Sympathetic to Chiron's plight, the gods allowed Chiron to cede his immortality to Prometheus. In that way, Chiron met death and was freed of his pain at last.

## The wounded healer

This ancient story does not appear to be a twin myth until we consider the concept of the "wounded healer". There are many womb twin survivors who are deeply wounded and who find healing for themselves by offering it to others. It seems that these are the multiple womb twin survivors, the sole survivors from a multiple pregnancy. Chiron's dark cave could represent the darkness of the womb. As a centaur he would have been what is biologically known as a chimera, with two very different sets of DNA in his body. He knew abandonment, rejection and loneliness. His life-long wounded-ness and his desire to be free of pain would be familiar to most womb twin survivors. The three characteristics of Chiron that are found among multiple womb twin survivors are related to creating communities, promoting healing and building relationships. We will explore each of these in turn, to see what can be learned from this comparison.

## Creating communities

In the Dream of the Womb of a multiple womb twin survivor, there is a group of embryos. If you are a multiple womb twin survivor, you probably gather around yourself a large group of acquaintances but have only a few friends. Even in this group you are still lonely and in pain but the energy of being in a group sustains you in the lonely hours after everyone has gone home. Any group will do, be it a social club, a choir, a church congregation or a special-interest society.

If you are a multiple womb twin survivor, you may have already noticed the great effort you make to hold communities together. You probably work hard to keep everyone in your family happy, at considerable personal cost. If you have no family, you are probably busy creating another one for yourself. The energy you are prepared to expend in maintaining communities is driven by a long-lost memory of being in a group of other embryos, where you were the strongest and most capable individual in that space. You may find being with other people exhausting because of your wish to enliven and sustain every group you enter, but still you keep trying. You are reconstituting the first group you ever knew, which lies in your Dream of the Womb.

*Over the last year, I have gone from strength to strength within myself. I used to let people overstep my boundaries. I was too generous with time and finances. Now my boundaries are strong and I am giving myself regeneration time doing what is right for myself. I have always given and given and given, ending up exhausted. Now I am not prepared to do this any more.*
*[Tasha, USA]*

## Promoting healing

Chiron knew what is was to be in pain but he was ready to share his wisdom with others to help them strengthen and grow. If you are a multiple womb twin survivor, you may have noticed in yourself a similar interest in assisting others to develop and learn. In the process of healing your own wounded-ness, you will have absorbed a great deal about the various methods of healing. You may have already discovered in yourself a natural healing gift, which provides you with a sense of mission - to "heal the world."

*I have a sense of being granted the mission of rescuing and saving injured and orphaned wildlife. I have a healing ability that seems to be meant for creatures other than humans. I also have other abilities - such as being able to read people's inner feelings by looking at a current photo of them. I avoid people, as it is too difficult, depressing and exhausting to try and absorb their feelings and bring them peace. I feel so different and alone in the world, but this is my mission and it brings me great joy and satisfaction.*
*[Terri, USA]*

## Building relationships

Multiple womb twin survivors are often the first to reach out and build new relationships with strangers. You may have discovered this tendency in your own life. You may be shy, but you are prepared to overcome your shyness to make and maintain connections with others. You often feel alone in a crowd, even among dear friends. Nevertheless, friendship is very important to you. Your tendency to absorb the feelings of others will hamper your progress occasionally, for you need plenty of private space to recover your energy.

*When I was a teenager I felt very different from other kids. We didn't share the same interests. But there was mutual respect, and friendship as well. I just felt very lonely and different. At the same time people often come to me when they need someone to talk to. I always felt happy to help someone or just listen to them. It made me feel "connected". I care too much. I want to make things right. I have always tried to "take care" of people. I have worked with disabled people, elderly people, mentally handicapped children, etc. Usually I only want to make things better for others, and tend to forget about myself.*
*[Gracie, USA]*

## Recreating your womb story

The Womb Twin Survivors Research Project has shown that, until someone's full womb story is made clear, his or her healing can be delayed indefinitely. You may already have some information about your own womb story that has come to you via the family, or you may have discovered some documentation about your twin. If you have no such information and can find none no matter how hard you try, then you will have to use your intuition.

As you will have discovered by now, recreating your Dream of the Womb is like trying to do a jigsaw puzzle without the larger picture. Some pieces seem to belong together but it is not be clear exactly where or how. At this early stage, as you struggle to understand what may be in your Dream of the Womb, you will probably reach faulty conclusions along the way. In time however, a sense of unease will arise which, if you listen to it carefully, will guide you towards the truth of what really happened.

## A two-egg womb twin survivor of the same sex

We are now not so much at a crossroads, as at the beginning of a short series of parallel tracks. The tracks all lead in the same direction and will take you forward, so feel free to consider them all carefully. The next step will explore what it feels like to be the sole survivor of two-egg twins of the same sex.

# 18
# Two-eggs, single sex

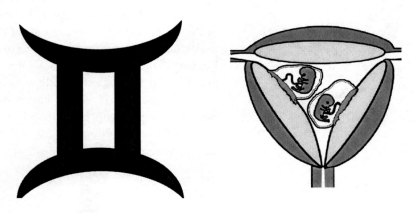

When a womb twin survivor is born from a two-egg (dizygotic) twin pregnancy, two zygotes (fertilised eggs) begin to develop, but at some stage of the pregnancy one of them dies or never develops at all. This particular step on the path concerns two-egg twins of the same sex, like Castor and Pollux in the Greek myth we considered earlier. So far, we have seen that the three characteristics of the two-egg womb twin survivor are the pain of abandonment, duality in difference and self-sacrifice. Now we will take a closer look at those characteristics that may be specific to two-egg womb twin survivors of the same sex. To establish the characteristics of a two-egg, single sex womb twin survivor, we will review the ideas discussed in previous chapters and see what can be found.

## Your Dream of the Womb

In your Dream there once was a twin sister or brother, the same sex as you, developing in a completely separate sac, with his or her own placenta. Your healing will be to try and work out exactly what your womb story was. You will find many references to and diagrams of two-egg twin pregnancies in earlier chapters of this book.

To help you, overleaf here is a diagram of a complete two-egg pregnancy that you can use to create your own diagrams. Even if you already have

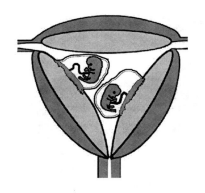

information about your mother's pregnancy, you may not have explored exactly what the real situation was, why your twin died and what happened to the body. All of these factors are critical to understanding how you have kept your Dream of the Womb alive, sometimes in extraordinary and very subtle ways.

Of course, if you have no information you will have to rely on your intuition to guide you.

## Life and death

If you are a two-egg, single sex womb twin survivor, the illness or death of someone the same sex would be hard for you to bear. Relatives of the same sex in your family are probably especially precious to you. If you have a child of your own who is the same sex as you, you may be excessively concerned about his or her health and welfare.

Your healing will be to understand that the people of the same sex as you in your family are not after all reincarnations of your fragile little twin, but strong and capable individuals in their own right.

## Craziness

You may feel as if you are "weird" or "different", especially in your very positive attitude to people of the same sex. You may find people of the opposite sex so strange that you think you will never understand them at all and you keep them at a distance. You may wonder if you are homosexual, but consider that "same-sex attraction" is a more-accurate term for your feelings. After all, there is no sexual element in the attraction you experience towards people of the same sex as you. Your healing will be to know you are not crazy. Quite naturally, you have been in search of a replacement for your lost twin sibling - a soulmate, not a sexual partner.

## Self-sabotage

Your chosen form of self-sabotage may include remaining in a state of arrested development, so that you never really grow up. This can mean living at home with your parents for many years, never marrying (or if you do marry, having little interest in sexual activity) and never wanting children. In middle age, you may find yourself sharing a home with another person of the same sex who is also a two-egg, single sex womb twin survivor - simply for companionship, nothing more. In that way, for both of you, the Dream of the Womb can come true. Your healing will be to allow your full gender energy to find expression. If you are male, you could begin to find and express in full the marvellous masculine side of yourself. If you are female, you could discover and begin to give full expression to your fabulous femininity.

## Addictions and compulsions

There do not seem to be any specific addictions or compulsions related to being a two-egg, single sex womb twin survivor. However, it is common in many two-egg twin pregnancies for the two placentas to fuse together. If this happened in your case and you got most of the blood supply, you may have guilt feelings about eating, which could have been enough to trigger an addiction to some foods. Your healing will be to recognise that you had nothing to do with the availability of blood in the womb. Gradually, you may come to accept that the privileged position which enabled you to survive was a great gift and need not be a lifelong burden.

## Self-isolation

The characteristic loneliness of the womb twin survivor is found among two-egg, single sex womb twin survivors, but with a subtle twist. As well as family members of the same sex as you, you will choose people of the

155

same sex to be your "best friends." The isolation will continue nonetheless, because of the separation of the two placentas and sacs that lies in your Dream of the Womb. It will keep your Dream alive if you create a distance between yourself and your friends and family, so that is what you do.

> *My childhood memories are rather lonely and somber. I usually made friends with one particular person, which now seems odd, and really took solace in having a best friend. I always kept my distance from the popular crowd. I don't keep in touch with any of my best friends today. My family is now broken up, parents divorced and remarried, and my sisters and I rarely talk. We've all gone our separate ways and have never been very close. I recall my mother mentioning to me that she had a miscarriage previous to my birth. She had expelled an unidentified mass into the toilet, and had presumed after speaking with her doctor that it was a twin fetus.*
> *[Sue, USA]*

Your healing will be to make your twin more real. That will enable you to re-experience that original sense of contact with *Someone* very near, that you had long ago in the womb, in company with your twin. By making some kind of tangible memorial to your twin, you may find you can rebuild a sense of that lost connection.

# Dual nature

You might be acting out your Dream of the Womb by creating a kind of "double life". For instance, you may "shop in twos" and purchase two of everything, as if you were buying for your twin as well as yourself. Shopping for two probably happens most when buying gender-specific personal items, such as handbags, clothing, hairbrushes or razors. Another way to "be yourself twice over" is to create two very different ways of being you.

> *I'm smart and literate, capable and appreciative, but yet I'm uninspired, unwilling, and unmotivated about a lot of things too.*
> *[Victoria, USA]*

Your healing will be to tease out which characteristics belong to you alone and which are borrowed from your twin. You may have already attempted the Me-Not-Me exercise detailed on page 107 but there may be more to do. As you let go of your Dream, you will begin to own your strengths.

## Unrealised potential

Your chosen way not to realise your potential is to refuse to allow yourself be a fully developed man or woman, as the case may be. You move gently through life, asking for very little from the world, but not giving much back from your own gender energy. You always hold back, just a bit, the expression of your talents. You may persistently fail to develop your gender role, so that you seem to be half the person you could be. Yet when circumstances require it, you can achieve much more than anyone expected. You may even surprise yourself. You keep forgetting that the potential is there inside you, but you just don't use it.

> *If I had a twin this would explain so much about why I feel incomplete.*
> *I have tried to do just about everything from college to art to music and*
> *I eventually fail at it. I always wanted a twin sister as a child and I now*
> *believe that is because I had one.*
> *[Summer, USA]*

Your healing will be to embrace your own gender energy and give it full expression in your life. Only then will you be truly whole and able to live as your authentic self.

## Something missing

The missing person in your life seems to be always someone of the same sex - a sister if you are a woman, a brother if you are a man. You miss your twin in those activities you would have shared, such as travelling, visiting the theatre or going out for a meal. For you, to travel or go out for an evening by yourself is painfully lonely, but this is how you must live, it seems. Someone to share experiences who is the same sex as you could make everything seem right again, even if you both hardly say a word. Just being together would be enough. Sometimes it happens that you have a companion and for a time life seems wonderful, but the friendship never seems to last. Once more your Dream of the Womb comes true and you are left abandoned.

Your healing would be to find more friends. The world is full of lonely people, many of whom are also two-egg, single sex womb twin survivors and would love to have you as their companion. You could also begin to notice the people of the opposite sex who are waiting to be your friends. So far, you have persistently ignored them, but think again - not every encounter with the opposite sex has to be sexual.

## Emotions

As in the Greek myth of Gemini that we examined earlier, the strongest emotions of a two-egg, single-sex womb twin survivor are focused on loss, grief, loneliness and longing. But those feelings are not so strong as to be overwhelming. You are well-able to control your emotions, almost to the point where you barely experience them at all. Your healing will be to waken up to your feelings and how deep they truly are. You will discover feelings of joy and gratitude, as well as anger or sadness.

## Your Black Hole

Your personal Black Hole has never been so bad that it cannot be endured. It feels not black, but like a grey cloud over your existence - an inevitable aspect of every day. The subtle shadow of your Black Hole is not always evident, so you may be enjoying a normal life, but deep down there is an all-pervading sense of Something Wrong.

> *It's like there's a grey cloud over me, something dampening my happiness, but yet deep down I'm grateful for such small things in my life, that other people take for granted all the time like love, food, laughter, sunshine. [May, Canada.]*

It's time for that cloud of negativity to go. It will disappear from your life when you awaken from your Dream and recognise that it is there in your mind simply because you created it and carefully maintain it to keep your Dream alive. You chose to put the cloud there, so once the womb twin work is done you will be able to allow it to depart.

## The Alpha-Beta gap

There does not seem to be any specific effect for two-egg, single sex womb twin survivors in terms of the Alpha-Beta gap. However, you may have had a lifelong sense of a vulnerable little "inner child." It may help to recognise that the little child who seems to be somewhere inside you is not a memory of a younger version of you. It is in fact a vague sense of your own Beta twin, who was another little girl or boy, as the case may be. Knowing who your "inner child" really is will help your healing.

## Personal boundary

As a two-egg womb twin survivor, your personal boundary style still echoes the arrangement of the membranes in the pregnancy. You and your twin each had your own space and that is how you like your personal boundary to be managed today. In a close relationship (usually with another person of the same sex), you prefer to keep your own counsel and maintain a reasonable level of personal privacy. You hold your friends at a safe distance, for your basic belief is that friendship and companionship are brief, elusive kinds of experience. As in your Dream of the Womb, you assume that close relationships soon break down, so it is best not to get involved. Your healing will be to allow people to come a little closer to you. You could risk letting them into your life and trusting they will not abandon you. You may begin to believe that when people do not seem to respond, it is not because they have gone out of your life forever, but because they are busy with other things. They are still willing to be your friend.

## Shame

Existential guilt is not a great feature of your life, unless the two placentas fused and you got the lion's share of the blood supply, causing your twin to die. That may leave you with acute survivor guilt. As for shame, you may be

159

reluctant to display your full femininity or masculinity, so that you remain only half of what you could be. As the womb twin work begins to take effect, you will accept full responsibility for who you are, including your giftedness and your failures - in fact, everything you do, believe, think or say. If you can reach that level of personal awareness, you could be a force for great good in the world. Never forget that the twin constellation of Gemini is among the brightest objects in the night sky.

## Resistance

Your resistance to healing is in your desire to do the impossible. Like Pollux, you wish to join your twin in death and you don't want to be here, in this life. You are, in a sense, only partially alive. That slightly detached feeling of not being fully engaged in life is the main way in which you prevent yourself from living as the strong survivor.

> *I know my twin was a girl and was given a funeral but from some things my mother said about the birth I don't know what state she was in at birth. I worry that this womb twin survivor idea is just an excuse to cover up feelings that a lot of people have. I don't think that many people are happy or free of inner demons. I worry this is so much psychological snake oil. But, then I know I'm carrying something around.*
> *[Natalie, USA]*

Until you awaken from the Dream, you will continue to block your healing and waste your time, talents and energy. You will drift through life, never truly happy and not letting very much touch you. Your healing will come very soon, when you wake up and start engaging in life.

## A healing bond

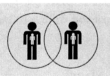

A specific characteristic of the two-egg, single sex womb twin survivor is making a "surrogate twin" bond with other people of the same sex. You probably prefer to be in the company of people of the same sex, such as in the armed forces or a single-sex school. As we have seen, this is a non-sexual, fraternal bond but it is emotionally intense and often dependent.

160

The healing bond for you, as a two-egg, single sex womb twin survivor, would be to find another sole survivor of a single-sex twin pregnancy. Then you could both consciously work out your feelings of dependency on each other and your mutual fear of abandonment. Gradually, each of you could allow your rigid personal boundary to relax. You could both try to let other people of the same sex enter your life as friends, thus reducing your dependency on one another.

### Katie and Sonia

Katie has two sons and her third child is Sonia, the longed-for daughter. Sonia received a great deal of attention as a baby, being the only female child in the extended family for a generation. As Sonia grew up, Katie became increasingly obsessed with her daughter and neglected her two sons as a result. This put a strain on Katie's marriage, especially when her second son, Mike, started stealing money from her purse. Katie and her husband asked for professional help and Katie began to pay more attention to her sons, but she was still unable to allow her daughter to grow up. When Sonia was 12 years old, Katie became depressed and incapable of running the home without her daughter's help. For three years, Katie was excessively dependent on Sonia, who was unable to go out with her friends like a normal teenager. Katie began to describe Sonia as her "soulmate." It is now clear that Katie is a womb twin survivor, and this may explain her dependent behaviour.

No single person can ever replace your lost twin, but each individual in your life could contribute some small part of what your lost twin may have provided. Once a support group of friends is in place, you and the person on whom you have been excessively reliant will each be able to let go of your emotional dependency on the healing bond with each other.

## The next step: two-egg twins of the opposite sex

The myth of Gemini fits well with the story of the two-egg, single-sex womb twin survivor. It is now time to consider what may be specific to the two-egg womb twin survivor when the lost twin was of the opposite sex. As we will see, this is a completely different story.

# 19
# Two eggs, opposite sexes

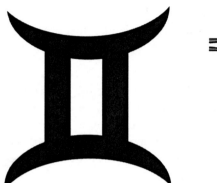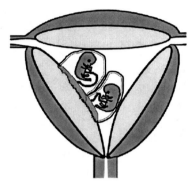

This chapter will discuss a different kind of two-egg womb twin survivor. As in the previous chapter, in a twin pregnancy two eggs are fertilised and begin to develop but by the end of the pregnancy one of them has died. In this case the twins are of opposite sexes. The result is very different from the ancient Greek tale of Castor and Pollux that we considered previously. The most important aspect of this kind of two-egg, opposite sex twinning is that the two placentas may fuse in some way. Two-egg twins do not implant at the same time, so inevitably one will implant before the other. There is a risk that the second zygote will come along after the placenta of the first has begun to develop and either implant itself so close to the other that the placentas fuse, or try to implant on the surface of the other, with fatal results. The following two diagrams illustrate this eventuality.

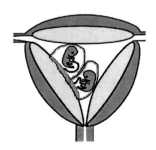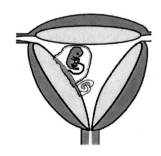

**TWO-EGG PREGNANCY WITH TWO FUSED PLACENTAS**

**ONE TWIN HAS DIED, AND ONLY THE DOUBLE PLACENTA REMAINS**

When a two-egg twin pregnancy develops with a fused placenta but one twin dies leaving a sole survivor, the single baby is born with a placenta that is extra large, has additional lobes, or has signs of the physical remains of the dead twin as a *foetus papyraceous* (the compressed body of the twin, still encased in the amniotic sac) still visible on the surface. Now we will take a closer look at what characteristics may be specific to two-egg womb twin survivors of the opposite sex by reviewing the ideas that we discussed in previous chapters.

## Your Dream of the Womb

If you are a two-egg, opposite sex womb twin survivor, in your Dream of the Womb there is a twin sister or a brother, the opposite sex to you, who was once there, but is now gone. If you are not sure about the gender of your twin, there may be some subtle clues if you know where to look. The idea may gradually grow in your mind, as a deep sense of certainty that once you had a twin sibling of the opposite sex.

> *As a child I asked my mum if I had a twin and she said no. Yet somehow I just knew that I was a twin and my twin has been taken from me. I had an imaginary friend, Casper, from the lack of true friendship. I would have constant dreams of him. He looked so familiar and it was like I knew him. I do have my doubts but behind every doubting moment is the voice of my twin brother telling me that it is the truth. [Shannon, Ireland]*

For your healing, you will need to develop that sense of certainty into something more real and definite. If you look at the diagrams on the previous page, or review the healing steps so far, you may find images that seem to reflect your story that you can use to recreate for yourself an image of your own Dream of the Womb, however vague it may turn out to be.

## Life and death

Your attitude to life and death may reflect the gender of your twin. For instance, you may feel very close to your opposite-sex parent. If that parent dies, your grief will be greater than when your same-sex parent dies. If you are wondering what gender your twin may have been, you could notice how close you are to family members or friends of the opposite sex. If you have some opposite-sex features, or if you show signs of the opposite sex in your character, this may be a sign that in your mother's pregnancy the two placentas fused. In that case, some of the sex hormones from your twin made their way into your bloodstream and have affected your character ever since.

## Craziness

The two seemingly "crazy" characteristics of two-egg, opposite sex womb twin survivors are known as "gender dysphoria" and "codependency."

### Gender dysphoria

"Dysphoria" means unhappiness and the term "gender dysphoria" includes gender identity disorder, gender incongruence, cross-dressing and transgenderism. It means you don't like the gender of your birth and feel as if you were somehow born into the wrong body. Gender dysphoria is not the same as homosexuality. If you are a two-egg, opposite sex womb twin survivor, you have every reason to want to adopt the manners and lifestyle of the opposite sex. Not only do you have a touch of opposite-sex hormone, which will affect how you look, feel and behave, but also you want to keep your twin alive in your life – even within your body.

### Codependency

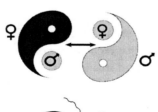

The term "codependency" describes the deep need for a soulmate to make you feel complete - your other half. If you find your soulmate in another womb twin survivor who also finds the equivalent in you, the result is a codependent relationship, where each party is reliant on the other for a feeling of wholeness. Clearly, in each case the soulmate is the missing twin. It is completely normal for a womb twin survivor to seek out a substitute twin in another womb twin survivor. Unfortunately however, the original tragedy of the death of one twin is also re-enacted. Conflict arises between the desire to keep the connection alive and the need to sabotage it to maintain the Dream. The relationship may break down, or alternatively each party will strive hard to maintain it. Either way, this is how they both keep their individual Dreams alive.

## Self-sabotage

Among two-egg, opposite sex womb twin survivors, codependency is a tendency that sabotages sexual and marital partnerships. When a womb twin survivor enters a sexual partnership with someone of the opposite sex who is also their "twin soul", he or she will try to create a specific style of relationship with the partner that resembles a sibling relationship more than a sexual one. That is fine so long as both parties are content to be together in this way, but for the conception and rearing of children, a different style of relationship is required. In short, your surrogate twin cannot be your lover or a parent to your children.

## Addictions and compulsions

Addiction can be defined as a "habit that hurts" and it is said that we can become addicted to love. Two-egg, opposite sex womb twin survivors do show signs of this kind of addiction and for them love hurts. They feel compelled to "rescue" others at considerable cost to themselves. In heterosexual relationships, both love addiction and the compulsion to rescue can cause a great deal of hurt to the parties involved, but it continues nonetheless. The following table may help you to spot love addiction and a rescuing compulsion in yourself:

| Signs of love addiction and rescuing compulsion | Yes | No |
|---|---|---|
| My relationships often involve people who need my help | | |
| I often find myself giving advice and counselling others | | |
| I have difficulty maintaining healthy relationships | | |
| It is difficult for me to receive praise or care from others | | |

| | | |
|---|---|---|
| It is hard to say "No" when people ask me for help | | |
| It is hard for me to ask for what I need personally | | |
| I often over-commit my time or make too many promises | | |
| It's difficult to believe that someone could truly love me | | |
| I am afraid of really allowing myself to love | | |
| I am afraid of being abandoned or being alone | | |
| When people hurt me I make excuses for them | | |
| I take responsibility, so things end up being my fault | | |
| Other | | |

Your healing will be to recognise that other people do not need to be rescued, because they can save themselves. They are not helpless, like your womb twin was, but strong and capable. The best way to help them is to encourage them to help themselves.

## Self-isolation

The biggest problem for the opposite sex, two-egg womb twin survivor is that sexual desire often, if not always, conflicts with the need for a surrogate twin relationship. As we have seen, when you are sexually attracted to another womb twin survivor with the same pre-birth story, relations between the two of you can easily tip into codependency.

In that case, the original abandonment in the Dream of the Womb will be lived out, leaving both parties forsaken and alone. On the other hand, if you are sexually attracted to another person who is not a womb twin survivor of any kind, your need for a constant close companion may conflict with the very different way your partner sees the relationship. He or she may want to see you occasionally and for the relationship to be almost entirely physical, while you want so much more companionship, shared experience and conversation. However, if in your Dream of the Womb your twin was physically there with you, but largely unresponsive, you may choose to stay with this person, as this kind of isolation enables your Dream to come true.

## Dual nature

As a two-egg, opposite sex womb twin survivor, you are both male and female and that is your dual identity. However, the degree to which you are carrying opposite gender hormones varies, according to what lies in your Dream. If the two placentas were completely separate, you probably do not carry any opposite-sex hormones at all. However, somewhere deep in your psyche you may have identified with your lost twin brother or sister and that may have affected your sense of yourself. So, for example, you may be a very masculine male, but enjoy the company of women and have a soft and sentimental personality. On the other hand, you may be a very feminine woman, but enjoy being with men and have a strong and aggressive personality. If the two placentas were fused together, you will probably have received some opposite-sex hormones (oestrogen or testosterone), according to the extent to which the two blood supplies were able to mingle.

### Chimera

A few days after conception, when you and your twin had each developed into a tiny bundle of cells called a *morula*, the two balls of cells may have combined, as this diagram shows:

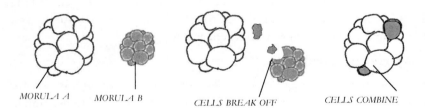

MORULA A    MORULA B    CELLS BREAK OFF    CELLS COMBINE

When two zygotes fuse together in this way, their merger produces a single embryo with two sets of DNA. This is called a chimera. If the two zygotes are of opposite sexes, the sole survivor carries both male and female DNA. If your twin merged with you like this, you may be a chimera, with two genetically different types of tissue in your body - some male, some female.

# Unrealised potential

Whatever lies in your Dream of the Womb, your healing will be to discover your true genetic make-up, if that is possible. If not, you can simply recognise that while you may be genetically a male, you once had a female twin. Your twin sister lives on in your Dream but she isn't you. Likewise, you may be genetically a female, though with a deep affinity with all things male. You once had a twin brother, but you are still a woman.

There are two kinds of energy that you may recognise as being male and female. To achieve your full potential, it is important to accept and honour your genetically imprinted gender energy. Of course, if you are a hermaphrodite and your DNA is so mixed that you are not sure if you are genetically male or female, you do not have to choose. You can simply express both sides of yourself equally.

## Male energy turned female

There are a variety of ways in which some people express their male energy in a female kind of way. If you are a male two-egg, opposite sex womb twin survivor with some feminine energy, you may be prepared to give away your strong, aggressive male power and let someone else (often a female) take control. Being everyone's servant, obsessing about cleanliness in the home or compulsive shopping for food or clothes could be seen by some as taking the female energy a bit too far, as could extremely long hair or even wishing you could bear a child your self. But of course, this is perfectly natural - you are looking for ways to express your female energy.

## Female energy turned male

If you are a female two egg, opposite sex womb twin survivor, it is easy for you to slip into a kind of male mode when the situation seems to demand it. Be warned, though - you will be much more powerful if you act within with your own genetic gender energy. Your female energy makes you naturally very good at gently confronting other people with the truth about themselves. With too much male energy however, the truth may be used as a weapon, to scold and criticise. Whether you are a man or a woman, living within your own genetically imprinted energy will make you more attractive as a person. Too much opposite-sex energy can make you appear off-putting.

## Something missing

The search for a soulmate of the opposite sex is characteristic of all two- egg womb twin survivors. In your own search for a replacement twin of the opposite sex you will never find the precise person, any more than you can find your twin.

You may have the idea that only when you find your perfect soulmate will you feel complete at last. Sadly however, your constant yearning for a partner of the opposite sex, who will always be there for you as your twin would have been, is never satisfied. You remain alone.

## Emotions

Two-egg, opposite sex womb twin survivors are easy to identify by the way they handle their emotions. The male with a great deal of feminine energy is often sentimental and easily moved to tears, whereas the female with male energy is more aggressive and does not cry so easily. Both sexes carry the pain of being a womb twin survivor, but they express it in different ways.

## Your Black Hole

For most two-egg womb twin survivors, the Black Hole is a place of desolation and abandonment. Because of the unfortunate conflation of sexual desire with the need for a twin soul, two-egg opposite sex womb twin survivors often marry or live together, and end up sharing the same desolate Black Hole.

They need each other for companionship but are disappointed every day that their partner or spouse does not meet their needs in the same way as they imagine their twin would have done.

## The Alpha-Beta gap

For two-egg, opposite sex womb twin survivors, the Alpha-Beta gap is very important in the development of sexual relationships. Where there was a big gap between you and your Beta womb twin and you have made your sexual partner into your own opposite-sex womb twin, you will perceive your partner as much weaker and more vulnerable than you. But if you constantly rescue your partner, then you will not expect him or her to take responsibility for his or her own bad behaviour. That will put you at risk of being squashed out of existence yourself as you adopt the role of your partner's Beta twin. The following case study may help to make this clear:

### Joan and Tom's story

Joan and Tom are married and they both share their home with Tom's hoard of possessions. For three decades, Joan has silently tolerated the fact that her home is extremely cluttered with things. She has tried to stay true to her marriage vows, but she is completely unable to use most of the rooms in their house. She now realises that her uncomplaining nature, far from being strong, has allowed Tom to dominate her completely. Meanwhile, Tom is gradually coming to understand that he has been too weak to decide what to clear out and has left all the decision-making to Joan.

## Personal boundary

The two-egg, opposite sex womb twin survivor becomes so involved in the emotional life of their opposite-sex surrogate twin that the personal boundary between them disappears. This means it is hard to know where personal responsibility lies. It is easy for each to take on the shame of the other. The first sign this is happening is when you feel guilty for what someone else has done. You had no part in it but believe it is "all your fault."

## Shame

Apart from carrying the shame of other people, two-egg, opposite sex womb twin survivors also feel ashamed of their own codependency, which is a style of relationship viewed very negatively by psychotherapists:

- Codependent people are needy, demanding and submissive.
  *(Of course. They are stuck in their Beta space.)*
- They are immature and cling to others for support.
  *(They need their surrogate twin in order to feel whole.)*
- No matter what abuse is inflicted upon them – they remain in the relationship.
  *(Being left alone is too close to their Dream of the Womb.)*

Codependency is generally assumed to be caused by some kind of emotional trauma, occurring long ago, probably in early childhood. That may well be true of some people, but a womb twin survivor's emotional wounds were inflicted before or around the time of birth. Whatever happens in their childhood and adulthood is a continuation of their womb story.

## Resistance

The two-egg, opposite sex womb twin survivor resists healing to such an extent that he or she may enter an abusive relationship and remain in it for decades, despite the efforts of friends and professionals to persuade the two people concerned to get help or to separate.

Each persons's Black Hole turns the relationship into a perfect replication of the shared Dream of the Womb. Neither party will admit that, if this goes on, their relationship is doomed. As any marriage counsellor will testify, the resistance to change is usually far to great to allow any changes to occur, so the marriage dies, bringing pain and suffering to everyone involved, especially the children.

## A healing bond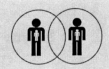

If you are a two-egg, opposite sex womb twin survivor and love hurts for you, it may be time to carefully consider the possibility that your partner is also a womb twin survivor. That may have been one of the reasons why you were attracted to each other in the first place. If your partner is unaware of this possibility, you will have to take him or her back to the beginning of the healing path, and walk it together. In that way you can transform a difficult marriage into a healing bond, to the benefit of both parties. In that joint venture, you will find your personal boundaries will strengthen as you each relinquish responsibility for the bad behaviour of the other. You can both reclaim more of your genetically imprinted gender energy within the partnership, while allowing for the fact that both of you may have some opposite-sex energy inside you. If the two of you work hard to create a new climate of personal responsibility and mutual acceptance, a strong and enduring relationship can be forged.

## The next step: one egg, two chorions

In the next chapter we will consider the characteristics of a particular group of one-egg womb twin survivors. Like two-egg womb twin survivors, they had separate placentas and amniotic sacs but when we look closer we will find many differences between the two groups.

172

# 20
# Two chorions, one egg

As we begin our exploration of one-egg (monozygotic) twins, we will need to remind ourselves of the biology of twinning. The many manifestations of one-egg twinning have been described in detail in the book *Womb Twin Survivors,* but for convenience we will consider here some of the more important aspects of this kind of twinning.

## Two separate chorions

Everything depends on the arrangement of the various membranes that make up the pregnancy. The amount of the original zygote (fertilised egg) that is shared between the twins varies according to the precise timing of when the zygote splits into two. That affects how the membranes develop. When the original single zygote splits in the first two or three days, the two resulting balls of cells implant themselves quite separately in the wall of the womb, each creating its own placenta. As part of the whole pregnancy, the placenta is enclosed in an outer membrane known as the chorion, within which are also the amnion or inner membrane, the amniotic fluid in the amniotic sac, the foetus and the umbilical cord. This diagram shows one-egg twins who have developed in this way:

**TWO CHORIONS**

PLACENTA

UMBILICAL CORD

FOETUS

CHORIONS

AMNIOTIC SAC

AMNION

This type of one-egg twin pregnancy is called dichorionic, because there are two separate chorions. When a womb twin survivor is born of a twin pregnancy of this kind, we will call the sole survivor a "two chorions, one egg" womb twin survivor. As we have seen previously, the three main psychological characteristics of all one-egg womb twin survivors are the Bubble of Oblivion, inwardly focused energy and contradiction. If you are a womb twin survivor you will already have realised that the impressions that lie in your Dream of the Womb are remarkably accurate.

## Your Dream of the Womb

In your Dream of the Womb you are alone in your own separate chorion, just like a two-egg womb twin survivor. However, for a very brief time you were united with your twin within the original zygote.

> *My mother told me as soon as I could understand that I would have been an identical twin, but the second heartbeat stopped at the beginning of the fourth month. She experienced bleeding and was ordered to bed rest for the remainder of the pregnancy. The doctor stretched out the placenta to show my parents that my half was huge and healthy and the half that housed my twin was black and dead.*
> *[Anna, USA]*

In your Dream of the Womb there is no sense of time and place. You feel both separated from and united with your twin, all in the same moment. You may like to make a storyboard to illustrate exactly how you came to be a womb twin survivor of this kind. Here is an example:

**1. SINGLE ZYGOTE IS FORMED**     **2. ZYGOTE SPLITS INTO TWIN MORULAE**

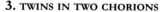

**3. TWINS IN TWO CHORIONS**     **4. ONE TWIN DIES**

## Life and death

The death of a person of the same sex with whom you have had a close relationship feels like the death of half of yourself. That will be your Dream of the Womb realised. There is a lifelong sense that in some way "half of you is dead".

## Craziness

You may create an imaginary friend to be your surrogate twin and accompany you everywhere. You may insist on being called by a different name. You may, even as a young child, constantly ask: "Where is my twin?" You may have spent years in therapy to make you "normal" again, but these ideas have persisted in your life. If so, be reassured that there are many seemingly "strange" behaviours that are easily and completely explained once the idea of being a one-egg womb twin survivor enters the equation. An important step towards healing therefore, is to describe yourself as a perfectly normal womb twin survivor, however the professional therapists may label you. There is a great deal more work to be done in understanding the psychology of womb twin survivors. This book can be only a small beginning. so expect that most people will not understand how you feel.

## Self-sabotage

One-egg womb twin survivors with two chorions mainly sabotage their lives in their search for a "kindred spirit." They constantly seek out someone exactly like themselves to make them complete again as half of a twin pair. Of course it is not possible to find anyone exactly like you, however hard you try. You may scan faces everywhere in your search and manage to find another person who thinks like you or looks a little like you. Even if you find someone who is so empathetic that he or she seems to know your thoughts exactly, this will not be your twin. You may become excessively excited about any similarity you find with an individual you happen to meet, but you will not have met your twin.

## Addictions and compulsions

A common characteristic of womb twin survivors is compulsive hoarding, and this may be related in some way to your Dream of the Womb. Let us suppose that identical twins begin to grow in separate chorions but one twin never develops beyond the earliest stages and so is never responsive in any way. The other carries a vague sense of being somehow connected to *Something Out There*. In born life, that Something can easily be translated into objects. A deep attachment to each object develops instantly, so it is collected and brought home, until there is a large hoard of possessions too precious to discard. Significantly, bags of various kinds, particularly plastic bags, are often found in a hoard of this kind. After all the lost twin was enclosed in a chorion, which is a translucent membrane like a plastic bag.

> *I have a lot of things that are of no use anymore but they are so hard to throw out. What hurts me the most is all the perfectly good, brand new things I have never used. To give away my new craft things would be to literally throw away my dreams and throw away my identity.*
> *[Fran, USA]*

## Self-isolation

You cannot feel fully alive when alone. To live life to the full, you must remain closely connected to another living being. You will reach out eagerly and make great efforts to establish a "surrogate twin" connection with anyone who is willing to provide it. This is how you try to "call your twin home."

YOU — YOUR SURROGATE TWIN

If they are unable to find a suitable friend, young womb twin survivors of this kind will invent an imaginary playmate of a similar appearance.

## Dual nature

One-egg womb twin survivors who developed in a separate chorion have a dual nature very similar to two-egg womb twin survivors. If this is your story, then you are probably identified with your own lost twin, who is *Somewhere Out There*. Your life is filled with a need for duality. You seek out pairs in every way you can. You often notice two similar objects, or seek out and notice pairs of one-egg twins. It feels as though you are merely half a person in many respects, for only your twin could make you whole again.

## Unrealised potential

There are many ways to be merely half the person you could be. You may wonder sometimes why you never seem to get things done or start on the amazing career you have planned for yourself. You may sit at home dreaming of what you could be, but are unable to muster the strength to make it happen. You may have a sense of great potential locked inside you, but somehow there is a gap between the dream and the reality.

*I am someone of great potential and ability but somehow seem to find ways to fall just short of success.*
*[Colin, UK]*

Two chorions one-egg twins have a sense of being only partially developed. You may feel this way and have an overwhelming sense of personal failure and painful disappointment. You have missed many opportunities and have not made good use of your talents. You fear that your whole life will be wasted if you continue to live in this way. You feel that somehow you could make a difference if only you could start moving forward. You stay where you are, because you are identified with your Beta twin, who never had a life. To allow yourself to live fully and develop into the person you were meant to be would be to betray your twin - the other half of you.

177

## Something missing

The missing twin in your life is *Somewhere Out There*, but there is also a feeling of dissatisfaction inside you. You know that in many ways you have been living half a life, but it seems there is little that can be done to change things or to fill that emptiness inside.

## Emotions

As we have seen, the emotional pain involved in being a monozygotic womb twin survivor takes different forms, according to how the pregnancy membranes were arranged. For the two chorion, one egg womb twin survivor, this is related to a feeling of emotional vulnerability and an extreme sensitivity to being overlooked, ignored or rejected.

> *What hurts the most is when people do not understand how vulnerable and sensitive I feel inside. It seems that no one is interested enough to look below the mask I have had to create to cover my feelings. It's easy to see, surely? No one even tries to guess how I feel. There is no empathy, no understanding. Even the people with empathy do not understand fully how I feel. I stopped a long time ago trying to get people to understand, it just hurts me too much.*
> *[Martin UK]*

If this is your story you are left sad and alone, but safe inside your Bubble of Oblivion. There you can dream of being with your twin and instantly understood, without the need for any explanations - just as it once was with your twin in your Dream of the Womb.

## Your Black Hole

In your Black Hole is a sense of being abandoned by your twin and left on your own. It seems you cannot possibly live without your "other half."

That would diminish you to the extent that there is no way you could cope alone. You just don't want to be here at all if it means you have to go through life all by yourself. It is important for your healing to admit openly that you are not engaged in life here on this planet, but would wish to be spirited away, just like your twin. This is a life/death choice, made out of longing and despair. It creates a kind of irritable and grudging compliance with the ordinary demands of your existence. Rather than be in the real world, you would much rather retreat into your Bubble of Oblivion where your Dream always comes true and you can create your own reality.

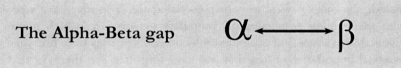

## The Alpha-Beta gap

If you think of the energies inside you, you will find that there are two very different ways of being you - one is aggressive and protective and the other is small, vulnerable and super-sensitive. These two sides of you are manifestations of your Alpha and Beta energies. If your twin never developed very far before being miscarried, then that little person inside you will seem very small indeed. If, on the other hand, your twin managed to grow larger, even to the point of being born - then inside you will be two very similar versions of yourself. One has a life but the other has no chance of life at all. For your healing, you will need to examine your Alpha and Beta energies and notice how they work in opposite directions. The expression of Beta energy diminishes you almost to the point of extinction. On the other hand, Alpha energy enables you to grow into the person you were created to become. If you are to develop your full potential, the expression of Beta energy must decrease. Your Alpha energy is strong and is helping you to grow, but in your Dream of the Womb you are allowing Beta energy to diminish you. How well you do in life will depend on the balance between these two energies. The healing work will be to give fuller expression to your Alpha energy.

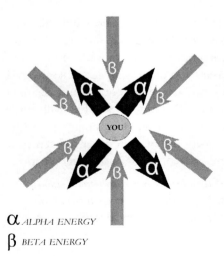

$\alpha$ ALPHA ENERGY

$\beta$ BETA ENERGY

## Personal boundary

Your personal boundary extends beyond yourself to include your lost twin. We have already seen how much effort you put into "calling your twin home." You eagerly reach out to others, drawing them into your life, holding them close and making them into your soulmates. This means the boundary you have between yourself and others is constantly being breached in order to include the other person in your personal space. You may have a problem with maintaining your personal boundary in any case, which makes you vulnerable to abuse and exploitation by others. You may have breached your personal boundary so often that you have forgotten it is there. In that case, you could become so caught up in the lives of other people that you have no life of your own. If this is your story, you will have almost ceased to exist as an individual. You are only allowing yourself to live through the lives of other people, whom you constantly rescue, care for and save from themselves. Your healing will be to rediscover your personal boundary. Then you will be able to reclaim your own space for rest and recuperation.

## Shame

For you the greatest area of shame is being the one who survived. Why should you be the one who lived? This is a hard question to answer. You may also feel ashamed of yourself for allowing other people to walk all over you, abuse you and exploit you. It is unpleasant and distressing and at some level you know you are letting it happen by not asserting yourself and claiming your rights. Healing shame will involve self-forgiveness. That will come when you understand that everything you have done to sabotage your life, your relationships and your personal growth has been in order to keep your Dream alive. The idea may have been misguided, but it is not a sin or a crime.

*Every year that passes, I find myself wondering more and more about my twin. I know she was there in the beginning, I know we would have been identical, I know her name and I know that there was nothing left of her when I was born.*
*[Angela, USA]*

## Resistance

Your greatest resistance to healing is to be found in your Black Hole. If you don't want to be here in this world in any case, you will not care how poor your life is and how far you are falling short of your potential. For you, the possibility of healing is a matter of choice. If you don't choose to live a full life, you will never choose healing. However, if you think that you would like to try, perhaps just for a while, to embrace life and all its possibilities, you will not be able to do it alone. You will need a healing bond with another womb twin survivor.

## A healing bond

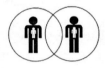

Someone of the same sex who is the same kind of womb twin survivor will be most able to help you, and you will be able to help him or her in return. As you both had separate chorions, you may be able to enter into a distant relationship by email or telephone. You may even be able to bring healing to each other without ever meeting in person. The main issue to work on will be your respective personal boundaries. You will have to try not to get too involved in the life of your surrogate twin. In time, you will learn to claim your own space and not constantly make personal sacrifices on behalf of the other person, however selfish that may seem at first. You can take as your ideal a precise 50:50 relationship. You can struggle to make sure that neither party is the greater and neither appears to be the more worthless. If you work together towards that delicate balance, you will both benefit greatly and grow in individual strength.

## The next step: single chorion, one egg

We now move on to the next type of one-egg twinning – where the twins share a single chorion, but have separate amniotic sacs. We will call the sole survivors of this kind of pregnancy "single chorion, one-egg" womb twin survivors.

181

# 21
# Single chorion, one egg

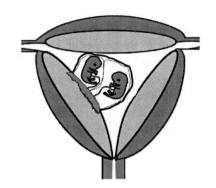

In the last chapter we saw how the character of a one-egg (monozygotic) womb twin survivor varies according to the timing of the split and the consequent arrangement of the membranes in the pregnancy. In the previous case there were two separate chorions or membranes enclosing the whole pregnancy, but if the zygote (fertilised egg) happens to split between four to seven days after fertilisation, a single chorion is shared between the twins.

It happens this way: Over the first week of life, the original single cell zygote divides countless times and forms a morula (a ball of cells) and then a blastocyst, which has different layers of cells. The outer layer of the blastocyst is known as the trophoblast. It is this layer that implants on the womb wall and forms the chorion and the placenta. For reasons no one understands, the inner cell mass may divide into two separate masses, which

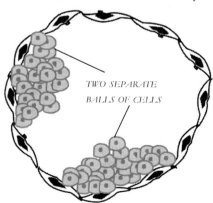

TWO SEPARATE BALLS OF CELLS

give rise to two sacs, two cords and two foetuses - one-egg twins. In this case and as a result of this split, the twins each develop in their own amniotic sac, but they share the same placenta and are enclosed by a single chorion. If this is your story, you are a "single chorions, one-egg" womb twin survivor and you and your twin spent almost a week as a single zygote before the split occurred.

## Your Dream of the Womb

If you shared a placenta with your twin, but had an amniotic sac all to yourself, that arrangement of membranes is there in the back of your mind as part of your Dream of the Womb. For your healing, you will need to be very clear about how these membranes were arranged. It would be good to make a storyboard of your Dream. Here is a set of diagrams to use as a guide:

**1. FERTILISATION**

**2. SINGLE MORULA**

**3. INNER CELL MASS DIVIDES**

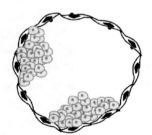

**4. SINGLE CHORION, ONE-EGG TWINS**

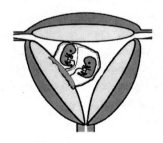

**5. ONE TWIN DIES**

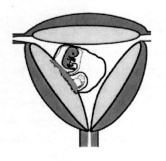

**6. SINGLE CHORION, ONE-EGG WOMB TWIN SURVIVOR**

*I used to think I might have a twin in the world when I was younger. That thought only came when my mom told me about how I was born. She was at home and in her bathroom when something came out of her and she thought it was me, being born. They rushed her to the hospital and it wasn't me. She doesn't know what it was that came. I do sometimes think about what it was too and sometimes look for people who look exactly like me or resemble me a bit.*
*[Cherry, USA ]*

## Life and death

If you shared a chorion with your twin and your twin died, you may have been left with the sense that you "killed your twin." You may be burdened by a sense of survivor guilt because you believe you somehow lived at your twin's expense. For you, the whole idea of death is very near, accompanied perhaps by a sense of being in some way "half-dead".

*I found out about my twin at six-years old after this one incident with my siblings. Feeling left out, I wrote my first poem, "When I was born, there was death to bear, because half my life, wasn't there." It was a random impulse. Later that night when I saw my mom, I had my notebook and asked, "Where's my twin?" She was shocked, but then sat me down and told me about my twin sister and how she died at the end of the second trimester.*
*[Shelly, USA]*

## Craziness

Your inner life is very important to you. Your inward search for your lost twin soul may include talking to yourself, which other people can find disconcerting. Your imaginary friend, should you have one, may seem bizarre to others and your constant scanning of faces can look like an obsession. You often feel as though you are two people with two distinct personalities. Your healing will be to forgive the people who do not take seriously the idea of your being a womb twin survivor.

## Self-sabotage

The main form of self-sabotage practised by single chorion, one-egg womb twin survivors is in their paradoxical attitudes to other people. The great need to find their lost twin in others is counteracted by a need to keep their Dream alive by remaining alone. You may have wondered why you can never get close to people - perhaps you have found ways of pushing them away.

> When I wake up in the morning I have a feeling of emptiness and loneliness, even though I am married and wake up beside my husband. I literally feel invisible to other people and people actually have pointed out to me that I act as though I don't matter. I have knowingly chosen relationships that are detrimental. I haven't acted as a person with a strong sense of worth yet I have a lot to be proud of. I have gone through much of my life not really knowing what I look like, not in the way other people seem to know.
> [Sonia, UK]

## Addictions and compulsions

Your major compulsion is probably towards finding the one person who will make you feel special, wanted and absolutely understood. Another common compulsion among one-egg twins who shared a chorion involves food and eating. The guilt that you got the major share of food in the womb and your twin died (possibly as a direct result) may lie behind an inability to eat normally. A common response to this kind of guilt is bulimia, where you try to fill that deep sense of inner emptiness with food, but then become too guilty to allow yourself to keep it, so you get rid of it.

Your healing will be to see your various addictions and compulsions are not some kind of strange disease that has no cure and which you are helpless to control. In fact, this behaviour and the feelings behind it are entirely of your own invention, to keep your Dream alive.

## Self-isolation

In your Bubble of Oblivion there is only you and your twin, feeding off the same source of food and oxygen. Cut off from the outside world, pushing other people way and demanding the highest level of empathy and understanding at all times, you are not likely to find a relationship that meets all your needs. It probably seems to you that this is how is always must be if you are to keep your Dream alive. The following diagram shows how you constantly make a great effort to "call your twin home" and try to reconstitute the original bond in the single zygote with the help of a surrogate twin.

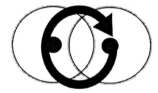

Almost all your reaching-out energy is focused on drawing other people to yourself. This is how you make sure the twin bond is kept alive, while at exactly the same time you are making sure you will be left alone.

## Dual nature

Your dual nature is best described as "split." When your body divided from your twin's, there may have been small deviations, leaving one side of you made up physically slightly differently from the other. You may also be conscious of being two people in one, and having a "split personality." You probably have marked mood swings, from excitement and liveliness to deadness and despair. You are living two lives at once. One life is yours as the strong Alpha survivor. You occupied the whole womb space, had the entire food supply and oxygen to yourself and were born into the world alive. The other life you try to live at the same time on behalf of your Beta twin. It is a brief and inconsequential existence, ending in premature death. If life seems pointless and you often consider suicide, this is why you feel that way. In the Dream of the Womb, if you are the Beta twin, you must die.

186

## Unrealised potential

**The most c**haracteristic way not to realise your potential is to be only half of what you could be. This can be done in a paradoxical way, especially among the one-egg group, and particularly among those who shared a placenta with their twin. You are only half as good as you could be, because you are trying twice as hard as you need to just to be the person you are. The following case study may illustrate this.

### Harry's story

Harry works and plays very, very hard. He has plenty of money, high standards and a comfortable lifestyle, but he strives daily to accomplish more and more. He has already forgotten how tired he is. He functions well below his abilities because he has no spare time and is always exhausted by over-work. Despite having a large number of associates, he has few friends. He sometimes feels as if he is the loneliest man in the world.

## Something missing

If you are a single chorion, one-egg  womb twin survivor, your sense of something lacking is very close to you, but not within you. You spent about a week united with your twin, so there is a missing half of yourself. There are two ways to try and live with a sense of "being half". Either you can wander through life in a kind of dream, or you can compensate for your missing half by seeming to be "larger than life" while secretly feeling a fraud.

*THE SAD BETA*          *THE CHEERFUL ALPHA*          *THE MASK OF NARCISSUS*

The symbol of Narcissus, discussed previously, sums up the double life of the single chorion, one-egg womb twin survivor. The sadness of losing your precious Beta twin and the cheerfulness you bravely assume in order to carry on are depicted by the two half faces. This is how the symbol, which is also the mask you wear, expresses the contradictory half-ness and duality that is so much a part of your nature.

## Emotions

A source of emotional pain for you is a lack of empathy in others. The twin bond is a strong, non-verbal connection, where mutual empathy and understanding are at their most accurate. You are so closely bound to your twin that you assume your inner feelings are perfectly obvious to others. If someone does not seem to realise how vulnerable and sensitive you are, your instant reaction is to be hurt by the lack of effort to comprehend how you feel. It is also painful when someone does not understand what you mean and demands a fuller explanation. You assume your meaning should be instantly obvious to anyone who really cares about what you say. That misunderstanding leaves you feeling ignored and rejected. Many single chorion, one-egg womb twin survivors express their private thoughts by talking to themselves. You might unwittingly voice those thoughts in a conversation with another person but not realise you have not yet explained yourself. When other people do not seem to understand you, the resulting painful sense of isolation arises once more out of your Dream of the Womb. For that reason, you probably find serious conversation emotionally draining.

## Your Black Hole

In your Black Hole there is nameless fear and a sense of dreadful darkness in which you are totally alone. Single chorion, one-egg womb twin survivors were still merged with their twin for a week after conception, so they are hard-wired for constant company. They are not able to cope alone at all well, particularly in the dark. If you are afraid of being on your own at night, this is entirely understandable. A lonely darkness is a terrifying reminder of the time when your twin died and was gone. Your healing will be to put a name to your nameless fears, and fit them into your Dream of the Womb.

## The Alpha-Beta gap

Your inward-looking energy, focused inside your Bubble of Oblivion, may make you feel "special" or "extraordinary" when compared with others. It is true that you were the stronger twin of the pair and therefore more able to survive. If your Beta twin was far weaker than you, your sense of personal strength and privileged existence will be that much greater in your life.

## Personal boundary

If you are a single chorion, one-egg womb twin survivor, your personal boundary is very vague and almost nonexistent. In the womb, only a thin membrane separated you from your twin, so in life your personal boundary is also very thin. You may not have noticed how weak it is, so you end up picking up and carrying other people's pain and shame, which feels like a knot in your stomach that will not go away. That will show you there is the thinnest possible dividing line between you and the people you care most about. Your healing will be to recognise that the painful feelings you are carrying are not your own. Other people must be allowed to take responsibility for their own pain. Your personal boundary can be strengthened by being more assertive in claiming your rights to personal privacy.

## Shame

There is a persistent vague sense there is something WRONG about you. Many single chorion, one-egg womb twin survivors feel as if they have arrived from another planet. As you walk the healing path, you will become more aware of the extent to which you have been borrowing guilt from other people, by taking responsibility for their bad behaviour. Your flimsy personal boundary will leave you very vulnerable to bullying or verbal abuse. If someone insists you are to blame for some unfortunate event that plainly has nothing to do with you, you will believe them.

You could learn to keep reminding yourself that you do not run the world single-handed. Never forget that when you get caught up in the life of another person, you are trying to re-enact your Dream of the Womb.

## Resistance

Your resistance to healing lies in the strength of your Dream of the Womb. The closer you are to it, the less able you will be to awaken to the real world that lies outside your Bubble of Oblivion. Your healing is a simple action, but very difficult to carry out. It requires a decision to stop trying so hard to keep your twin alive, resolving the contradictions inside you and turning away from the Bubble of Oblivion. In the bubble all is death and stagnation. Outside, in the real world, there are life, growth and all kinds of wonderful new experiences and opportunities. To choose to wake up from the Dream is to choose life, but that is where your main resistance lies.

## A healing bond

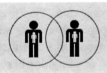

It may seem to you that your bond with your twin is unbreakable and you will always be half of a pair. To create a healing bond is not to break that tie with your twin, but to make another one elsewhere. You can take some of the elements from that original bond and apply them in a new friendship with another womb twin survivor who is of the same sex as you. As a result of being this kind of womb twin survivor, you are highly sensitive and empathetic. These are very attractive qualities in a person. You also value intimacy and companionship very highly, so that would make you an excellent friend to someone. You do not have to be like Narcissus, forever transfixed by the image of your twin. Even if you cannot replace your twin, you can find companionship and love from those people around you.

## The next step: single sac one-egg womb twin survivors

In the next chapter we will explore the form of one-egg twinning that arises out of a split in the zygote that happens a few days later. This creates twins who share a single placenta and occupy a single amniotic sac.

190

# 22
# Single sac, one egg

 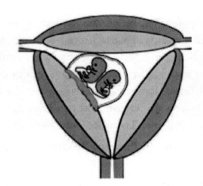

If you are a single sac, one-egg womb twin survivor, this is your womb story: By the ninth day after fertilisation, a blastocyst (cell cluster) has developed. It has floated down the Fallopian tube into the cavity of the womb and is beginning to implant. By this time it has formed into three layers. The outer layer of the blastocyst has begun to create a placenta, the middle layer is developing into a single amniotic sac and the inner mass of cells will eventually form the foetus. For some unknown reason, that inner mass of cells sometimes divides into two and creates a pair of twins who will share the same amniotic sac.

**1.** BALL OF CELLS IN SINGLE AMNIOTIC SAC

**2.** BALL OF CELLS SPLITS

The later the split occurs, the more of the original ball of cells is shared between the twins. If the split occurs after the 14th day, the foetal body is beginning to form and the twins share part of it they are said to be conjoined twins. If you were once conjoined and your twin was surgically removed, you can consider yourself a single sac, one-egg womb twin survivor.

191

# Your Dream of the Womb

In your Dream of the Womb, there was a relatively long time when you and your twin were united as a single zygote, or fertilised egg. That sense of being merged with your twin is still an important part of your character, but with slight variations depending on exactly how and why your twin died. Different histories can arise when the inner cell mass in the blastocyst divides between the eighth and the 13th day after fertilisation, as the diagrams that follow show. To make your own storyboard, here are some diagrams:

### Creation of "mirror "twins

When the split occurs in such a way as to create two mirror images, one twin is left-handed and the other right-handed. The sole survivor can be either left- or right-handed.

### Unequal split

When the cell mass divides, this may not be precise, so one twin has more cells than the other. The difference may mean that your twin failed to grow and eventually died.

### Chromosomal abnormality

As a direct result of an imperfect split or because of some other misfortune, the cell mass that would grow into one twin has damaged chromosomes, causing immediate death or fatal abnormality.

### Developmental failure

One half of the cell mass fails to develop at all while the other half develops normally and completely.

## Flaws in the DNA

After the cell mass begins to divide, the DNA in the two masses differs very slightly. This creates fatal flaws in one mass of cells. A few damaged cells are taken up into the body of the survivor. The survivor thus has some of the other twin's cells, which contain the slightly altered DNA. This creates an auto-immune reaction in the body of the survivor as the immune system constantly tries to reject the "foreign" DNA.

## The twin within

Some stem cells from the Beta twin pass into the body of the Alpha survivor and start to develop. The Beta twin dies and the body disintegrates. The stem cells develop into a dermoid cyst, teratoma or foetus in foetu within the body of the Alpha survivor.

> *I had a grapefruit-sized dermoid cyst removed from my left ovary when I was 18. It was in later years that I read that pathology report in my chart. The report said the cyst had hair, teeth and skin. I have always felt as if I have a very dual personality and nature, like there are two very different people inside of me.*
> *[Pam, USA]*

## Parasitic twin

The two balls of cells develop until they are almost united. In that case, at birth you may have had some small parts of your twin's body attached to your own, such as extra fingers, extra toes or an extension to your spine.

## Twin-twin transfusion

Even if both twins continue to develop normally in the shared amniotic sac, it is still a dangerous situation for both of them. If the blood supplies become connected, twin-twin transfusion may begin. This means that when one twin dies, the blood from the living twin pools in the body of the dead twin and causes fatal anaemia in the survivor. If the transfusion begins early in the pregnancy, it may resolve naturally when one twin dies, leaving the survivor anaemic, but alive. This may be the origin of cerebral palsy.[1]

193

## Life and death

As your twin has always been so close to you - and may still remain inside you as a cyst of some different DNA - death is so near it holds no fears for you. Living a full life is the bigger problem. This is particularly so if your twin never developed a completely functioning brain or body. In that case, despite the fact that your twin could hardly be described as an individual, somewhere in the Dream of the Womb there is a deep sense of being bonded to whatever remained of him or her. Your Beta twin never had a life at all so you feel you must not have a life either.

## Craziness

In your Bubble of Oblivion you are identified so closely with your virtually non-existent womb twin that it feels as if you are the one struggling to survive. You persistently try to make an impression on other people, to prove you truly exist and have not vanished like your twin. When you speak about your fear of non-existence or your overwhelming need to win in every competition, other people do not understand how it is to be you. They do not know what it is like to feel brainless, formless and so vulnerable that you could be easily snuffed out. You must go on proving, day after day, that you are not your own Beta twin. Your healing will be to grasp the truth, which is that you are not your little Beta twin at all. You are the strong Alpha survivor.

## Self-sabotage

You may believe you can make your own rules inside your Bubble of Oblivion, but your way of life would then conflict with what is considered normal behaviour and set you at odds with other people. You will quickly become an outcast from society if you continue to do whatever you like in your own way. Your healing will be to notice that living only by your own rules is not clever or strong, but a sign of immaturity. This is how, safe in your Bubble

194

of Oblivion, you keep yourself fixed in a state of arrested development, just like your Beta womb twin.

## Addictions and compulsions

The main compulsion of the single sac, one-egg womb twin survivor is most obvious when the lost twin never developed a fully functioning brain. If this is your story, you feel compelled to regard yourself in every situation as the only person present with a brain. This is not appropriate behaviour when dealing with people who have perfectly good brains of their own. However, all that matters to you is to be constantly reassured that your brain is functioning well and you have not yet disintegrated into a brainless object like your Beta womb twin.

## Self-isolation

There is no sense of isolation inside your Bubble of Oblivion, for in it is everything you ever wanted. The following diagram illustrates what little effort is required to keep the original twin dyad, or pair, together in your Dream, for the two of you are so closely entwined.

There is little need to "call your twin home" or find a surrogate, for your lost twin is already part of your own identity.

*I knew she was dead, yet she was within me. I feel her now in my heart physically, an ache that is physical, heavy, painful, I can hardly breathe. Yet it is so much a part of me I know that it will be there until I die. My mother told me that I had an imaginary friend, and that I had even gave her a name Natha. I once told my mother that she was the little girl that had died. Knowing her is like knowing me; we were one,*

*from one cell that split into two. Part of her was within me for the first 18 years of my life, and then surgically removed without me knowing that part of her had been there all the time. Was that the reason for my searching for something I just could not find? I have this feeling of being isolated, and being so alone. Even when there are many people around me, this feeling takes hold of me.*
[DEE, South Africa]

## Dual nature

As a single sac, one-egg womb twin survivor you feel like a single individual but there is also a sense of another *Someone* inside you who is much smaller and less mature than you, a part of you that never grew up. If you once were are a mirror twin, your sense of duality will be strongest when you look at your reflection in a mirror.

*My twin sister and I were totally identical - not just identical but mirror identical. We had similar moles on our noses, just like in a mirror. I think that's why I look in the mirror and think, "Wow! That's what she would probably look like".*
[Bernice, USA]

## Unrealised potential

As you strive to keep your Dream alive, you are prepared to sacrifice a large part of your development as an individual for the sake of some kind of "fairness". Because the inequality between you and your twin has been the cause of your pain, you probably have very strong feelings about justice, equity and general even-handedness. You are so tightly bound up with being fair to your twin that your potential is never reached. For example, you may have an exaggerated idea of how clever you are, but you carefully keep it secret because at the same time you are wondering if you have a brain at all. Sooner than put this to the test you don't try too hard, so if you fail you can always use the excuse that you were not striving your utmost. In this way, however great your potential may be, the world never sees it fully realised.

Until you manage to sort out in your own mind what incapacities belong to you and what you have taken on from your womb twin, you will continue to live a long way below your potential.

## Something missing

That sense of things being unfair extends to recognising that you have had less of a life than you believe you should have. It seems that you are in some sense always denied, betrayed, let down or disappointed. If there is anything missing in your life at all, it is the life you could have had, if only you had been able to manage it. But somehow the energy to move on is never there - or not for very long, anyway. Your healing will be to discover why that energy fades away so soon, every time you make an effort to grow and develop. When you awaken from the Dream to the outer reality of where you fit into society, then the inner reality of your own natural capacities will become clearer.

## Emotions

The emotions of the single chorion, one-egg womb twin survivor are intense, very painful and mainly associated with disappointment. Deep down, there is a feeling of a broken promise and the death of hope. It probably seems to you that life itself has wounded you to the core. What is worse, no one seems to understand how much you suffer, however hard you try to explain. Your healing will be to recognise the extent to which your intensely painful emotional state is a self-inflicted wound. In your Bubble of Oblivion you work hard to keep the pain alive. In your Dream there is a deep sense of once being a single unit, which was wrenched apart, torn in two, broken, damaged and rendered incapable.

## Your Black Hole

Your Black Hole is a terrifying place. In it you are very, very small, vulnerable and confused. In your Dream you are being split into two and falling apart.

197

If your DNA differs slightly from that of your twin you may be very sensitive to rejection or being different.

## The Alpha-Beta gap

If your twin never developed very far at all, then the Alpha-Beta gap will be expressed in the way you do not achieve your full potential. If your twin lived into the third trimester there will be no Alpha-Beta gap between you, because single chorion, one-egg twins are the most-closely identical to each other of all one-egg twin types.

## Personal boundary

The very idea of needing a personal boundary can seem strange to you, for in your Dream there were no membranes between you and your twin. You may find that you are often rebuked for interfering in other people's lives, or being too eager to take charge. On the other hand, you could find you are too open to other people's feelings and have to fabricate some artificial means to protect yourself, such as spending a great deal of time in total isolation.

## Shame

The kind of shame that single chorion, one-egg womb twin survivors experience is existential - that is, being ashamed of yourself in terms of your own existence. You are so ashamed at being alive that you fail to fulfill your genetic potential and then feel guilty about wasting your life. You hide in your Bubble of Oblivion where you can imagine you are invisible, just like your vanished twin. To explain to yourself why you are hiding away so carefully, you may believe that deep down you are a very bad person, which is why no one wants to relate to you. The best way to heal existential shame is to notice the many paradoxes in your life. You feel a vague sense of guilt, but you know you are innocent. When you conceal your vulnerability with defensiveness, you reveal it clearly to the world. Most importantly, you could notice how shame is blocking your healing. It will do so indefinitely until those paradoxes are resolved.

## Resistance

You have probably spent a lot of money on all kinds of different therapies, with little or no result. The therapies are not working because you don't want them to work. You resist healing because you think being the sole survivor is so very unfair. Notice how much effort and money you are prepared to spend on treatments of one kind or another in the hope there will be something out there that will fix you. You are putting a great deal of energy into healing, but you are also working hard at not being healed.

## A healing bond

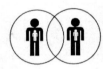

The bond that will heal is within you. It would be good to find another single chorion, one-egg womb twin survivor, if you can, and make a healing bond with him or her. However, the best way to heal yourself would be to rediscover your twin and make him or her into a real person. People may say you are crazy or even psychotic to try and turn something like a dermoid cyst into a real person, but don't worry. Once you have a sense of your lost twin as a separate individual, you will be able to relate to him or her as you would to somebody real. That will be your healing bond. Then your whole life will begin to make sense, your inner confusion will begin to clarify and you will be ready to make some changes.

## The next step: A multiple pregnancy

This chapter concludes our exploration of one-egg womb twin survivors. In the next chapter we will take the Greek myth of Chiron that we examined previously and explore in detail how it feels to be the sole survivor when more than two embryos were present at some stage in the mother's pregnancy.

# 23
# Multiple

 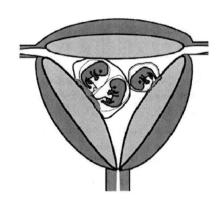

This chapter will concentrate mainly on triplets, but of course multiple pregnancies can involve many more than two or three embryos. An unexpectedly large number of people who volunteered to participate in the Womb Twin Survivors Research Project eventually came to understand that they are multiple womb twin survivors. If you are still unsure about the nature of your twin, it may be that you too are the sole survivor of a multiple pregnancy. We will begin my examining some of the physical signs and indications of a triplet pregnancy that ends in a single birth. A triplet pregnancy is formed in one of three ways:

### THREE EGGS (TRIZYGOTIC )

Mother ovulates more than once in a month and three eggs are fertilized to form three zygotes

### ONE-EGG PAIR PLUS ONE (MONOZYGOTIC-DIZYGOTIC)

Mother ovulates twice in a month, two zygotes are formed and one of them splits at some stage into two monozygotic twins

### DOUBLE ONE-EGG (MONOZYGOTIC-MONOZYGOTIC)

A single zygote is formed that splits in the first few days into two monozygotic twins. A few days later, one of the one-egg twins splits a second time into a pair of one-egg twins

In a multiple pregnancy, a huge variety of events can occur that eventually result in a single survivor being born. This chapter describes a few of the many possibilities. If you are a multiple womb twin survivor, there may be enough detail here to help you to discover the story that lies in your Dream of the Womb.

## Your Dream of the Womb

To demonstrate how varied the outcomes are, here is a list of five different multiple pregnancies:

**THREE EGGS**

Two of the triplets have died

**ONE-EGG PLUS ONE**

Both the one-egg twins have died, leaving the third triplet

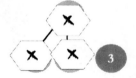

**ONE-EGG PLUS ONE**

One of the one-egg twins has died, also the third triplet

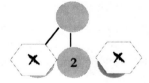

**ONE-EGG DOUBLE**

The triplet of the first one-egg split has died, also one of the second set of one-egg twins from the second split

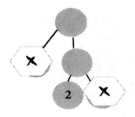

**ONE-EGG DOUBLE**

The two MZ twins of the second split have died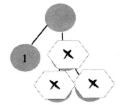

Now we will explore the signs and symptoms that may help you to diagnose yourself as a multiple womb twin survivor.

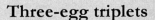

**Three-egg triplets**

**THREE EMBRYOS WITH DIFFERENT GENES**

If you are a three-egg womb twin survivor, here are some of the signs:

- There may have been three or more gestational sacs visible on an early ultrasound, but at a later scan only one was left and that was you.

- There may have been visible signs of your two co-triplets when you were born. If there were no tiny bodies to be seen, there may have been one or more extra cords, extra sacs or extra lobes on the placenta.

- If you were the sole survivor of multi-foetal pregnancy reduction, the tiny bodies of your triplets would have remained beside you until birth.

- Your mother may have had two miscarriages or two episodes of vaginal bleeding during her pregnancy. Each time, this was a sign that one of your co-triplets had died.

- If your same-sex fraternal twin died close to birth, but you have some opposite-sex energy in you, that may also be a sign of a missing opposite-sex co-triplet.

## One-egg plus one

**TWO EMBRYOS WITH THE SAME GENES, PLUS ONE WITH DIFFERENT GENES**

In this case, a set of one-egg twins is accompanied by another individual embryo. If you are the sole survivor of this kind of pregnancy, you may notice that you have one or more of the signs of a lost one-egg twin, as described in the previous three chapters, coupled with one or more of the signs of a lost two-egg twin as detailed in chapters 18 and 19. If so, you are a two-egg plus one womb twin survivor.

There are many eventualities but here are just two examples

- Your two-egg twin died at birth, but in your body there is a dermoid cyst or a teratoma, which are signs of a one-egg twin.

- You have indications of opposite-gender energy in you, which is a sign of an opposite-sex DZ twin. You are also left-handed, which is an indicator of an MZ "mirror" twin.

## One-egg double

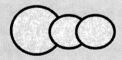

**THREE EMBRYOS WITH THE SAME GENES**

In this case, a single zygote split into two one-egg twins and one of the twins split again a little later. If you are the sole survivor of this kind of pregnancy, you may notice that you have some of the signs of a two chorion, one-egg twin plus some of the signs of a single chorion, one-egg twin. Again, there are many eventualities, but here are some two examples:

- Your one-egg twin died close to birth and had extra fingers or toes.

- Your one-egg twin was stillborn and you have a dermoid cyst or teratoma.

It may take a long time to establish if you are a multiple womb twin survivor or not, but it is always worth bearing the possibility in mind as you move along the healing path.

> *I know that my twin sister died at around four months in the womb, but my older sister told me that she remembers quite clearly that Mum was bleeding quite heavily at around the two-month mark. She remembers this exactly, as that was the day that JFK was shot.*
> *[Judy, USA]*

## Chiron and the multiple womb twin survivor

As we have seen previously, in Greek myth the centaur Chiron's three main tasks were creating communities, building strong relationships and promoting healing. These three tasks are crucial to the healing of all multiple womb twin survivors. They all involve reaching out to others. In doing so, multiple womb twin survivors can become part of the community they create, be enriched by the relationships they help to build and be healed by bringing others to healing. Driven by a deep sense of mission to heal the world and everyone in it, they seek to ease pain wherever it can be found. They are on a rescue mission through which they can also be saved. If you are a multiple womb twin survivor, but so far you have not yet undertaken any healing tasks, be aware that until you do so wholeheartedly, you will not be fully healed yourself. Multiple womb twin survivors put particular emphasis on using their reaching-out energy. How that emphasis is placed depends on what is in their Dream. There are many different possible womb stories. To help you explore them further and perhaps find your own, there is a chart in Appendix B, setting out most of the possible combinations. The rest of this chapter will briefly sum up what we know of the character of the sole survivor when a pregnancy begins with three embryos, but ends with the birth of one baby. The Chiron character can be seen in all of them.

# Three eggs

In this particular Dream, to begin with there are three separate embryos, as depicted above. If two of them die, the main task of the sole survivor is to reconstitute that group of individuals in order to keep his or her Dream alive. Three-egg womb twin survivors love to bring groups of people together. They are good at creating teams or organising events involving large numbers of people. They are at their very best in groups.

## Reaching out

The following diagram shows how the reaching-out energy of the three-egg womb twin survivor is often applied. In the Dream two embryos have died and the survivor reaches out to other people in order to reconstitute the original group

**ONE OF A THREE-EGG PREGNANCY DIES**

The sole survivor reaches out to two other people to try and recreate the original triplet set.

## The different variations in a three-egg pregnancy

Apart from the different manifestations of the Alpha-Beta gap, there are also differences in gender between the embryos. You will find a complete chart in Appendix B. Take the case of a female sole survivor who had once been part of a three-egg pregnancy along side two brothers. To keep her Dream alive, she will find various ways of reconstituting the original group. She may find it most pleasing to be in an exclusively male environment. Her additional male energy would help her to be "one of the boys".

> *I always felt my twin grew up with me psychically. If I do healing journeys, then my twin is usually there as an adult man and he helps me. But lately I feel like "many" and not just two. Not only do I feel like two people but I also feel androgynous, or even hermaphrodite - both sexes at once; yet I am physically female. I am a person first, and feel I*

*am both male and female together, although in body female - yes it gets complicated.*
*[Therese, USA]*

## One-egg plus one

In this particular Dream there is a pair of MZ twins and another embryo developing, as depicted above. Live-born triplet sets often consist of two babies who look identical and another who looks quite different. One-egg plus one womb twin survivors combine the characteristics of one-egg and two-egg survivors. The general effect varies, according to whether the individual was the sole survivor of the one-egg pair or if the entire one-egg pair was lost before or around birth.

### Reaching out

For this kind of multiple womb twin survivor there are two very different ways to reach out in order to re-enact the Dream of the Womb. One attempts to recreate the one-egg twin pair and the second tries to "call home" the other embryo. The two ways are mutually exclusive, because the Bubble of Oblivion in which the one-egg twin pair is recreated has no room for the other, although he or she must be included in some way if the Dream is to be realised. The following set of diagrams shows how the reaching-out energy is exercised in each case.

#### 1. ONE-EGG TWIN PAIR DIES PLUS ANOTHER

The sole survivor tries to recreate the one-egg bond with a similar person, and also reach out to another person less similar, in order to reconstitute the original triplet set.

> *As a boy I grew up with one best friend, since I was five. Now he has moved on and married. Since we've been distanced, I've felt an ever-increasing sense of not belonging, of not letting anyone in, that nobody knows the real me. Although a man, I'm very emotional and tend not to understand other guys very well; in fact, I get along much more easily*

*with women. I keep pursuing something, although I don't know what it is. I am always drawn to wanting to rid the world of suffering as much as possible, which is why I've entered a helping profession: first social work then nursing. Failing to achieve that goal of reducing suffering is painful for me because at times my empathy is too strong. I love making people laugh and seem to be really good at it, but I feel this is the person everyone sees, but not the person I am. The other side of me is very serious and analytical.*
*[Stephan, Belgium]*

This womb twin survivor, Stephan, shows two signs of being a one-egg plus one multiple survivor, as he had one very close best friend and his character has two very different sides, but he also displays elements of female energy in his choice of career. These characteristics are very subtle, but they can be meaningful and significant in the character of a womb twin survivor.

### 2. WHEN BOTH ONE-EGG TWINS DIE

The sole survivor tries to connect with two people who are similar to each other and may be of a different gender to the survivor.

**Different genders**

The diagram above describes a pregnancy where the one-egg twins are female, but of course every variation of gender mix is possible (see chart in Appendix B). In the case depicted above, the male sole survivor will have a double dose of female energy. To re-enact the Dream of the Womb, he will often seek out the company of women.

**Hypersensitivity**

One-egg plus one womb twin survivors are the most complex of all, because of their characteristic hypersensitivity. They have a strong intuitive sense and a deep capacity for empathy. If you are a multiple womb twin survivor of this kind, your mind constantly races, filled with a stream of fresh ideas. You are highly creative and imaginative. You can sense subtle changes in atmosphere and often answer unspoken questions or carry out unspoken requests. When with other people you readily become attuned to their feelings. In a desire to heal their pain, you may carry it away from an encounter as if it were your own. You constantly scan the body language of other people, as your way to reach out.

## Double one-egg

It is thought that double one-egg triplets are formed when one of the one-egg twins splits again into two, as depicted above. In this case, if there is to be just one survivor, one of two things could happen:

- The second twin pair dies
- Only one of the newly created one-egg twins manages to survive.

Very little is known about how triplets are formed. In the Womb Twin Survivors Project so far, no double one-egg triplet survivors of this kind have been identified. It has been suggested that this type of splitting does not actually occur, and that monozygotic triplets are in fact formed from an original one-egg twin pair, in which each divided into two to make quadruplets, but one quad then died. The theory that triplets are formed from quads is borne out by a report about monozygotic triplets, two of whom were left-handed. As left-handedness arises from "mirror" twinning, it follows that this set of three babies must have once been four, but one of them died - presumably the right-handed twin of the second split.

**DOUBLE ONE-EGG QUADS**

For there to be a sole survivor of a quadruplet pregnancy only one thing can happen: one complete one-egg twin pair dies, plus one of the second pair.

**A ONE-EGG TWIN PAIR DIES**

The sole survivor reaches inside to reconstitute the original group of four.

If this is your story, then to keep the original group together you must search constantly inside yourself for the missing three. That may mean you are forever preoccupied with your own feelings. You may have spent many years believing there are several "versions" of you. You are probably searching for your womb mates and trying to keep them alive in your Dream of the Womb.

### Multiple personalities

If there were several versions of you in your Dream of the Womb, this may explain "multiple personality disorder." If you are the sole survivor of a double one-egg pregnancy, you do not reach out towards others. Rather, you reach inside yourself to create relationships and build a sense of community. The community you construct consists of the different parts of your inner self. They are your lost womb twins, whom you are trying to keep together.

> As a child I had "head mates". I've always been like that. I assumed it was normal. When I was a teenager I used plural pronouns and confused people, particularly my teachers, and they complained to my parents about this. My mother dismissed it as just the way I always spoke. I have other people in my body but I don't think that I'm mentally ill. If you naturally have more than one person in your body or you naturally hear voices, there's nothing wrong with that. You just have to learn how to harness it. I've been actively working with my Others since I was 12. I'm 27 now. I don't need curing, I am not sick. My body is just a bit crowded.
> [Linda, USA]

## The next stage:  Awakening from the Dream

The next stage of healing will help you to reach a place where you can begin to make major changes in your life. The next step will show you how you can move along the healing path from grief towards new growth.

Overleaf there is a space for you to draw a diagram of your womb story, now that you have explored twinning in detail. There have been several opportunitites in previous steps along the healing path for you to try and recreate your own womb story. By now, the full story should be clear enoug to make a decision about what exactly happened to you in the womb. Intuition is a wonderful thing and we now know it is remarkably accurate, so don't worry about getting it wrong - just try it.

# STAGE FIVE

# Awakening from the Dream

You died for me, that I might live.
You are the driver of my dreams,
The force behind my leaping,
The wind beneath my wings!

Stay with me awhile
Lest my energy and dreams
Should leave me as you did…

Your voice tells me a new thing now,
That you live on in me;
That you are the added element to all that is mine
- That is MINE!

I know now that I may receive and take,
I may assimilate this gift into my muscles and bones,
To grow strong in the life we have together
And live.

# 24

# From grief to growth

As we take our final steps along the healing path, we will explore how you can transform some of the negative aspects of your life as a womb twin survivor into positive energy to take you into the future. By the end of this chapter, you will see how carrying out certain actions could channel your grief into personal growth.

**Triggers to grief**

When a loved one dies, the people who are left behind begin to feel grief. Womb twin survivors think about death a lot and are easily triggered into a state of grieving, but sometimes they experience grief even when no one has died. Perhaps that has happened to you. Here are some triggers to grief that many womb twin survivors have mentioned.

| Triggers to grief | Yes | No |
|---|---|---|
| Redundancy | | |
| Moving house | | |
| Moving to a different country | | |
| Disability | | |
| Loss of earnings | | |
| Death of a pet | | |
| Divorce | | |

| | | |
|---|---|---|
| Relationship breakdown | | |
| Loss of personal possessions | | |
| Other: | | |

*When my breakdown crept up on me at age 35, it was the last thing I ever thought could happen to me. But in retrospect, it could have been predicted. I had lost several close friends in the space of three months; before I could grieve for one, another would be dying. I buried myself in my work. I acted as if their deaths didn't affect me. At the same time, the person I was dating decided that it was time to leave me. Although I am fine alone, intellectually I could cope with losing friends in death but could not understand somebody just leaving. I started to grieve for all my friends at once. This led to an all-out collapse, or nervous breakdown.*
*[Tara, UK]*

### Excessive grief

Some people remain for many years in a kind of perpetual, low-level grief. If these people are womb twin survivors who have not yet realised the true nature of their bereavement, then their state of mind may be mistaken for depression. After the loss of a loved one, such as a parent, partner or sibling, a womb twin survivor may grieve excessively. The sense of sorrow cannot be fully processed because it is not properly understood. If you grieve excessively when a loved one or a pet dies, it could be that you have not yet grieved for your lost twin. Some experts have described excessive grief that does not heal as "complicated grief disorder", which may describe your feelings. Among the diagnostic criteria for complicated grief disorder are:

| Diagnosing complicated grief disorder | Yes | No |
|---|---|---|
| Intense intrusive thoughts | | |
| Pangs of severe emotion | | |
| Distressing yearnings | | |
| Feeling empty | | |
| Feeling excessively alone | | |

### Reasonable grief

Womb twin survivors have every reason to grieve, for they are born knowing at a deep level that something very precious is missing. Unfortunately, because of the widespread ignorance of the effects of the loss of a twin before birth, womb twin survivors are not helped to see that their feelings of grief are completely natural and reasonable under the circumstances. Perhaps you often felt very sad as a child and would burst into tears for no particular reason. Death and loss are probably very sensitive subjects for you. You may find it hard to let go of the past. All this could be because you have not yet connected your feelings of sadness and grief to the loss of your twin.

> *I found out about vanishing twins about nine years ago. I am convinced that I had a twin sister who died in utero, but I have no actual evidence. I cried a lot as a baby and even cried myself to sleep frequently throughout my childhood. Even though I was not an only child, I often felt very alone and longed for a sister to share my life with. When my first intense romantic relationship ended in my teens it felt like I had been through the same kind of loss before and took me a long time to recover.*
> *[Kath, USA]*

You have been grieving for your twin all your life. Even if you have only recently realised that this is why you have always felt so sad and depressed, it is time to begin a period of mourning for your twin. Mourning helps to heal grief.

## A process of mourning

We will now explore six steps in the process of mourning for your womb twin (and any other womb mates.)

1. **Help on the journey**
2. **Speaking openly about your loss**
3. **The company of other womb twin survivors**
4. **Feeling free to grieve**
5. **Saying goodbye**
6. **Letting go**

### Help on the journey

There are people who could help you on this journey, including bereavement counsellors and other therapists. They may not understand how it feels to be a womb twin survivor, so do ask them how much they know about the subject before embarking on a course of therapy. The best kind of help would be another womb twin survivor who has made the journey already, but at present they are rare. In time, as the womb twin work heals more and more individuals, it will be easier to find such people. For the moment, therefore, your best source of help is probably the advice in this book.

## 1. Speaking openly about your loss

You have probably kept your twin a secret until now because your family never wants to speak about it. The idea of grieving for a twin you never met in your born life may sound very strange to some people. If you have tried to mention the loss of your twin to others, you have probably found it extremely hard to discuss. The best people with whom to talk about your twin are other womb twin survivors. There are many ways to do this online - blogs, groups and forums where womb twin survivors are able to speak their minds and open their hearts without fear of ridicule. Telling your story to other womb twin survivors is a wonderful way to heal yourself, because it makes your twin more real. It also heals others, by showing them that they are not alone.

## 2. The company of other womb twin survivors

Being in the company of other womb twin survivors is healing in itself. Attending a meeting where they gather, such as a seminar, therapy group or conference, would be of great benefit to you. The highly empathetic, intense connection that most womb twin survivors crave is found in abundance in a group of people with similar histories. A common emotional reaction to being in such a group is overwhelming grief, perhaps felt in full for the very first time.

## 3. Feeling free to grieve

In the company of other womb twin survivors and supported by them, you can become free to grieve openly. Even when you are on your own, now you understand your grief you can cry your tears knowing that you are not going crazy, but experiencing a completely normal feeling. If you are the parent of a womb twin survivor and your child is sad and tearful, seemingly for no particular reason, you may guess that the lost twin is the problem. Then you can talk about the twin and openly cry together for the little person who would have been part of your family. To outsiders, an open display of emotion over a tiny twin lost before birth may seem excessive and over-sentimental, but until your tears flow there can be little or no movement towards healing. It may be that for a long time your feelings have been pent up, while you have been seeking a reason and an appropriate outlet. Now you know the true cause of your grief, it can find full expression.

## 4. Saying goodbye

It is very important to say goodbye to your twin. When he or she died you were too tiny to know what was happening. You did not even realise your twin was dead. All you knew was that the Someone who was very near stopped responding to you. Very soon, as part of your healing journey, you will be able to say goodbye, but first you must greet your twin by name. You probably gave him or her a name at an earlier step on the healing path, but if not, see if one comes to you now.

## 5. Letting go of the Dream

For a very long time, you have been keeping your twin alive in your Dream of the Womb, even though you may have only recently become fully aware of his or her existence. Perhaps, in some subtle way without fully understanding why, you always knew that something precious was missing, but until now you had no words to describe it. You have greeted your twin by name and acknowledged with your tears the extent of the bond that existed between you. A loving and beautiful farewell ritual would be the best and most healing way to let go.

# Rituals

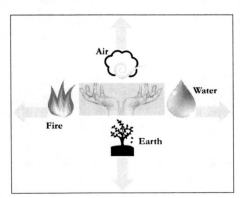

Special farewell rituals vary greatly and are created intuitively by womb twin survivors to try and express their Dream of the Womb in as much detail as possible. The Womb Twin Survivors Project gathered together a large number of very different rituals carried out around the world. It seems that there are no rules, so anything goes. A ritual is a symbolic action.

217

Every part of your ritual will symbolize what your twin means to you and what it means to let go of him or her. Use your intuition to decide when it is time for your ritual and do not allow anyone else to force the pace. You may spend some time planning it or do the whole thing on the spur of the moment but do not start until you feel a clear sense that "now is the time." The matter of letting go is a big problem for some womb twin survivors and you may find yourself resisting the whole idea. The extent of the difficulty varies with zygosity, the biological nature of the twinship, and the number of womb mates.

## Two-egg womb twin survivors

There are three main principles to a letting go ritual for a two-egg womb twin survivor:

- **Twin symbol:** A meaningful item of some sort, one that already exists or one that you have created for yourself.
- **One or more of the four elements:** Earth, water, air or fire.
- **A ritual action:** Burying, sinking/floating away, blowing away or burning the twin symbol.

The basic idea of the ritual is to symbolise the fact that your twin was once with you, but has now gone away.

*Yesterday I said goodbye to Thomas. I had a symbolic funeral with my therapist. I made drawings for him. I put some special things in a box: poems, a crane bird made with origami and a little stone. I burned a light and I listened to "Fly" from Celine Dion. I read a poem. It was a very special, emotional day. I let him go. I am glad that I have let him go. He must live his own life now, and it is time for me to live my own life now. [Nancy, Holland]*

## One-egg womb twin survivors

For a one-egg womb twin survivor, the letting go happens as part of a three-stage process. Two things are needed and can be planned in advance:

- **A half-twin symbol**: Any object consisting of two identical (or almost identical) halves that can be detached from each other.

- **A celebration of twinship**: Any action that brings you joy about being a twin.

You may be concerned that letting go means eradicating your twin for all time. You may be worried that you will forget him or her completely and never be able to rediscover that comforting and strengthening one-egg twin bond. Rest assured that the memory of your twin is firmly imprinted in your mind forever. You will always be a twin and nothing can change that. In fact the letting go process, once completed, will bring you closer to your twin.

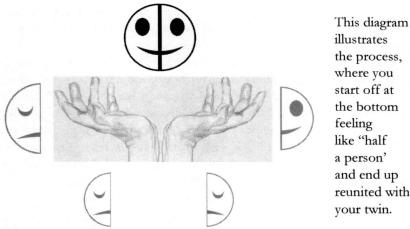

This diagram illustrates the process, where you start off at the bottom feeling like "half a person' and end up reunited with your twin.

The letting go process will take us back in time, beginning with today.

**1. Today**: We will start with how you feel at this moment – full of sadness and only half the person you could be. The first stage is to acknowledge that you are indeed half of a whole. For this, you will need an object that has two similar or identical halves. Decide which half could represent your twin. Look at the object often and keep it near to you, constantly reminding yourself of your twinship. When you feel that you have got to know your twin and he or she has become a real person to you, it will be time to move on to the next stage.

**2. The death of your twin**: In the second stage of letting go, we will recall the silence that fell when your one-egg twin died. It may help to make a little ritual of separating the two parts of your chosen twin symbol and placing them side by side, with some distance between them. This can represent how it was after your twin died. When you have fully felt and acknowledged your feelings of grief, you may like to make some kind of farewell ritual for your twin. The simplest way to do this is to light two candles, one large and one small, to represent you and your twin. When you are ready, you can blow out the small one as you say "Goodbye." Having made your farewell, you may wish to create a memorial to honour your twin. There is a special online womb twin memorial site, which many people have found helpful and healing.[1]

**3. Reunited**: In the third stage of letting go for one-egg womb twin survivors, we move back to the time of your conception. We can rediscover the original zygote, where you were one with your twin for a brief time, before the first split in the original zygote occurred. Using your twin symbol, you can make another little ritual of bringing the two halves of your twin symbol together again. This is depicted at the top of the diagram on the previous page.

Finally, you can celebrate your twinship in whatever way seems best for you. It would be good to time this part of the mourning process to coincide with the anniversary of the probable date when the split occurred in the original zygote. To work out the date of your conception you would need to know how long your mother's pregnancy was, but this information may not be accessible to you. In that case, see if there is a point in each year when everything seems to be new and fresh and you feel invigorated. The anniversary of your conception can often feel like a special time.

## Multiple womb twin survivors

Your womb mates may include one-egg or two-egg womb twins, so you will need to consider more than one kind of letting go - but which womb twin is best to focus on first? The way to handle this confusing situation is to go with your instincts and see where the greatest problems lie. So, for example, you may have had a two-egg twin who was there for many weeks, but your one-egg twin left you so early that you have no special sense of being a one-egg twin, even though you may carry a physical sign, such as a dermoid cyst or left-handedness. Because your two-egg twin had the greater part to play in your Dream of the Womb, it would seem sensible to start with him or her and move on to your one-egg twin later. If you trust your intuition and just let the ideas arise in your mind, you will make the right decisions.

# Growth

The growth that arises out of grief is paradoxical. When you say goodbye to the twin in your Dream, the bond grows stronger and more real. When you let go of your other half, you are made whole again. If you are a multiple womb twin survivor and work hard to heal the world, you will find that when you have let go of your womb mates, you will allow the world to heal you.

When you let go of your womb twin, you will gradually find yourself letting go of your emotional baggage. This may include pain, survivor guilt and resentment. Now that you have found a way to grieve fully and naturally for your womb twin, you will find yourself growing, but not in the way you may have expected. This kind of growth is not about being enlarged in any respect, but about casting off one burden after another. Eventually you will be stripped bare of all the negative aspects of your life that have arisen as a result of being a womb twin survivor. It will feel as if you are being "pruned", in the same way as a vine must be pruned if it is to bear plenty of fruit. Every time you cast off something negative you make room for more and more Alpha energy.

## The next step: Towards hope

Along with all your other burdens, you have been carrying the Beta energy of your womb twin all your life. The helplessness and extreme vulnerability of your Beta womb twin has become yours, so it is time to separate the two kinds of energy and become the strong Alpha survivor once more. The next chapter will take you from helplessness to hope.

# 25

# From helplessness to hope

In this chapter you might find some of the reasons for a paradoxical sense of helplessness, even though you are perfectly capable of helping yourself. We will focus mainly on womb twin survivors who had a womb twin who never developed a fully functioning brain. This chapter will help you if you are stuck in your Black Hole, rendered helpless by Beta energy. Once you have discovered why you feel so helpless, you will be able to take charge of your life. In order to keep your Dream alive, you have become a "False Beta."

If your Beta twin never developed a fully functioning brain, then despite the fact that you have normal intelligence, you will often act in a "brainless" kind of a way. In that case, you will have turned yourself into a "brainless" False Beta. Below are some of the many reasons why a womb twin may never develop a brain:

- **Failure to implant**: One zygote does not implant at all and is lost via the cervix

- **A blighted ovum:** One zygote implants, but all that develops is an empty amniotic sac, because of major chromosomal abnormalities

- **Hydatidiform mole:** Because of major chromosomal abnormalities, one zygote develops chaotically into a watery mole that looks like a bunch of grapes.

- **Developmental failure**: One embryo stops developing in the first 25 days from fertilisation

- **Chromosomal abnormalities**: The chromosomes that control the development of the brain of one twin are missing or damaged

- **Anencephaly**: One twin develops fully, but the brain does not form.

- **Chimera/mosaic**: A few days after conception, stem cells from the Beta twin that fails to develop are incorporated into the body of the Alpha twin, so the sole survivor has two sets of DNA.

- **Dermoid cyst:** A few embryonic cells from the Beta twin are absorbed into the body of the Alpha twin and develop into a dermoid cyst (often containing teeth and hair.)

- **Teratoma**: A few embryonic cells from the Beta twin are absorbed into the body of the Alpha twin and develop into a teratoma, (consisting of a mixture of various of tissues, sometimes containing bone.)

- **Foetus in foetu**: A few embryonic cells from the Beta twin are absorbed into the body of the Alpha twin and begin to develop into a foetus, (usually malformed and only partially developed.

- **Parasitic twin:** Embryonic cells from the Beta twin are partially absorbed into the body of the Alpha twin. Body parts protrude from the body of the survivor.

## Living "brainlessly"

"Brainless" False Betas are womb twin survivors of normal intelligence who live "brainlessly." They are cleverly and carefully doing two things at once. This is particularly so if you are a one-egg womb twin survivor. In that case, in your Dream of the Womb, half of you has no brain. Here is an example of an intelligent one-egg womb twin survivor who lives brainlessly:

### Ian's story
Ian is an intelligent man who always stands by when there is a philosophical debate. He will readily adopt an opinion he has read in the newspaper or heard from an expert, but he is not usually able to justify it. When pressed for his personal view, he never seems to have one. He has a few entrenched ideas, which he borrowed wholesale from his parents and has not deconstructed or examined. He is not shy about sharing his opinions, but they come across as coarse judgments rather than refined statements.

A detailed examination of Ian's thought processes reveals that he is deliberately handicapping himself in terms of his ability to think. He has a high IQ, a grammar school education and is widely read, so he should be able to discuss any topic at any time. Yet in discussions he tends to be devoid of thought or anything to say. When pressed for an opinion or explanation, he becomes mentally paralysed. He is aware that in that moment his mind is a blank and he has become a brainless False Beta.

## Self-defeating behaviour

Self-defeating, self-harming behaviour is essentially brainless. If you are an addict, you probably feel like the puppet person depicted at the start of this chapter. For example, over-eating without thinking of the consequences has been described as "mindless."[1]

> *I'm ashamed to admit that I have only been able to make it for a number of hours without falling victim to my addiction to food. I feel like a total failure and long to feel lighter in body and spirit. I know that I am slowly killing myself with my unhealthy consumption of food. I feel some pretty uncontrollable urges, almost like I am watching myself eating and picking up certain foods. It's almost like having an out of body experience and watching myself fixing this treat or getting that second helping of food. I feel completely powerless and feel that food is completely running my life and not in a direction I want to go in!* [Katie, USA]

It seems that there is only one motivation behind addictions and compulsions and that is to become your own brainless False Beta. It may feel like some irresistible force is manipulating you, but in fact you have chosen to give all your power away to your chosen fix.

## A highly intelligent way to become "helpless"

If you truly had no brain, you would be unable to think. Of course you do have a brain, which functions perfectly well. You may choose to use your brain to create all kinds of clever and subtle ways of being your helpless Beta twin while managing to look intelligent. One egg, brainless False Betas are particularly gifted at this. They skilfully manage to be two people at once - one with a brain and the other without. You may spend a lot of time and energy trying to recruit the help you need without ever having to ask for it directly. This is a subtle and clever strategy that keeps both your Alpha and Beta energies in play at all times. You can wait helplessly for rescue, insist you need no help at all or drop vague hints and hope that someone will offer to help.

## Waiting helplessly

You keep your mind a blank about the possibilities of improving your situation and simply wait helplessly for rescue. If it comes, then you have achieved one object, which is to remain a False Beta. If it does not come, you can succumb to the original fate of your Beta twin and are unable to live a full life. That result keeps alive your Dream of the Womb.

### Dick's story

Dick has filled his house with so much garbage that he is unable to function at all. He became ill and was treated for an acute chest infection in hospital. When he returned home, a kind neighbour offered to help him move the rubbish to prevent further illness. Dick sat helplessly in the midst of his stuff while his neighbour worked. He required every item to be carefully checked over before it was discarded, in case it was potentially valuable. After a great deal of wasted effort to help him, the kind neighbour lost patience and abandoned Dick to his fate.

## Denial

You may choose to deny that you need any help and claim you can manage everything perfectly well on your own. At first glance, that may seem to be an intelligent and sensible response. People who need help may not appear to be as strong and autonomous as people who can manage completely alone. However, it is widely known that human beings are all stronger as individuals when working together. To deny yourself the support of a group is to render yourself helpless, should your personal resources become exhausted.

### Peter's story

Peter was always a very independent child and grew into a self-sufficient man. Once he no longer needed financial support from his parents, he refused an offer to work in his father's firm, broke all forms of family contact and left his home country. He prospered at first, but some years later he was in so much debt that he had to sell his home and was left with nothing. He was officially categorised as "indigent", having no means of subsistence. His parents were contacted by the authorities to pay for his repatriation. Delighted to discover that, after so long a silence, their son was alive and well, his parents paid for him to return. Peter is now working for his father, living at home and totally dependent upon his parents.

### Dropping a hint

You may have a habit of dropping a hint about your need for help rather than asking, because asking may make you look helpless. In this way, you can manipulate another person into willingly offering to help you. You may be so skilled at this that a significant glance or gesture will usually get you the assistance you need. Some people, however, do not like being manipulated, they prefer to be asked for help outright. Consequently, if you tend to drop hints to get help, you will often be left without it. Behind this self-defeating behaviour is the lost relationship with your one-egg twin. Between one-egg twins, empathy is so strong that a slight hint is all that is needed for a positive response. Expecting the same level of unspoken understanding from other people as you may have received from your twin, is doomed to disappointment. Nevertheless, you continue to silently try to recruit assistance, largely without success.

Dropping hints to get help rather than asking outright ensures that most of the time there will be an inappropriate response or no response at all. This is how you keep your Dream alive, for if your one-egg twin had no brain there would have been no response. Whenever there is little or no reaction from other people, your Dream comes true. So all is exactly how you want it to be.

### Being a helpless helper

Multiple womb twin survivors are natural helpers because they always want to make the world a better place. Highly empathetic, they easily read body language and readily respond to any sign that aid is needed. If you often find yourself manipulated into assisting someone who drops hints to get help, you will know how it feels to lose control. You become like a slave to the other person while you are helping him or her. In this case it is very hard to know who is in charge at any given moment. The Alpha energy that lurks beneath the False Beta behaviour dominates the helper, who becomes the Beta twin. Meanwhile, the seemingly "helpless" individual is firmly in control.

## Losing yourself

If you live most of your life as a brainless False Beta, you are probably unsure who you really are. Using your natural intelligence, you know you are not "brainless" - even if you do feel that way sometimes.

If you often say, "I do not know who I am" you are being like your Beta twin in the Dream, who never had enough of a brain to know who he or she was. If you persistently deny your true self in this way, it will leave you feeling empty and isolated.[2] What would have to happen for you to humbly accept your true intelligence and giftedness and no longer be a brainless False Beta? Clearly, your habit of emulating your Beta twin has to go.

## Negativity

If you have completed the healing steps so far, you will have celebrated your twinship, held a memorial ritual and sent your twin to the Place of the Dead. Yet perhaps there is still something holding you back from expressing your full Alpha energy. It is probably rooted in negativity, the kind that paralyses. When you abdicate your Alpha power to others in order to remain a False Beta, you are left helpless and unable to change anything about yourself or your life. You are almost certainly filled with negative thoughts such as:

- *I suppose I have to put up with this...*
- *I didn't know what to do, so I did nothing...*
- *I don't know what I am supposed to feel...*
- *Somehow I just didn't get round to doing anything...*
- *I can't help being the way I am...*
- *I want you to accept me unconditionally....*

## Out of prison

If you feel helpless and powerless, you are in a trap. You have locked yourself into a prison of your own making and you are waiting for someone to release you. You could wait a lifetime. Now is the time to find the key to your prison. It is already in your hand, but you have been a False Beta for so long you have forgotten it is still there. The key to your prison is a powerful combination of choice, responsibility and willingness. All these are Alpha qualities and you already possess them.

- **Choice:** You can simply choose to be free. You chose to build your prison so you can choose to destroy it. You can be the one who knocks down the walls.

- **Responsibility:** You are responsible for your own pain. Only you can change the world you have created for yourself. Are you truly a helpless victim? Is everyone really out to get you? Do other people truly wish to hurt you? None of these is true. You are not helpless and brainless at all, but a perfectly normal, intelligent, capable individual.

- **Willingness:** No matter how many positive and hopeful ideas are presented to you by others, you will never believe them. If things are to change, you will have to accept these ideas can be true. But you are just not willing to take those binoculars of hope and focus on the good things to come.

Perhaps you will not embrace hope and use it to make changes in your life because you simply don't want to be here, on this planet, living your life on your own without your twin. There can be no action without willingness, and there can be no willingness without a wish.

## Do you DARE?

How **much do you wish** for freedom from your Dream of the Womb?

**Do you really want** to stop living out the life of your Beta twin along with your own?

**How prepared are you** to close the door on your self-imposed prison?

Do you DARE to take a step forward into your new life? Do you DARE to move:

FROM THIS          TO THIS?

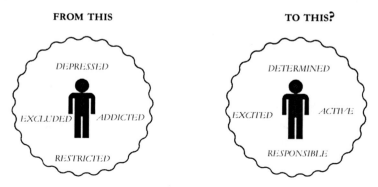

As you DARE to put aside your old life as a False Beta, you will move from

228

depression, addiction, restriction and exclusion to a new life of determination, action, responsibility and above all, excitement.

Here is a space in which you can write what you wish for now with all your heart. Until you know what you truly wish for, you will never be willing to set yourself free from the Dream.

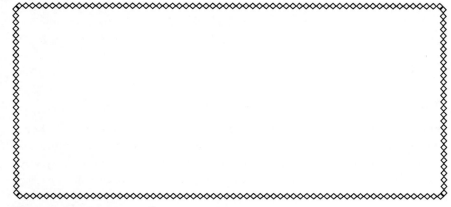

## Open your eyes to reality

Essentially, if you dare to set yourself free, it will be like opening your eyes to the reality of your situation. You could imagine you have walked all your life with your eyes closed and your mind stagnating in dreams of the past. You have been holding on to the illusion that somehow you can become your Beta twin. You have been living the life of your "brainless" Beta twin, despite the fact that you are perfectly capable of intelligent thinking. The "brainlessness" is only an illusion. Intelligent thinking is the reality.

## Alpha thinking

Now is the time for intelligent thinking and insisting on the freedom to be totally yourself. You will have to use Alpha energy to fight against your tendency to retreat to your comfort zone. You keep forgetting that this is voluntary imprisonment. Using Alpha energy means turning your back on passivity and being as active as possible in every way, making use of all your gifts. It requires you to claim all your personal space, for it is within that space that your freedom lies.

## Towards hope

Being hopeful will require the full use of your intelligence. Without thought, we have mindlessness and negativity. Without imagination, we cannot believe in a different future. Using your intelligence, you will be able to make more-considered decisions, which will put an end to self-defeating behaviour. If you keep developing your brain by constantly setting yourself challenges, you will deepen your understanding of yourself and the world.

> *I am over sixty and I am the surviving twin of a 1940s illegal abortion. I have been depressed most of my life and frequently have suicidal thoughts. We lost everything in the recent financial downturn and we are living on food stamps. I have always felt "different" from others and now I know why. I am not sure of what lies ahead for me but there is renewed hope.*
> *[Graham, USA]*

## The next step: From stress to serenity

In this chapter we have seen how you can move from helplessness to hope. We are now ready, with a more positive attitude, to face the difficulties that life often presents. In the following chapter we will explore the many ways in which you have chosen to reduce your capacity to cope with life. The next step will take you from stress to serenity.

# 26

# From stress to serenity

This chapter will focus on an aspect of the Dream of the Womb that is more of a process than a specific event. We are going to explore exactly how and why your twin died. That may be reflected in how you are living out your Dream of the Womb, with particular reference to how you cope with physical and psychological stress. With the help of that understanding, your next step to healing will be from stress to serenity.

**What is stress?**

There is physical stress, which is related to "wear and tear" on the body, and psychological stress, which is a reduced capacity to cope with life. The process of adapting to stress has been described as the "General Adaptation Syndrome".[1] It has four stages - alarm, recovery, adaptation and collapse.

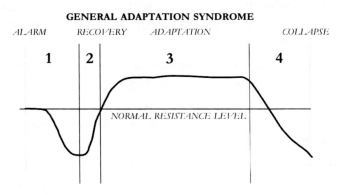

GENERAL ADAPTATION SYNDROME

| ALARM | RECOVERY | ADAPTATION | COLLAPSE |

NORMAL RESISTANCE LEVEL

1: **Alarm:** Things are normal and you can cope perfectly well with what is going on, until some sudden change or trauma sends your body into a state of alarm.

2: **Recovery:** You begin to recover from the initial alarm and you manage to adjust to the changed environment.

3. **Adaptation:** To continue to adapt to the new stressful situation, you have to draw on more and more energy to cope. Your body adjusts sufficiently to enable you to function reasonably normally.

4. **Exhaustion:** The bodily resources are completely depleted by the continual stress. The individual is no longer able to cope and exhaustion results.

## Fatal stresses in the womb

We will now discover what fatal stresses your womb twin may have experienced and how they may be reflected your own life. First of all, we will focus on the four principal reasons why one or more embryos or foetuses may die during a twin or multiple pregnancy, leaving a single survivor at birth. These are: chaotic development, inherent weakness, failure to thrive and environmental threat.

### Chaotic development
Development is so chaotic in one zygote or embryo that it does not form into any recognisable structures.

- **Hydatidiform mole:** One zygote develops only as far as forming a placenta, which evolves abnormally, looking like a bunch of grapes.

- **Blighted ovum**: One zygote forms a placenta and an amniotic sac, but the embryo fails to develop.

- **Chromosomal abnormality**: Some chromosomes are missing or damaged in one zygote, so that normal development is impossible

- **Inherent weakness:** In one twin (or one of a multiple set) there is some inherent weakness that eventually proves fatal.

232

## Developmental failure

One or more of the major organs (heart, brain, kidneys etc) of one embryo fails to develop and death results, either during pregnancy or around birth.

- **Imperfect split of a single zygote**: A single zygote splits unevenly, so that one twin does not receive enough of the cell mass to develop normally.

- **Congenital abnormality**: One twin inherits a specific gene, or there are extra or missing chromosomes, resulting in fatal abnormalities or weaknesses.

## Failure to thrive

One twin or multiple is unable to obtain sufficient vital external resources (blood, nourishment, oxygen, for example) to maintain life.

**Failure to implant**: Following the very early split of a single zygote into two one-egg twins, one twin does not manage to implant. This can also happen to one of two-egg twins, or more in a multiple pregnancy.

**Lack of nourishment:** An embryo implants successfully, but is not able to make good contact with the mother's blood supply and slowly starves to death.

**Lack of oxygen**: An embryo implants, but is unable to get enough oxygenated blood to survive. In a single sac one-egg pregnancy, one twin may be strangled by the umbilical cord of the other, if they become twisted together.

## Environmental threat

Bacteria, viruses or toxicity pass the placental barrier and affect one or more developing embryos or foetuses, but one survives.

- **Viruses:** If the mother has a virus such as influenza, it can affect the performance of one or both placentas, and one twin may not survive the pregnancy. This can also apply to one one-egg twin, while the other remains healthy.[2]

- **Bacteria:** A bacterial infection such as listeriosis can cause the foetal death of one twin, leaving the other healthy.[3]

- **Toxicity**: If the mother takes drugs or medicines that are toxic to the foetus, one twin may be more badly affected than the other and may die in the womb or around birth.

As we continue our search for serenity, we will look at some of the ways you put yourself under stress and see if there are any parallels with the four main causes of pre- or perinatal death detailed above.

# Chaos

You may have some vague idea in the very back of your mind of your twin gradually disintegrating into chaos. An associated thought would be chaos is life-threatening. If this is your story, here are some examples of how it might be lived out in your life:

**Meticulousness**

You are very sensitive to chaos and find it hard to cope with any kind of disorder. Maintaining a neat and tidy environment is extremely hard work but you persevere to the point of exhaustion. Misplacing some trivial item such as a pen or a handkerchief sends you into a state of alarm. To stay calm you must have order, but life is essentially disordered. Therefore you are in a constant state of stress, being "on guard" for any slight sign of incipient disturbance in your highly organised existence.

**Rigidity**

Chaos and disorder may be so disturbing for you that you dare not even think "outside the box." You may need a set routine for your day. Anything out of the ordinary is enough to precipitate you into alarm. As a result, owing to the usually unpredictable nature of things, you are always stressed. To remain calm, you prefer to be in a place where you can maintain some control of events.

**Perfectionism**

If disintegration into chaos lies somewhere in your Dream of the Womb, then anything that is not perfect is to be avoided. The creation of a perfect world would seem to be the best route to a more-peaceful existence but, sadly for the perfectionist, the world is essentially imperfect. Consequently, all perfectionists are under stress as they try to impose some sense of order upon an uncertain and ever-changing environment. If you are a perfectionist, you may have decided that yours is surely a better way to live than "always being in a mess."

**Self limitation:** You are probably already aware of how your attitude is greatly limiting your life and creativity. The diagram on the opposite page of a

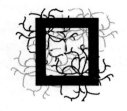

neural network reveals the chaotic mess of neurons that make up your brain. If you try to impose your concept of "How Things Should Be" (the black box in the diagram), a great deal of your brain capacity will not be available .

## Disappointment

In your quest for a perfect world you will always be disappointed. Being let down lies in your Dream of the Womb, so perhaps it is natural for you to continually expect the impossible.

# Inherent weakness

Somewhere in the perpetual present of your Dream of the Womb is the idea that your Beta twin is too weak to survive. Weakness and death are inextricably mixed, so weakness is to be avoided at all costs. Enormous amounts of energy may be spent in an effort to overcome any kind of frailty, either in oneself or in others. How you do this depends on the biological nature of your womb twin and how many zygotes were involved.

## Two-egg womb twin survivors: rescuing others

Any request for help triggers in two-egg womb twin survivors a desire to rescue others. If you are a two-egg womb twin survivor, you may work very hard at being strong for other people. This behaviour has been misunderstood as an addictive need to control others.[4] In fact, it is yet another way to keep your Dream alive, for in your mind the person you are rescuing has become your weak little Beta twin.

> When I was a kid, I felt like I should have had a close friend or brother that I could relate to one-on-one. I felt like he was there once but left and will never come back again. I've always felt that if someone close to me was sad, I felt their pain and even if I wasn't at fault felt a need to make amends or boost their spirit. When I can't, I'm devastated.
> [Eric, USA]

## One-egg womb twin survivors: afraid of weakness

If you are a one-egg womb twin survivor, you put on a brave face at all times, to convince other people that you are much stronger than you feel inside.

> *I've always tried to put up a front to say that I am an independent and determined individual, but the fear of failure or rejection has always prevented me from succeeding. I've always felt lost, like there is supposed to be someone else there with me for support.*
> *[Liz, USA]*

## Multiple womb twin survivors: healing the world

The lifelong task of all multiple womb twin survivors is to heal the world and everyone in it. If you are one, you are driven by a conviction that you are the strongest person in any given group and everyone else is depending on you to improve the situation.

> *I've had the feeling that something is missing. I always feel that there is something I should be working on - never fully relaxed. There is always some mysterious, long-term task that needs to be done.*
> *[Ed, USA]*

## Failure to thrive

Perhaps the following is your story: In the womb, your twin was unable to survive because there was not enough food or oxygen. This is possibly the reason you live in an unhealthy way. Despite your frequent efforts to develop a healthier life, you constantly relapse. The right kind of nourishment and plenty of fresh air are not for you, for in your Dream your twin had neither.

### The right kind of nourishment

Some womb twin survivors know very well they are eating too much of the wrong kind of food. They need no diet books or healthy eating plans to tell them so. The way food is being used reveals what is in the Dream - not enough good food to maintain good health. Keeping the Dream alive at considerable personal cost is the perpetual task of the womb twin survivor.

> *At my birth, there was a second placenta that showed evidence of a second fetus. I use food to comfort me. I especially overeat when I feel sad. I guess I am trying to fill this void I'm feeling inside of me. I use food to forget this sadness I always have inside me.*
> *[Helen, USA]*

## Fresh air and exercise

Information about healthy living is everywhere to be found but some womb twin survivors seem not to notice it and allow themselves to become so unfit they can barely climb the stairs to bed. Such an unhealthy life does not happen by accident. It is being deliberately chosen to keep the Dream alive, for in the Dream there was not enough oxygen to enable your twin to thrive.

# Environmental threat

As we have seen previously, the three commonest environmental threats found in the womb are disease, infection and toxicity.

## Disease

If your womb twin died of an infectious disease, then you would associate illness with death. As you are so closely identified with your twin, you would naturally assume there is something wrong with you that is potentially fatal. This assumption can fuel a long-term anxiety state about all kinds of personal disease.

## Infection

To maintain good health, it is obviously a sensible idea to avoid contamination, but some people make over-strenuous efforts to prevent any contact with germs. This is highly stressful. Such people wash their hands many times a day, take frequent showers, worry about how clean their house is and check their food very carefully in case it is going bad. If your womb twin died as a result of a bacterial infection or a virus, you may associate contamination with death. In that case, it is not surprising if you now take vigorous steps to avoid infection by bacteria or viruses.

## Toxicity

If you were once in a toxic womb environment that was associated with the death of your womb twin, then you would naturally assume you must avoid all toxins at all costs, or you too may die. As a result, you would go to great lengths to avoid any kind of poison, such as pesticides, food additives or the chemicals in toiletries or cleaning fluids, for example. To obsessively follow an additive-free diet and create a chemical-free home is very exhausting.

## Self-perpetuating stress

If you are to move towards serenity, it is important to see how far you are caught up in a stress-making cycle, so you can break it and live a more peaceful existence. Basically, the main cause of stress in your life is the inner conflict between your Alpha and Beta selves. This badly affects your ability to reach your potential, find your level of capability and be your authentic self.

### Self-actualisation versus not reaching your potential

There is probably one all-pervading stress for you as a womb twin survivor, that arises from choosing to be so much less than you could be. In the 1950s, Carl Rogers, a psychotherapist, recognised that every individual has an innate basic tendency towards self-actualisation, or fulfilment.[5] It follows therefore that deliberately choosing not to achieve your potential is to go against your most basic instincts to develop fully as a person, contributing to psychological stress.

> *It feels fantastic to finally identify why I have always felt different, why I have always been searching for something, why I run on half steam and seem unable to reach my full potential, why I sabotage relationships, work and projects. I am surrounded by half-finished projects!*
> *[Alice, Canada]*

### Seeking challenge versus feeling incapable

To grow and develop as an individual you need challenges and tests. If you are keeping alive a tiny Beta twin, however, you will not have sufficient confidence in your capacities to challenge yourself. That inner conflict creates a sense of on-going frustration and distress, particularly if no one seems to understand how much of a struggle life is for you.

## An end to stress?

It may feel as if you are trapped in a very stressful life, but in fact it is possible to put an end to stress. The two main principles involved in doing so are truth and surrender.

## Truth

The truth is that you are not as weak and incapable as you imagine. Also, you are not as strong as you believe you can be. It's time to know the reality of your own limits. It's time to admit your inadequacies and acknowledge your strengths. You can learn more about what these are by setting yourself challenges you might fail to achieve. If you do not fail, you have not tried hard enough. Keep going, trying harder and harder, until you begin to fail. Then you will have found the limit of your capacities. The scale of your achievements will probably surprise you. The truth of who you really are will become manifest when you awaken fully from the Dream.

## Surrender

The fastest way to serenity is to stop trying to make the world a different place. Accept it just the way it is and relax. There are some changes that can be achieved, but only in how you choose to see the world. You have no power to change the true nature of how things are.

> *I don't want to be this sad, pathetic shadow of a person. But there is nothing that will change the past. I got to live, my twin didn't. That's it. I am trying to confront my problems but this is not easy. I guess I just have to get there one day at a time.*
> *[Felicity, UK]*

A useful exercise would be to imagine that you are like a weather vane, which swings easily into the wind. It sits on a loose connection that enables it to change direction. If the seating becomes rusted and locks tight it will be unable to turn. The next strong gale will blow it off the roof and destroy it. The capacity to surrender to the course of events is a wonderful way to save energy. Self-imposed stress drains energy away and achieves nothing. If you decide to go with the flow, you will stop wasting time complaining about the way the world is made or how other people are. Just follow the natural direction of events, like the weather vane, and your capacity to adapt to situations as they occur will save you from possible destruction..

# The next step: From captivity to courage

If you awaken from the Dream you will not waste any more energy trying to keep your twin alive. Rather, you will have available to you all your natural creative drive and personal power. The power of the Alpha survivor is yours to use. The next chapter will show you how owning and using all your Alpha power will set you free.

# 27

# From captivity to courage

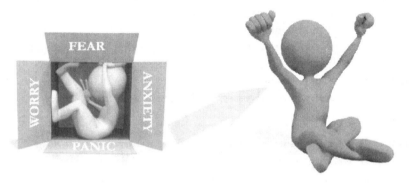

Now we will concentrate on a very common form of self-imposed stress, which is a perpetual state of self-induced anxiety. Many womb twin survivors are held captive by some unknown fear that is all the more terrifying for being mysterious. This step on the healing path will set you free from this imprisoning cycle of constant, nameless terrors by the simple process of naming them.

## Self-induced anxiety

A state of self-induced anxiety is a series of irrational worries, phobias and panic attacks that use up energy and block the healing process. There are

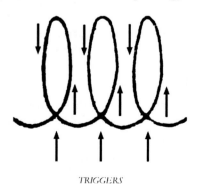

TRIGGERS

countless places to which you can attach any floating feelings of fear. Womb twin survivors fear what might happen. The thought of some dreadful prospect is enough to trigger a state of alarm, which is followed by a brief period of recovery before the next trigger takes effect.

**Triggers:** According to the results of Womb Twin Survivors Research

Project, the commonest fear among womb twin survivors is that they may be crazy. Rest assured you are not. You are looking for an explanation for why you are always so anxious about nothing and everything.

**Alarm:** A state of alarm is triggered by some real or imagined threat. This diagram shows how a state of alarm can be repeatedly triggered. A flood of adrenaline is produced, which increases your pulse rate, diverts blood to your muscles and puts your whole system into high alert. This is known as the "fight or flight" response, for it can enable you to stay and fight for your life or have the strength to run away.

**Recovery:** It takes a single rush of adrenaline about 20 minutes to disperse, so recovery from a state of anxiety will occur quite naturally if you just wait a while. Unfortunately, however, another dreadful thought can trigger another rush and prevent this recovery.

# Naming your fear

For a permanent change in your mood from fear to courage, we must solve the mystery of why you continue to live in a state of self-induced anxiety. We need to put a name to your fears. Below are a few of the many reasons you may justifiably feel anxious, and which are related to your Dream of the Womb. They are death, trauma, being alone, ageing and pain.

### Death

As a womb twin survivor, your life is somehow bound up with death. It is entirely reasonable that you should often think of it. The memory of your twin's death may be very real to you. You may believe that, like your twin, you will also die prematurely. That is a rational assumption but not a prophecy.

### Trauma

Post-traumatic stress disorder (PTSD) is a complex of symptoms that constantly recur after a major trauma. They include generalised anxiety, flashbacks to the original experience (often as nightmares) and a tendency to avoid anything associated with the traumatic event. Many womb twin survivors have been diagnosed with PTSD by psychologists who do not know about womb twin survivors.

*I am a womb twin survivor. So far, I have been labeled as having Dissociative Identity Disorder, Bipolar Disorder and Post Traumatic*

*Stress Disorder. They all presume the experience of a traumatic event in childhood that would trigger the condition. I have a good memory of events in childhood and can remember back to just about the age of three and a little before. I don't have any recollection of any traumatic event other than the trauma I suffered at birth from being born prematurely.*
*[Nat, USA]*

## Fear of being alone in the dark

Being alone in the dark is probably a little bit too close to your Dream of the Womb. As a child, it may have been very difficult for you to sleep in a room on your own and that fear may have continued into adulthood. Alone in darkness, you are reminded of death and abandonment, which lie somewhere in your earliest memory. It may be hard to access but it is still there and easily triggered into life by a similar experience.

*Five years ago I was rushed into hospital with abdominal pain and nausea (also a hugely distended stomach) and was operated on. They found a mature dermoid teratoma containing teeth, hair, cartilage and skin. I had imaginary friends up until age six and even to this day I am scared of sleeping alone in the dark.*
*[Victoria, USA]*

## Fear of ageing

Some womb twin survivors fear growing old, losing their faculties and becoming helpless. This may be related in part to a sense, common among womb twin survivors, that their life has some mysterious purpose. If you feel this and you are not sure what your "mission in life" is, it would of course seem vitally important that you live long enough to fulfill it, whatever it may be. Meanwhile, losing your faculties and becoming helpless would be uncomfortably close to becoming your own Beta twin.

## Fear of pain

The pain of being a womb twin survivor can be an inner torment that lasts a lifetime until it is understood. If you fear being hurt in any way, you may go to great lengths to avoid all sensations of pain, whether physical or emotional. That is very restricting, for it is impossible to ensure that you will always be treated kindly or that relationships will last forever.

*What hurts me the most is when a love relationship ends or if anybody rejects me in one way or another. I feel abandoned afterwards. Every time I think I have worked a lot to heal these feelings of abandonment*

242

*or existential fear, the pain is still there. I need to find out how to stop the screaming inside to be acknowledged and to be seen in my feelings. [Anne, Belgium]*

## Three fundamental fears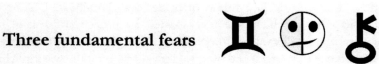

There are countless examples of imagined disasters to which womb twin survivors may attribute their feelings of anxiety, but there are just three fundamental fears that drive them all. Which one of them is your own greatest fear will depend on the nature of your womb twin.

### Two-egg twins: The fear of being left alone

If you are a two-egg womb twin survivor, your deepest fear is that somehow the original scene in the womb, when you were abandoned by your twin, will be repeated once more and you will be left alone for the rest of your life. Here are a few of the ways in which this fear can hold two-egg womb twin survivors captive in a self-defeating cycle. Do you recognise any of these in yourself?

| Particular fear | Yes | No |
|---|---|---|
| Clinging to other people | | |
| Remaining in an abusive or exploitative relationship | | |
| Pushing people away to pre-empt abandonment | | |
| Dependency on other people for companionship | | |
| Feeling distressed when alone | | |
| Excessive self-sacrifice to maintain friendships | | |

*It was my father who told me that it could have been possibly a miscarriage of my twin although he wasn't sure. Another thing that gave it away was the fact that I have constantly felt alone, as if it didn't matter if I was loved by every single person in the world, because I would still feel alone. I also had an over-active imagination that I knew I used as a way to cope with things in my life. I also cling to people. I am not trusting at all and am VERY difficult in relationships. [Eva, USA]*

## One-egg twins: The fear of annihilation

If you are a one-egg womb twin survivor, you are totally identified with your weak and very vulnerable womb twin. You may have many reasons to feel anxious, but your deepest fear is of being totally annihilated. Your twin is dead and gone, as if he or she never existed. Your deepest fear is that you - like your twin - will vanish without trace. Every day you have to prove your own existence to yourself and others. Here are a few of the ways in which the fear of annihilation holds one-egg womb twin survivors captive in a negative cycle. Do any of these apply to you?

| Sign of a fear of annihilation | Yes | No |
|---|---|---|
| Needing to always prove my own worth | | |
| Needing always to be the strongest, cleverest, etc. | | |
| Needing to be noticed and highly visible to others | | |
| Denial of my faults and failings | | |
| Denial of my own vulnerability | | |
| Excessive feelings of shame | | |
| Needing to constantly test my capacity to survive | | |
| Denial of my strongest feelings | | |

*Even though I have been working on the issue of being a womb twin survivor for the last six months, I still feel that I am not making any progress. The deepest fear seems to be one of annihilation and my terror in the face of that leaves me stuck in a place where I'd rather feel nothing at all than face it.*
*[Faye, USA]*

## Multiples: Soothing the fears of other people

If you are the sole survivor of a multiple pregnancy, you may have already identified with some of the descriptions mentioned above, according to the whether your fellow womb mates were one-egg or two-egg twins. You can also be held captive by the fears you pick up when relating to anxious people. As a multiple womb twin survivor, your need to soothe the fears of other people is strong. You are a highly empathetic individual who carries around the feelings of others without even noticing it. Thus, you spend your time unconsciously soaking up people's anxieties while doing your best to heal them where you can. Characteristically, if you are unable to help another person in distress, you become very distressed yourself. Are there any signs in your own life that you are carrying someone else's emotional baggage?

| Soothing other people's fears | Yes | No |
| --- | --- | --- |
| Unable to ignore a person in distress | | |
| Being excessively calm when with an anxious person | | |
| Feeling compelled to offer advice and counsel | | |
| Becoming very stressed by being with others in distress | | |
| Unable to ignore requests for help or support | | |

*Fear and anger gives me an eternal tight knot feeling in the stomach and the "butterflies" as well. I was carrying so much internal garbage with me I had to say "enough". I can't run away, it's inside. So how do I get it out? First I worked on getting my body out of the claustrophobic deadlock I found myself in - full to the brim with adrenalin.*
*[Hannah, USA]*

# The courage to heal

Many womb twin survivors are afraid of healing, and that may include you. Your fear may be one of the reasons why you remain stuck, even at this stage, when we are a long way along the healing path. It is possible that, even though you have followed all the steps in this book to this point, you are afraid to go any further. There are three ideas that may help you to move on:

1.  Complete healing is possible
2.  There is nothing to fear in being healed
3.  You already have natural courage

## 1. Complete healing is possible

A favourite way to stay stuck is to believe that this is the only kind of life you can ever have - how it must always be. Perhaps you feel lost and confused about the way forward, even after taking so many healing steps. Perhaps you feel guilty about being freed from your self-imposed captivity. All it takes for healing to come is to believe healing is possible. If you find that idea hard to accept, it may be because you lack the courage to let it happen. Perhaps this lack of courage has locked the door to your freedom. You know that on the other side of the door is something for you, but you cannot allow it to open. If you truly wish to be healed, letting the door open would be a start. The key is in your hand. That wish to be healed may become a willingness, if you stop blocking the process.

> *I see my twins' male energy working through me, helping me go forward and being the driving force, yet at the same time being a handicap and a life of illusion nonetheless. I am now here at the crossroads. I can't wait to discover what I am truly like.*
> *[Charlotte. USA]*

## 2. There is nothing to fear in being healed

Rest assured that being healed is not like entering a strange country or becoming a different person. Once you are healed, in many ways life will be as it always was, but it will be less stressful and certain barriers will have disappeared.

**MUSTS AND SHOULDS**

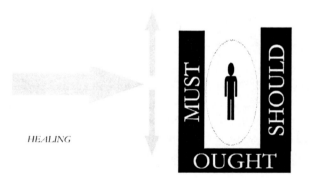

HEALING

The two main blocks to your healing are the MUSTS and SHOULDS that have been driving your behaviour. They have created a comfortable prison into which you have locked yourself.

246

**WILL AND SHALL**

HEALING                      HEALING

CAN      WILL      SHALL

The healing process can move freely through these transformed barriers. Once the constraints on your personal development have been removed, you will be able to grow and develop into the person you were meant to be.

## Your natural courage

You have more courage than you can know. Most of it lies latent inside you, waiting for the moments of crisis that will inevitably occur. Your courage is part of the way you are made as a human being. You may love a physical challenge, in which case you enjoy calling on your natural courage to carry you through. Perhaps you like taking risks, such as driving too fast or taking hard drugs, just to see how far you can push yourself. On the other hand, perhaps you do not believe you have any natural courage. In that case, you may go to great lengths to ensure that you have a peaceful life where crises are kept to the minimum. Of course, wars and natural disasters test everyone's courage to the limit. If you have experienced either of those, you probably remember being amazed at how well you coped at the time. In other words, your natural courage has always been there.

Womb twin survivors are often the kind of people who do not believe in their capacity to cope, but can act boldly if necessary to their survival. That boldness calls for Alpha energy, which is your natural capacity to survive. It explains why you are the sole survivor of your mother's pregnancy.

Any sense of helplessness, incapacity, weakness and cowardice in your life has been generated by your tendency to adopt the characteristics

247

of your weaker and more vulnerable Beta womb twin. Until now, your true courage has been obscured by too much Beta energy. It is time for that to change. This image illustrates how excessive Beta energy has eclipsed your Alpha self:

**Letting go of Beta energy**

You have let go of your womb twin, but have you also let go of the Beta energy that you have retained for so long? Perhaps you need to do that now. Here is an image of a balloon marked with Beta energy, floating away. Perhaps you can make a similar little ritual about allowing your Alpha energy to be revealed in this way:

When you have learned to recognise all the various forms of Beta energy that remain in you and let them go, what will be left is you. Now you can acknowledge that you have always been filled with Alpha energy, the source of your natural courage.

## The next step: From poverty to potential

Once you have let go, not only of your twin but all the Beta energy that has been lurking in your Dream of the Womb, what remains? You may believe that the loss of your twin or other womb mates has left you impoverished. You may believe that you are much less than you could have been, if only your twin or other womb mates had survived. The next step on the healing path will show you how to turn that sense of inner poverty into great potential.

# 28

# From poverty to privilege

The double image above illustrates the paradox of being a womb twin survivor. The poor little person on the left is burdened in many ways with riches of various kinds, while the person on the right is free of any burden and can stand strong and tall. For every womb twin survivor, there are two simultaneous feelings. One is based on an assumption that you are much less than you could have been if your twin or other womb mates had survived. The other is related to the fact that you are the fortunate sole survivor.

A deep sense of personal poverty is a constant distraction. You have probably been working so hard on finding external ways to heal your inner feelings of lack that you have not had the energy, or the time, to live a full life. Furthermore, it is likely that you have been bowed down under a heavy load of guilt and resentment.

Growth will be achieved in this healing step through an exercise of being gradually stripped bare of these burdens. The image of personal poverty depicted above carries six symbols, for status, money, food, sexuality, work and possessions, together with resentment and guilt. These burdens are self-imposed in a failed attempt to heal a feeling of inner emptiness.

As we take this step along the healing path, we will explore each one in turn and see how we can transform a sense of personal poverty into one of privilege, by letting them go, one by one.

## Status

You may have a feeling that you lack social standing or personal worth. This is usually summed up as "a lack of self-esteem" and is a self-inflicted sense of worthlessness. In reality you are worth exactly the same as everyone else. In your desire to raise your own self-esteem, you may have become dependent on the support, praise and acclaim of others.

To compensate for an inner sense of worthlessness you may have become arrogant, as you try to convince others you are someone of great importance. No matter how hard you try to be a well-respected person, you will still feel worthless. This is a self-imposed kind of poverty. You would feel richer if you stopped trying to be someone better and settled for who you are.

If you were to remove your top hat of status you would be better able to look up and show your face to the world instead of keeping it hidden under the brim of your hat.

*I don't like people but I hate to be alone. Sometimes I just prefer to be in the company of one (real) friend to accompany me. My self-esteem always falters, no matter what; I have no confidence in myself although I try to smile and be happy and cheerful. Sometimes, I wonder if I truly exist, is this reality or am I some machine realizing my presence? [Shantal, USA]*

## Money                                  £ $ €

Money is of course important, but it is a symbolic thing. It consists of pieces of metal and slips of paper that have no value except what we decide to put upon them. Money buys options, above all. It gives you choices and - to a certain extent - power. A shortage of money is a source of anxiety for some womb twin survivors, who feel unsafe without it. Being short of money can also increase a sense of inferiority in any womb twin survivors who have already decided that they are unworthy.

The result can be a preoccupation with money that fills your head with thoughts of how to increase your wealth in order to feel safe and important. To feel rich in financial terms seems to be a perfect way to heal a deep sense of emptiness and impoverishment. Sadly, no matter how much or how little money you have, the sense of poverty remains. Some womb twin survivors make themselves poor when they do in fact have money. They spend it all or gamble it away. To have plenty of money and throw it all away may seem foolish, but to a womb twin survivor, money can be a burden. A deep feeling of being undeserving is well-expressed by wasting what money you do have, until you have none.

If you could stop thinking about money, your head would feel clearer. You would realise that there are many wonderful things in life that are available absolutely free of charge.

*I know that if I tried I could do many great things but there's always something holding me back like money, time or other people. For some reason the question about having irrational feelings of nonexistence really stood out because when I was little (and even now) sometimes in the mirror I look and think to myself, "Is this the person that everyone sees? Is this me?"*
*[Lesley, USA]*

# Food

As we have seen in previous steps, some womb twin survivors find it hard to eat healthily, and that may include you. For years you have probably been eating too much of the wrong kind of food and too little of the right food, and wondering why you do so.

Experts who study obesity have yet to establish clearly why some people are thin and some are fat. In countries such as Britain or the USA, we live in a time of plenty and food is cheap, so if food availability makes us greedy, we should all be fat but we are not. Some of us eat far too much, to try and fill the emptiness inside, and that is what can make us fat.

251

That sense of nutritional poverty that changes how we eat has nothing whatever to do with hunger, or the availability of food. Anorexics eat hardly anything and just manage to survive, like poor, starving people. Meanwhile, the morbidly obese feast daily on copious quantities of junk food and starve themselves of healthy meals. The very fat and the very thin are equally poor, for they are using food to tell themselves stories from long before birth, about *having too much to eat* and *starving to death*.

If you can recognise that the hunger you feel inside is in your heart and not your stomach, you would be able to eat the food your body needs in sufficient quantity for optimum health.

*I've always had a sense that I don't deserve food. To this day, I get those feelings sometimes, like I'm completely unworthy of food. Sometimes I'll be eating and out of nowhere I'll think, "Why am I eating? Why should I of all people, get food?" I have a very weird relationship with food. [Shula, USA]*

## Sexuality

Inner emptiness and a general sense of deprivation can be mistaken for sexual frustration. Some womb twin survivors make sure they remain sexually unsatisfied. They move rapidly from one sexual relationship to another in search of intimacy and satisfaction. Opposite-sex, two-egg womb twin survivors, in particular, sabotage their sexual relationships. As a result, when they finally find a suitable partner they are too old to have children.

Some one-egg womb twin survivors yearn so much for an intimate friend exactly like themselves that they choose another person of the same sex for a sexual relationship. Many of them - mostly males- enter into a series of brief homosexual contacts, never allowing time for the relationship develop. This is sexual poverty - a state of mind in which every sexual activity is empty and meaningless, bringing only the briefest moment of connection and fulfillment. Almost as soon as the sexual encounter is over, whatever form it takes, the loneliness and emptiness return.

If you can freely express your sexuality in terms of your genetically-imprinted gender energy, you will recognise sexuality for what it is and not a means to fill your inner emptiness.

*For the past year I have been working on taking responsibility for my thoughts and behaviors. I have been able to recognize the relationship between your inner state of being and how your reality is simply a reflection of that inner state of being. I feel a constant emptiness that I have always thought was Daddy issues and wanting a man.*
*[Viv, UK]*

## Work

Some womb twin survivors feel they must earn their place on this planet. Others believe the harder they work, the better things will be - more money, more security, higher status. Another group are so busy saving the world, healing pain wherever they go and rescuing people in distress, that they become totally exhausted and burn out.

Work can be rewarding, fulfilling and fun, but it important also to keep a reserve of energy for enjoying relaxation and rest. It may seem strange to say that you need energy to rest, but there is a sort of hyperactivity that comes from the exhaustion caused by rushing against the clock from one crisis to another. Some womb twin survivors do not want to slow down, because in stillness they experience the painful emptiness that haunts them. To have no time to reflect or even to rest is to be spiritually impoverished.

If you can acknowledge that extra effort does not add anything to your personal worth, you will be able to slow down, recover from your exhaustion and live more effectively.

*I found out my twin was stillborn when I was 12. I felt guilty for a long time then I felt I had to fill my life with as much experience as possible.*

*This only served to ruin my life, looking for love and acceptance and making more than double my share of mistakes.*
*[Jenny, USA]*

## Possessions

The desire for possessions is a kind of greed that is constantly stimulated by the consumer society. Advertisements persuade us to buy bigger, better, more prestigious things. There is a way to be surrounded by an abundance of possession and yet be spiritually impoverished, and that is hoarding. Collecting and hoarding items of various kinds takes up a great deal of time, money and energy. As the abundance increases, so does the spiritual poverty. To be an extreme hoarder is to live like a pauper in a house full of your possessions. If you are always shopping, even when there is nothing you truly need, then the chances are you are trying to fill up the emptiness inside yourself. If you feel somehow impoverished, then that is how you will remain, however many possessions you accumulate.

 If you can realise that having a great many possessions cannot replace your lost twin, you could begin to make good use of your possessions, which will enrich your life.

*I seem to be a bit of a hoarder - clothes, knick-knacks, everything. I always think I'll need it later. I really would feel better if I could just get rid of some stuff and deep down inside, I want to be a minimalist! I also think that my hoarding is my way of giving myself something to do, so I won't think about bigger, scarier issues.*
*[Janie, USA]*

## An end to resentment

Resentment creates a pool of negative energy that will easily swamp any joy or fulfillment in life that you may manage to experience. Resentment is a kind of childish petulance, like winning second prize in a competition, getting indignant that you did not come first, refusing to collect your prize and insulting the organiser of the competition. The closer you are identified with your own Beta twin, the more fragile you feel and the more resentment is required to make you feel stronger. To help you to see if resentment is present in your life, here is a checklist of some of the ways in which it can show itself:

| Ways to feel resentful | Yes | No |
|---|---|---|
| Being a bad loser | | |
| Feeling animosity towards others | | |
| Feeling hatred towards someone | | |
| Hating people who reject you | | |
| Finding it hard to forget a hurt, even after many years | | |
| Ruminating on a humiliating experience | | |
| Needing to be right all the time | | |
| Holding a grudge | | |
| Feeling bitter | | |
| Maintaining a family feud | | |
| Being unfriendly towards certain people | | |
| Feeling that life is unfair | | |
| Feeling angry with God | | |
| Other | | |

To let go of resentment you need to practise acceptance. This means learning to take life just as it is, rather than in the way you feel it should be. It is a fruitless task to try and impose on the world your ideas about how things ought to be, for you are not powerful enough to do that - no one is. There is a paradoxical arrogance in resentment, for it arises out of your sense of inner fragility, but has all the confidence of wanting to control events and other people.

Resentment is painful and continues to hurt, as if you are picking at sores and not allowing them to heal. As it fades away, your burden will be lighter and you will be able to look about you more easily. Then you will see the beauty and kindness that is there for you, if you would receive it.

If you can see that resentment creates nothing but negativity, you will also be able to see that no one has been trying to hurt you and there is another reason for your pain.

*I had an identical twin sister in the womb, but due to Twin-to-Twin Transfusion Syndrome she died approximately three months before we were due to be born. Ever since I found out about the existence of my sister, I've felt many different things. Grief primarily, but also anger at my parents for not telling me, and anger at the hospital for not being able to stop it.*
*[Tina, USA]*

## An end to guilt

It should be clear by now that all the burdens you have been carrying have just one root cause - survivor guilt. The death of your twin was not your fault. It was no one's fault but a perfectly natural process. Your twin was too weak to survive in any case and was doomed to die. It was not your choice. The death of a twin or other multiple foetuses is never caused by any action on the part of the sole survivor. Survivor guilt is quite different from any other kind of guilt or shame, however hard you may try to confuse the two. You may have felt guilty about everything for most of your life. A pervasive sense of guilt is a deep feeling of shame about *Something Wrong* that you have certainly done but would never wish to do. As a result you have a sense of somehow being punished, despite the fact that you are innocent. Survivor guilt has impoverished you but that is exactly how you want it to be.

The answer to survivor guilt is to forgive yourself for what you think of as the sin of being alive. You are innocent of all crimes against your twin. You had no control over events in the womb, any more than you can control most events in born life. There were reasons why your twin died that have absolutely nothing whatever to do with you.

If you can forgive yourself the sin of being alive, you will be able to forgive your twin or other multiples for being weaker than you and unable to survive to keep you company.

*When I hit my teens I felt an overwhelming sense of guilt like I shouldn't be here and I had done something terrible to get here. My mother told me she had a miscarriage whilst pregnant with me. I realised that the guilt was because I had deprived my twin of something she needed in the womb and as a result she isn't here beside me today.*
*[Amber USA]*

## From guilt to gratitude

Your life as a womb twin survivor has been very difficult and it may seem ridiculous to be grateful for such a bad experience. However, if you are to be fully healed you must allow yourself to experience some sense of joy that you are alive. That simply means acknowledging that your life, albeit difficult, has been a gift. However much you may wish to join your twin in death, as the sole survivor you occupy a privileged position.

Privilege brings responsibility. Privileged people enjoy benefits denied to others. They are differently gifted and set apart. They are granted an unlooked-for advantage that arrives quite by chance. Privilege has nothing to do with being deserving, it just happens to you. It is a free gift that nevertheless comes with instructions for proper use. You could have a rich and fulfilling life, but have you chosen to live in spiritual and/or material poverty? Is survivor guilt preventing you from recognising that you have made that choice? Are you truly thankful that you were born alive?

# The next step: From victim to victor

Letting go of the various ways in which you have made yourself poorer will leave you face-to-face with an important truth. Growth towards healing means losing everything in order to gain a richer, fuller life. You may be smaller, but you will be stronger. That is something to be thankful for. Now you have been stripped bare of the illusion of personal poverty, you are faced with the true extent of your own strength. The next step will reveal the power that is part of your own nature as the sole survivor.

# 29

# From victim to victor

We are very close to the end of our journey together, but as part of this step we will go back to the very beginning. We will discover the truth of who is responsible for your life. Are you the victim of circumstances or have you used your personal strengths to gain victory over them? By exploring your prenatal origins, you will rediscover the amazing power that lies inside you, largely untapped.

You are only a fraction of the person you could be. For much of your life you have focused on your Beta twin and the limitations you have been imposing on yourself to keep alive your Dream of the Womb. This healing step will not dwell on your Beta side - your perceived lack of capabilities. It will explore your potential power - what you can do.

The following chart shows the route from victim to victor in four stages, which together spell out the phrase, "I can!"

| I | Intelligent thinking |
|---|---|
| C | Calm in spirit |
| A | Alpha energy |
| N | New life |

We will now explore in a little more detail what each of these elements may mean in your life. Every time you say to yourself "I can!" you will be reminding yourself of them.

# Intelligent thinking

Your brain is an amazing organ, but you are only using a small fraction of it. There are four ways in which you can begin to apply your brain in a more effective way, so that the Dream of the Womb will no longer rule your life.

## 1. Truth - not illusion

The Dream feels like an alternative reality, but it is very important that you learn to distinguish truth from illusion. Every time everyone seems to be getting at you or your world seems to be falling apart, carry out a reality check. Perhaps the criticism was fully justified and the world is just being chaotic - as usual.

The best way to discover the truth about yourself is to ask another person what they think of you and listen carefully to the answer. If this person says you are someone with much to offer, but you hide yourself away, he or she may be right. If the reply is that you are good at your work, but no better than anyone else, you may need to recognise your own shortcomings.

## 2. Awake - not dreaming

To awaken from the Dream of the Womb is the same as waking from any dream. In the morning, it will fade only after you begin to be active. If you lie in bed all day in a reverie, your dreams can become more and more real to you, so you are unable to tell if you are awake or sleep. If you are to practise intelligent thinking, you will take steps to make sure that you are fully awake to the realities of your own existence. This means:

- **Fitting** yourself into society
- **Taking** responsibility for your own welfare
- **Maintaining** your personal boundary.

In the Dream of the Womb, there is only you in your lonely little world, clinging to the memory of your lost womb twin or other womb mates. In born life, you are just one little person among many millions of others. Nevertheless, all your actions and inactions have consequences.

## 3. Facts - not assumptions

As we have seen, the fabric of your Dream of the Womb is constructed from foetal assumptions. As a tiny foetus, incapable of coherent thought, you were only able to learn by a primitive process of trial and error. You gradually built for yourself an assumptive world, that you took for granted. It included ideas such as: *To be with my twin is the Way Things Are.* Hard-wired into your neural network, these assumptions today feel like facts. They have been there from the beginning and are the bedrock of your personality.

How to tell an assumption from a fact? One way would be to consider the opposite view and see what is to be learned. It may feel stronger to be angry but it takes courage to admit your fear. When you are feeling attacked, perhaps no one is getting at you. If you are feeling fragile, perhaps you have forgotten your inner strength. Every time you experience that familiar feeling of anxiety, say to yourself, "It's that Dream again!"

### 4. Alpha - not Beta

Almost all of the steps on this healing path have been designed to help you to separate yourself from your Beta twin. Until you discover your distinct identity as the sole survivor, you will continue to hold on to vestiges of your Beta twin, which will diminish you.

The self-defeating behaviour that has characterised your life to date, has not been clever. All in all, your life as a re-enactment of the Dream has required you to switch off your natural intelligence and mindlessly repeat the same foolish conduct with the same negative results. Next time you feel a desire to fix your emotions by doing some harm to yourself, try intelligent thinking and say to yourself, "That is a stupid idea". Flooded with intelligent Alpha energy in that moment, you will find yourself making the sensible decision, which is to look after yourself and protect your own welfare.

## Calm in spirit

A calm spirit is one at peace with itself. That means allowing a moment of surrender, where you recognise that there is absolutely nothing you can do to change the world. Impossible dreams are fuelled by impatience - the idea that you can have everything now and you don't have to wait. Healing requires you to let go of your impossible dreams, slow down and let things happen. Impatience can make you force the pace of your own healing, which is a great mistake. Healing is something you allow, not something you can create. Trying too hard to heal will delay your healing indefinitely.

## Courage - not timidity

To remain calm under duress needs the kind of courage that quietly endures. Some people mistake the bravery it requires to remain calm in the face of a threat. An aggressive, angry reaction may seem to be more courageous than keeping quiet, but only a strong person can remain calm enough not to be triggered into a response. You may habitually avoid confrontation, but that is not the same as being calm in spirit. You may have been too afraid to make a riposte, but perhaps none is needed. In the face of threat, if you stand strong within your own space, there will be no need for some smart comment or aggressive response. If someone acts in a threatening way or attempts to breach your personal boundary, you can remain outwardly and inwardly calm but determined. That will be enough to end the conflict.

## Acceptance not control

To keep your Dream alive in the face of reality, you have probably tried to control events and other people, in an attempt to make them conform to how you have assumed the world must be.

- **If you assume** that everyone else except you is virtually brainless, you will have to lead the conversation.

- **If you assume** that intimate relationships lead to rejection, you will have to make sure no one comes close to you.

- **If you assume** that you are very fragile and could easily be annihilated, you will have to elicit constant feedback from others, so you can know you exist.

Awakening to the Alpha power within you will enable you to relinquish your need to control others and let them be themselves. If you accept the way things are, there will be no impulse to take control of people and events. The world will continue to function perfectly well without your influence.

## Forgiveness - not resentment

Resentment will interfere with your wish to be calm in spirit, for the negative energy it generates will keep you angry and restless. If you can forgive yourself for picking at sores to keep the pain alive, you will see at once that no one has been trying to hurt you. All the pain you have endured has been self-inflicted. You may feel that life has let you down badly, so it is very hard to remain calm. However, you know you have sabotaged your opportunities in life because of your guilt at being alive. No one has taken away your chances, robbed you of openings or rejected you. You have made sure that your life is much less that it could have been. Forgive yourself for living and the peace of mind you seek will soon be yours.

# Alpha energy

Your position as the sole survivor of a twin or multiple pregnancy was not simply a matter of luck. It was because you had the stronger constitution. You possess a particular kind of energy that has certain characteristics. We will now explore some aspects of Alpha energy so that you can recognise it in yourself.

## Vivacity

You are full of energy for life, but to what extent have you diminished it by working yourself to exhaustion or denying yourself a healthy lifestyle? You have a quality of intensity about you - a desire to squeeze as much as you can out of every moment. That is your innate vivacity, which helps you to survive illness and hardship. You are a natural survivor. No matter how hard life turns out to be, you will be determined to embrace it.

## Interest

You have a na**tural** curiosity about life. You may have sabotaged your education by not applying yourself in school, but your fascination with life remains. You are interested in everything and everyone and want to know more and more about all kinds of things. However, you may have deliberately ruined the effects of your learning by not thinking intelligently.

Alpha energy is not experienced to the full until you harness action to your ideas, for they could be useful and may make a difference. It is often said that the people who bother to turn up to get the job done, end up running the world. As long as you restrain your Alpha energy the world must do without the benefit of your ideas.

## Confidence

You could have the natural confidence that comes from being held safely within a strong personal boundary. Sadly, you have allowed other people to take away your personal space. Your self-confidence would still be there if you were prepared to assert yourself. In future, if you are ever subjected to bullying or exploitation, remember that you are full of Alpha energy. Use it to hold your boundary and stand your ground. Once the power of your Alpha energy is visible to others, no one will ever bully or exploit you again. Rather, they will begin to respect the way you stand up for yourself.

## Truth

Alpha energy enables you to speak the truth with love and to hear it told about you. By speaking the truth in a loving way, you will be able to help other people to see how they are behaving without hurting their feelings. The way to use the truth is to help, not to hurt. When someone makes a mistake, notice not the mistake itself, but why it happened. Then you can speak to them about that. To hear the truth spoken about you to your face requires Alpha energy. What you learn may be uncomfortable, not necessarily because it is negative. To hear your own gifts praised and publicly acknowledged, when you know you have not been fully using them, can make you feel ashamed of yourself. Alpha energy will help you to listen to these remarks, acknowledge them and admit the truth of your un-lived life. That will contribute to your healing and growth.

## Ordinariness

Womb twin survivors feel different from other people, but they are ordinary humans nonetheless. Alpha energy will help you to recognise how ordinary you are. You are a perfectly normal human being, despite the fact that various professionals may have attempted to label you as having some kind of "personality disorder" in order to explain your feelings and behaviour. Your Alpha energy is an added element that is unusual, but does not set you apart from others. That extra *Something* does not make you better or more important than anyone else. You may be conscious of your special gifts, but Alpha energy will help you maintain your sense of normality. It will enable to you to relate to all people in the same way, for we are all of equal worth.

## Release

Alpha energy is not something to be developed or worked at. The moment it is forced, it is blocked. The only way to express it is to simply acknowledge it is there and allow it to be released, but take care:.

- **If can be misused** if it is forced in any way.
- **It is strong,** but it can be used to dominate.
- **It is powerful**, but can be used to abuse others.
- **It gives you a sense of mastery** but could make you controlling.
- **It creates a sense of personal autonomy**, but could separate you entirely from the people who love you.

Alpha energy must be handled with care. If it is deliberately used it will immediately be eclipsed by that familiar Beta energy. It is Beta energy that has sent you in search of healing, rather than waiting patiently for it to come.

To release Alpha energy you have to own it, acknowledge it and just set it free. The way in which this form of energy works is mysterious. It arises when you don't look for it and heals you faster than you could ever imagine, once you have stopped working at it and have surrendered to the healing process.

## New life

Now you have awakened fully from the Dream, you have liberated the energy inside you that has been suppressed all these years. Questions may remain, so we will consider a few of them here:

### Will I be a different person?

The changes that will take place over the next few months and years will be immense yet subtle. Inside, you will feel completely different, but you will seem just the same to other people. You will be more like yourself, the person you were born to be. If you are still not sure exactly who you are, try giving yourself a new name, a new look or a new hairstyle, to symbolise the new you.

- **You have let go** of your twin
- **You have stripped yourself** of illusions and false assumptions
- **You have cast off** all the fragments of your Beta twin and any other womb mates

All that is left now is you, the sole survivor.

> *All through my childhood, I felt like I was alone, very much on my own even though I patently wasn't. I never felt like I fitted in, was painfully shy and mostly preferred to be on my own or with my dog. It is only becoming clear to me now that I had practically no sense of my own self, my life, my dreams, my entitlements. I was like a shadow moving between others and trying to make sure that everybody else was happy. I am at the beginning of some journey but I cannot see what the first step is, not to mention the destination!*
> *[Norma, Ireland]*

## Will I be happier?

Happiness is one aspect of Alpha energy that is almost impossible to pin down. The more you pursue it, the further away from it you will be. You have felt sad for a very long time because you have been grieving for your twin. Your period of mourning is over now. You have remembered, greeted and honoured your twin and that is enough. The day will come soon when you emerge into life again and start to enjoy it. One thing is certain – if your personal definition of happiness is to be reunited with your twin, you will remain in that familiar, dark place of sorrow for the rest of your life.

> *I want nothing more than a twin, someone who would be my soulmate and stop my mad search for someone to complete me. I always imagine little details of how our relationship would work - she would hold me when I was sad and vice versa, I could do her hair and she mine, we would hold hands when we walk and sit side pressed to side on sofas. I someday wish to see her - meet her here, in heaven, somewhere, for if she is nothing more than my imagination and even in heaven I am told I have no twin, I will not want to exist.*
> *[Mimi USA]*

# The next step: Onward

Until now, the meaning of your life has been the search for answers to why you have had strange feelings and ideas about being a twin. Now the search is over, it may seem as if everything that ever mattered has been stripped way. In fact, the whole issue of the loss of your twin has been like a smoke screen obscuring the view of your own future. In a little while, things will clear in your mind and you will begin to discover the meaning of your life to come. The next and final step on our healing path together may help to make this clear.

# 30

# Onward

We have come to the end of this set of healing steps, but this is not the end of your journey. The meaning of your life from now on will be to continue on your healing pathway, with a much-clearer view of how to make the best of the life you have, even if your destination always remains unknown. There will be no magical moment when you can pronounce your healing complete. It is an ever-developing, continuous process.

As you reach the end of this first and most important phase of healing, you may like to know that there will be plenty more revelations and surprises along the way ahead. You have probably noticed already that, once you took the first step on this healing path, there was no going back. For those who truly want to heal, an unstoppable process has begun.

> *I heard about the Vanishing Twin Syndrome for the first time yesterday. I have not married, have no children, and have not had any family events of my own. I always hoped for the future, but when reaching 50 years old my life really came to a halt. The last half year I have been searching for what it is that holds me back in every aspect of life. I have enough talents, ideas and projects to have an interesting life. I have come short in all matters where it is about including other people in my life - romantic relationship, friends and work. This thought that there could have been a twin brother together with me when life started, is so moving and touching. I am curious to find out if this will lead to an ease of my passivity. I am longing to use my talents and find out what is holding me back.*
> *[Lynda, USA]*

# A new perspective

At the end of any life-changing experience it is important to carry out a review. If you look back over the previous steps you will see that the process of womb twin healing has six stages:

| | |
|---|---|
| **Exploring the Dream of the Womb** | An exploration of the Dream of the Womb, which you have re-enacted throughout your life in a variety of ways. |
| **Ending self-sabotage** | An exploration of various self-defeating behaviours in the form of addictions and compulsions. |
| **Clarifying identity confusion** | Deciding who you are. Are you the Alpha survivor or your own Beta twin |
| **Healing difficult relationships** | Learning how your usual pattern of relationships today echoes the original connections you made in the womb |
| **Letting go of your womb twin** | Acknowledging with a ritual that your twin has died and is no longer with you |
| **Moving forward** | Discovering the true meaning of your life journey. |

There are three questions that you could ask yourself now, to fix the total healing experience in your mind:

1. What was the most difficult phase of the journey for you?
2. What stands out as a peak experience?
3. What particular ideas will you always carry with you?

Here is a space for you to record your answers.

**Most difficult**

**Peak experience**

**Particular ideas**

## Your Alpha gifts

To equip you for your onward journey, we will now discuss the many gifts and talents that arise out of your Alpha energy. You have them simply because you are a womb twin survivor.

## Connection

Out of your desire to restore the lost connection with your twin, you have always been concerned with relationships and how they should be created and maintained. You may have spent much of your life sabotaging your chances of having the close relationship you crave so much. Now, with the use of intelligent thinking, you are allowing more people into your life. Your concern for relationships is a great blessing - people who need people are highly gifted in that respect. You believe in the healing power of love. That belief will help you to gather friends around you.

### Positive energy

Alpha energy is positive. It fuels a sense of mastery and self-confidence. Being able to discern the positives in the direst situation will be one of your greatest gifts.

- **It will see you through** the dark times and enable you to survive.

- **There will be Black Hole moments** when all seems lost, but your Alpha energy will pull you out of them.

- **When things do not go as expected** and your way forward seems to be blocked, your positive energy will help you to realise you may have been going the wrong way.

- **It will give you the perspective** to reconsider what you want and where you want to go.

It is a truism that there is no such thing as disappointment, only too-high expectations. Likewise, there is no such thing as a mistake, only an opportunity for personal growth. As for regrets, they are a waste of energy. The only thing to do with regrets is to turn them into lessons. Such a positive attitude will keep you moving forward, almost always in the right direction.

## A spirit of calmness

If you carefully develop the practice of remaining calm, it will continue over the years to strengthen and develop your Alpha energy. With a calm spirit, you will be able to meet every situation with a clear mind and make sensible choices. You will be like the still centre in the storm and others will look to you for reassurance. You will be able to soothe people in distress and help to bring resolution to fractured relationships. All this will be done effortlessly, simply by being yourself.

## The ability to wait

Impatience is a Beta quality. The patience that arises out of being a womb twin survivor is related to trust and understanding. Coming to hasty, ill-informed conclusions is a sign of unintelligent thinking. Trust in a stable future is hard for the traumatised, but now you have emerged from the trauma of losing your twin, you can see the world is a much safer place than you ever imagined

You can wait calmly for things to work themselves out, simply because you trust that they will. If things do not work out, you can handle disappointment more easily, now that you have come to terms with being let down by the death of your womb twin. You have discovered the ability to wait by not striving to heal, but allowing the healing to slowly change you.

## Respect

Of all people, womb twin survivors who have walked the healing path naturally show respect for everyone they meet. This probably applies to you, too. In order to recover your own self-esteem, you have had to face the fact that you are no better or worse than anyone else. Intelligent thinking will show you the truth - that we all have equal worth. Respect arises naturally out of that insight.

The meetings that were arranged by the Womb Twin Survivors Research Project demonstrated that an atmosphere of emotional support and mutual respect prevails among womb twin survivors. Even the most difficult individuals, who had not at that time realised they were no more important than anyone else, were treated with respect. For these people, receiving respect turned out to be an important factor in their healing.

## Benevolence

Womb twin survivors are among the most compassionate people in society. They have all known suffering and are highly empathetic. The characteristic response to suffering is to reach out and try to help alleviate it if you can. Womb twin survivors have had to forgive themselves for living and that makes them acutely aware of how much other people may be hurting.

Womb twin survivors are to be found in great numbers in the caring professions. For example, they may become healers, teachers, nurses, doctors or carers. A good day for a womb twin survivor is one where he or she has made a difference in someone else's life. A loving touch can have a positive effect on someone in despair. If that other person is also a womb twin survivor, but is not yet aware of that fact, a simple gesture of friendship can be the beginning of healing.

## Trustworthiness

Womb twin survivors are naturally loyal. You were so loyal to your womb twin you held yourself in your Beta space for many years. That made your life very difficult. Even when we had walked several steps on the healing path together and it was time to let go, it was hard for you to imagine no longer being responsible for your womb twin, such had been your loyalty. Womb twin survivors love the truth and are often painfully honest. They will sacrifice a friendship for the sake of exposing the truth. That combination of honesty and loyalty makes womb twin survivors very trustworthy.

When your twin died, your world fell apart and your first trusted relationship ended unexpectedly. Consequently, it has been extremely difficult for you to learn to believe in a benevolent universe and to trust other people not to leave you. Learning to trust has been a hard lesson, but now you insist on other people being trustworthy and you practise it yourself. That is a great gift.

## Surrender

To be able to align yourself to the natural course of events is an important element in patience and calm, but it has been something you have had to learn in order to walk the healing path. You have surrendered yourself to the healing process and noticed the Alpha energy rising in you.

For you, surrender is now associated with new life and seen as strong and positive. Before your healing came, you probably regarded someone who was meek and mild as rather pathetic and weak. Now you can see the strength it has required from you to stop forcing events to a conclusion, but let life carry you forward.

## Self-mastery

For many years you have been easily overcome with emotions and your behaviour has been driven by compulsions and addictions. You have realised Alpha energy is the kind that stays calm in a crisis and helps you to practise intelligent thinking. This means you have now learned to master your emotions and behaviour. Self-mastery is different from self-control, which is a strong exercise of willpower.

By walking the healing path. you will have discovered there is no effort at all for you in self-mastery. All that is required is to develop and use your

Alpha energy, which will keep you calm and clear-headed in almost every situation. Your family and friends may not notice the difference, but you will. You will be more focused and waste less energy on fruitless tasks.

This gift will make you stronger and much happier, for you will feel more equal to challenges and be better able to rise above losses and disappointments. It may take a while for the change to become apparent, but if you look back, you will be able to see how much more you are accomplishing these days than before.

## Going forward

The way forward is to continue to heal yourself and the culmination of your healing will be to help other womb twin survivors to heal. There can be no better way to honour your womb twin than to save others from the pain and suffering that you have endured, simply because you didn't understand what was wrong with you. Even when you did know about your twin, you probably had no idea what to do about it.

Now you know, you can tell others. There are many millions of womb twin survivors who need help, almost all of whom have not yet found an explanation for their feelings. If you can promise yourself to help just one other womb twin survivor along the healing path, that decision would give your life meaning and purpose.

If you have ever asked yourself, "Why was I the one to survive?" perhaps this is the reason. You will probably be most effective when helping people with a similar Dream to yours.

### Two-egg:

*Learn to stand alone*

For the two-egg womb twin survivor, one lesson that is worth taking forward from this experience is how to be independent. Your Alpha energy will make sure you are no longer reliant on others to bring you happiness or help you to achieve your dreams. From now on you will walk alone, responsible for your own welfare and personal growth. Secure in your Alpha space, you will be able to tell the truth of what it means to be a two-egg womb twin survivor.

You may have learned to stand alone, but your capacity for warmth and friendliness guarantees you will never walk alone.

Other unaware two-egg womb twin survivors will spontaneously come to you, intuitively sensing that you will understand. If you simply tell your story whenever and wherever you can, the womb twin survivors you encounter will benefit greatly. There will be no need to do anything further, for hearing your story will be the start of their own healing journey.

### One-egg

*Reach out to others*

As a one-egg womb twin survivor, the one characteristic that has caused you the most difficulty is your tendency to brood on your problems. As a result, your energy is directed inwardly. Having walked this healing path, you will have learned that your problems are similar to those experienced by many other one-egg womb twin survivors. You could use this knowledge to help others like yourself.

Because you once had a monozygotic twin, you are an extremely sensitive person and acutely aware of other people's body language. You probably already know someone who seems to feel as you do about life and could also be a one-egg womb twin survivor. Reach out to this person and invite him or her to share his or her feelings with you. If you do that, not only will it help your friend, but it will also help you. Between you and a fellow one-egg womb twin survivor, you will have created a deep and empathetic relationship - that is exactly what you miss so much.

### Multiple

*Let the healing come*

As a multiple womb twin survivor who has walked the healing path, your mission in life will remain as it always has been - to heal the world and everyone in it - but with a difference. Because you have learned to keep a strong boundary and hand back every day any feelings you have picked up in empathy from other people, what remains of the pain is entirely yours.

You are now free to heal your own pain. There is no more need to try and heal other people so that you no longer feel their pain. You are someone who is healed and who believes in the process of self-healing. You have been there and done it. All you have to do now is to tell the story of your own healing path. Explain how it was for you, wherever there is someone to listen. Inspired by your example, others will soon follow and that is how your healing journey will continue.

## A healing fable

On the next few pages is a healing fable, which may help you to continue on your own healing path through the years to come.

# Epilogue:

# Out of the Box

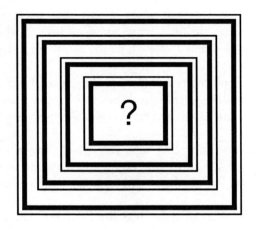

I was in a place of complete darkness. It was a country I knew well, but I was visiting it with my awareness for the first time. I opened my inner eye and saw a set of Chinese boxes, made of dark, dark wood with one packed inside the other. I was where I had always been: in the outermost box, hemmed in on both sides. I did not care. I had just enough for my needs.

I could manage this for a lifetime. I had no connection with the outside world for this was a prison. I was on a life sentence. I was resigned to never being let out or escaping - in fact I had long since given up on the possibility. I settled for what I had. I was content. I was alone. Yet somewhere, faintly sounding in the back of my mind, I heard a child cry out.

Something deep in my heart awoke and responded to that cry. I began to listen carefully to that tiny little voice. It seemed to be coming from the other side of the wall. My listening drew me inwards, to wonder about what was on the other side of the dark, inner wall of my prison.

I realised that, in the place where I was, all I had ever managed to do was to walk in circles. If I stopped walking round and made a hole in the wall, what would I find there? I made a very tiny hole in the wall and dared to look through. It was very dark in there and it was filled with fear. I feared that I was stepping into a void, would vanish from the world and never find that little voice.

The crying sounded a little louder. In my heart I knew the child was lost and alone in the dark. I felt very sad that this lonely little person had no friend. So I stepped into the dark and fearful place to be the one to bring comfort, but I did not know where I was or what to do.

I felt helpless and sad that the child was lonely. I realised then that I did not wish to be alone. I walked round in that new space, which was much smaller than my former prison. Very soon I came back to where I had started walking. Round and round I walked, many, many times, but there was no way out.

The child was still crying and alone and I grieved for that child. I began to wonder how this thing had come about. Why was I was sad and alone and grieving for a little child who cried out endlessly in the dark but no one came?

I wondered who the child was, and why I had always been alone. I wondered if the child and I could be friends. I wanted to shout out, but I had no voice. I was left in silence with only the sound of sobbing to guide me.

Then I realised that the silence was all around me. The child's crying had stopped. I tried desperately to call out and found an unaccustomed voice of my own. I cried out in a whispery tone: "Where are you? Why will you not talk to me? I want to be your friend!" There was only silence.

There in my dark wooden prison I felt more alone than ever. The silence of that child's cry spoke to me of the death of hope.

My heart broke open at last. The pain was terrible. I was racked with it and clutched at my own body for I knew the pain of true desire at last.

And out of that desire came rage and power - I would have what I wanted! I smashed the wooden walls of my prison until they lay about me like matchwood. I stepped towards the centre into the silence where the child had been.

There was no sign. The child was gone. The wind blew gently around me and I knew freedom. But there was no one there. There was only myself, staring into the space at the centre of the ruins of my wooden prison.

So I piled up all the wood and made it into a great beacon and set it alight with the new fire of life that was burning inside me. The flames leapt high and the light of the beacon shone out over all the land.

In a distant place, after many long years of waiting, the child saw the light I had made and came home.

# APPENDICES

# Appendix A

## Statements about personal psychological state

*(Extract from the Womb Twin Survivors Research Project questionnaire)*

I suffer from depression

I have a problem with food and eating

I fear abandonment

I fear rejection

I have wanted to commit suicide more than once in my life

I am afraid of being alone in the dark

I have been searching for something all my life but I don't know what it is

I get very intense and involved at the start of a relationship but then I sabotage it somehow

I am a woman, but I have a strong male side

I am a man, but I have a strong female side

I frequently feel unable to cope with life

I grieve deeply and for a very long time after someone close to me, or a beloved pet, has died

Deep down, I feel very vulnerable, as it would not take much to totally annihilate me as an individual

I am easily bored

I think a lot about death and dying

I am addicted to substances or behaviours that are potentially damaging to my health, wealth or wellbeing

All my life I have been "putting on a show," pretending to be someone else, and I know its not my authentic self

I feel the pain of others as if it were my own

Deep down, I feel alone, even when I am among friends

I easily get into a love/hate relationship with individuals I want to get close to

I compulsively self-harm

It upsets me if I am unable to reduce the suffering of others

I often find it difficult to fall asleep, even when I am very tired

I know I do not rest enough

There are two very different sides to my character

All my life I have felt as if something is missing

I spend a lot of time talking to myself in a mirror

I find disappointment very painful

I think I am psychic

I am a perfectionist

I find it hard to forgive people who have hurt me

I have been in an exploitative relationship with another person

All my life I have felt empty inside

I don't let other people get close to me

I am paranoid

I get extremely upset about silly little things

I feel driven by "musts" and "shoulds"

I feel different from other people

I feel guilty about everything

I always feel in some way unsatisfied, but I don't know why

I know I am not realising my true potential

I have strong, inner imaginary life that I use as a coping mechanism

Deep down, I somehow know I experienced death before I was born

I find it hard to let go of unfinished projects: I am always going to finish them one day

I have a strange, irrational feeling that somehow "I don't exist" or "I'm not really here".

I feel very privileged, simply to be alive

There is at least one room (including shed or garage) in my home that is completely full of stuff

I generally lack energy and motivation

I have a problem with expressing anger - either there is too much or too little

I suffer from low self esteem

I often feel torn in two between two decisions

I have suffered for a long time from feeling vaguely unwell, as if I am slowly dying

I make a lot of effort to protect my privacy

I am so intuitive and empathetic that it is a problem for me

All my life I have felt restless and unsettled

All my life I have carried deeply felt emotional pain that persists, despite all my efforts to heal myself

I have a deep desire to heal the world and everyone in it

I feel guilty about being alive at all

I want to succeed in life, but I always end up somehow sabotaging my chances of success

# Appendix B

### Possible combinations of a triplet pregnancy
### (showing gender differences)

**TRIZYGOTIC (THREE-EGG) TRIPLET PREGNANCY**

**ONE-EGG, TWO-EGG TRIPLET PREGNANCY**

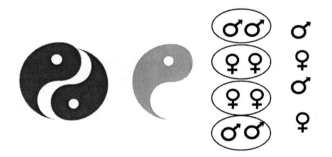

**DOUBLE ONE-EGG TRIPLET PREGNANCY**

# Glossary

**Amniotic fluid**  The fluid surrounding a foetus within the amnion

**Amniotic sac**  The sac in which the foetus develops, also known as the bag of waters

**Anaemia**  A condition in which the body does not have enough healthy red blood cells

**Anorexia**  An eating disorder characterised by self-starvation and irrational fear of gaining weight

**Arrested development**  Not growing up, remaining childlike in adulthood

**Auto-immune**  An inappropriate immune response of the body against substances and tissues normally present in the body

**Blastocyst**  An embryo that has developed for five to six days after fertilisation

**Blighted ovum**  A fertilised egg implants in but no foetus develops

**Bulimia**  Binge eating followed by induced vomiting or purging

**Cerebral palsy**  A group of neurological disorders caused by damage to the brain during the pregnancy

**Chimera (chimerism)**  An individual whose body is composed of two or more different populations of genetically distinct cells

**Chorion**  The outermost membrane around the embryo

**Chromosome**  A string of DNA molecules in a thread-like structure

**Clomid**  Clomifene citrate (clomiphene, also known as Clomifert) taken as tablets to increase ovulation

**Codependent**  Passivity, feelings of low self-worth and the need to constantly "help" or rescue others

**Congenital abnormality**  Abnormal development of a foetus because of a genetic defect

**Dermoid cyst**  A non-cancerous growth found on any part of the body, that contains skin and other tissues such as hair and teeth.

**Dizygotic**  Formed from two zygotes

**DNA**  Deoxyribonucleic acid, a self-replicating material present in nearly all living organisms as the main constituent of chromosomes. It is the carrier of genetic information

**Egg**  The ovum, the single cell female gamete

**Embryo**  An unborn child aged between 14 - 57 days.

| | |
|---|---|
| **Fallopian tube** | The tube that connects the ovaries and the womb |
| **Foetus (also foetus)** | An unborn child older than 12 weeks. |
| **Foetus papyraceous** | A twin foetus that died after 12 weeks of development and has been pressed flat against the uterine wall by the growth of the living foetus |
| **Hermaphrodite** | An individual with both male and female sexual characteristics |
| **Hydatidiform mole** | A growth in the wall of the womb which looks like a bunch of grapes |
| **Hyperemesis** | Excessive vomiting |
| **Hyperovulation** | More than one egg released from the ovaries in any month |
| **Immune system** | A network of cells, tissues and organs that work together to defend the body against attacks by "foreign" invaders |
| **Implantation** | An event that occurs early in pregnancy in which the embryo adheres to the wall of uterus |
| **Intrauterine** | Inside the womb |
| **IVF** | Harvesting and fertilisation of several ova (eggs) outside the body; any resultant embryos placed into the womb |
| **Membrane** | In pregnancy, a thin, film-like structure enclosing various parts of the pregnancy. |
| **Monoamniotic** | Sharing an amniotic sac |
| **Monozygotic** | Formed from one zygote |
| **Morula** | Embryo at an early stage of embryonic development, consisting of a ball of cells |
| **Mosaic (mosaicism)** | An individual with cells of two genetically different types |
| **Multifoetal pregnancy reduction** | In a multiple pregnancy, one or more foetuses are selected for termination by lethal injection |
| **Multiple birth** | A pregnancy when more than one baby is conceived and survives until birth |
| **Multiple personality disorder** | At least two distinct and relatively enduring personalities existing within the psyche of one individual. Also known as Dissociative Identity Disorder (DID) |
| **Oestrogen** | A group of steroid hormones that maintain female sexual characteristics |

| | |
|---|---|
| **Ovulation** | When one or more eggs are released from the ovaries |
| **Ovum** | The egg, the female gamete |
| **Placenta** | A flattened circular organ in the uterus which nourishes the foetus through the umbilical cord |
| **Psychotic** | Unable to distinguish reality from fantasy |
| **Secondary sexual characteristics** | The physical signs that indicate gender - ie. genitals, breasts, body shape, facial hair etc.. |
| **Self-actualisation** | The process of developing one's personality to full maturity |
| **Stillbirth** | The birth of an infant that has died in the womb or is born without breathing |
| **Surrogate** | A person taking over the role of another |
| **Teratoma** | A non-cancerous growth that contains a wide variety of different tissues in a disorganised mass |
| **Testosterone** | A steroid hormone that stimulates development of male secondary sexual characteristics |
| **Toxicity** | Poisonous, potentially damaging |
| **Trizygotic** | A multiple pregnancy arising from three separate zygotes |
| **Trophoblast** | A layer of tissue on the outside of the developing embryo which forms the major part of the placenta |
| **Ultrasound scan** | A visual image produced from an ultrasound examination also known as a sonogram |
| **Umbilical cord** | The tissue linking the foetus and the placenta, containing blood vessels to maintain the life of the foetus. |
| **Vagina** | The muscular tube leading from the external genitals to the cervix |
| **Vaginal bleeding** | Bleeding from the vagina |
| **Vanishing twin pregnancy** | A twin pregnancy is seen on an early ultrasound but on a later scan one twin has disappeared. |
| **Womb twin survivor** | The sole survivor of a twin or multiple conception |
| **Zygote** | A large cell created from the fusion of an egg and a sperm |

# References

**1. Your dream of the womb**
1. Hayton, A., (2011) *Womb Twin Survivors - The Lost Twin In The Dream Of The Womb*, Wren Publications, p.183
2. Boklage CE, (1995) *The Frequency And Survivability Of Natural Twin Conceptions* Chapter in Keith, L.G., Papiernik, E., et al. (eds) *Multiple Pregnancy: Epidemiology, Gestation and Perinatal Outcome,* Parthenon.

**3. How crazy are you?**
1. American Psychiatric Association (1994) *DSM-IV-TR: Diagnostic and Statistical* Manual of Mental Disorders, American Psychiatric Press Inc.
2. The Womb Twin Kids Project [www.wombtwinkids.co.uk]
3. Laing, R.D., (1972) *The Divided Self,* Penguin Books

**4. Self-sabotaging behaviour**
1. Zonnevylle-Bender, M. J.S., van Goozen, S. H.M., et al., (2004), Emotional Functioning In Anorexia Nervosa Patients: Adolescents Compared To Adults. *Depression and Anxiety,* No.19 pp. 35–42.
2. Sampson, H.A., MD (1999) Food Allergy. Part 1: Immunopathogenesis And Clinical Disorders, *The Journal of Allergy and Clinical Immunology,* Vol. 103, No.5, pp 717-728
3. Brostoff, J, & Gamlin, L., (1989) *The Complete Guide To Food Allergy And Intolerance*, Bloomsbury, p.156

**5. A matter of choice?**
1. Le Fevre, R.(2000) *Kick the Habit,* Carlton Books p.11
2. Jeffrey A. Schaler (1999.) *Addiction is a Choice,* Open Court Publishing Co., U.SA
3. Goodman, A. (1990.) Addiction: Definition And Implications. *British Journal of Addiction*, No. 85: pp.1403–1408.
4. Sobell, L.C.,T.P. Ellingstad, M. B. Sobell (2000.) Natural Recovery From Alcohol And Drug Problems: Methodological Review Of The Research With Suggestions For Future Directions, *Addiction* Vol. 95, No. 5, pp. 749–764
5. Hayton, A. (2000) *Food and You,* Wren Publications, England
6. Corwin, R.L., P. S. Grigson (2009) Symposium Overview - Food Addiction: Fact or Fiction? *Journal of Nutrition,* Vol. 139 No. 3, pp. 617-619
7. Kennedy, J.(2007) *Weight Loss Surgery The Age Of Consumer Diligence And How It Affects You, Free Report,* [http://blog.weight-loss-surgery-secrets.com, retrieved Feb 2012.]
8. Frosch, W.A. & H. Milkman, (1977) *Ego Functions in Drug Users,* Chapter 10 in Blaine, J.D., D.A. Julius (Eds.) *Psychodynamics of Drug Dependence*, Jason Aronson Inc. Publishers.
9. Selby, S (1985) *A Look at Cross-Addiction,* Hazelden Information & Educational Services
10. *Ibid.* p 10

11. van der Kolk, B.A., (1989.) The Compulsion to Repeat the Trauma, *Psychiatric Clinics of North America*, Vol. 12, No 2, pp: 389-411
12. Hayton, A. (2011.) *Womb Twin Survivors - The Lost Twin In The Dream Of The Womb*, Wren Publications, p. 256

## 6. Self-isolation
1. Hayton, A., (2011) *Womb Twin Survivors - The Lost Twin In The Dream Of The Womb*, Wren Publications, p.128
2. The Lone Twin Network - www.lonetwinnetwork.org.uk
3. Goode, B.,(2007) *A Woman In Her Thirties Who Lost An Identical Sister At Birth*, Chapter in Hayton, A. (Ed.), *Untwinned: Perspectives on The Death Of a Twin Before Birth*. Wren Publications, p 19-20
4. Fraga, M.F., et al. (2005) Epigenetic Differences Arise During The Lifetime Of Monozygotic Twins, *Proceedings of the National Academy of Science USA*, Vol. 102, No. 30, pp.10604-10609
5. Kantor, M.,(2003) *Distancing: Avoidant Personality Disorder*, Praeger, p.35

## 11. Making friends with your Black Hole
1. Aron. E. (1999) *The Highly Sensitive Person*. Thorsons, p.236

## 12. Bridging the Alpha-Beta gap
1. Bryan E.M., (1995) The Death Of A Twin. *Palliative Medicine*. Vol.9, No.3, pp.187-9

## 13. Maintaining your personal boundary
1. Hall J.G., (2003) Twinning. *Lancet*, No. 362 p.736

## 17. Twin myths as an aid to healing
1. Graves, R.,(2011) *Greek Myths,* Penguin

## 22. Single sac, one egg
1. Pharoah P.O.D & Cooke T (1996). Cerebral palsy and multiple births. *Archives of Disease in Childhood-Fetal and Neonatal Edition*, 75, 174-177

## 24. From grief to growth
1. Womb twin memorials page [http://www.wombtwin.com]

## 25. From helplessness to hope
1. Wansink, B., & J.Sobal (2007) Mindless Eating. The 200 Daily Food Decisions We Overlook. *Environment and Behavior,* Vol. 39 no. 1 pp. 106-123
2. Besser, A., Gordon L Flett, Richard A Davis (2003) Self-Criticism, Dependency, Silencing The Self, And Loneliness: A Test Of A Mediational Model. *Personality and Individual Differences,* Vol. 35, No.8, pp. 1735–1752

Lightning Source UK Ltd.
Milton Keynes UK
UKOW05f1809240515

252207UK00005B/155/P